BUDDHIST LEARNING AND TEXTUAL PRACTICE IN EIGHTEENTH-CENTURY LANKAN MONASTIC CULTURE

BUDDHISMS: A PRINCETON UNIVERSITY PRESS SERIES

EDITED BY STEPHEN F. TEISER

A list of titles in this series appears at the back of the book

BUDDHIST LEARNING AND TEXTUAL PRACTICE IN EIGHTEENTH-CENTURY LANKAN MONASTIC CULTURE

Anne M. Blackburn

PRINCETON UNIVERSITY PRESS
PRINCETON AND OXFORD

Published by Princeton University Press, 41 William Street,
Princeton, New Jersey 08540
In the United Kingdom: Princeton University Press, 3 Market Place, Woodstock,
Oxfordshire OX20 1SY

Library of Congress Cataloging-in-Publication Data

Blackburn, Anne M., 1967–
Buddhist learning and textual practice in 18th-Century Lankan monastic culture/
Anne M. Blackburn.
p. cm. — (Buddhisms)
Includes bibliographical references and index.
ISBN 0-691-07044-X
1. Buddhism—Sri Lanka—History—18th century. 2. Monastic and
religious orders, Buddhist—Sri lanka—18 century.
3. Tipiòaka—Criticism, interpretation, etc. I. Title. II. Series.

BQ372.B53 2001
294.3′657′095493—dc21 00-049186

This book has been composed in Sabon

The paper used in this publication meets
the minimum requirements of
ANSI/NISO Z39.48-1992 (R 1997)
(*Permanence of Paper*)

www.pup.princeton.edu

Printed in the United States of America

2 4 6 8 10 9 7 5 3 1

For my parents

WHO MADE ME READY FOR THE OPEN SEAS

AND

In memory of Godwin Samararatne

TEACHER AND FRIEND

Contents

Author's Note viii

Acknowledgments ix

Abbreviations xi

Chapter One. "Destroying the Thick Darkness of Wrong Beliefs" 3

Chapter Two. Contextualizing Monasticism 23

Chapter Three. Marks of Distinction 41

Chapter Four. "They Were Scholars and Contemplatives" 76

Chapter Five. "He Benefited the World and the *Sāsana*" 107

Chapter Six. Readers, Preachers, and Listeners 139

Chapter Seven. "Let Us Serve Wisdom" 197

Appendix A. Contents of the Monastic Handbook Attributed to Saraṇaṃkara 205

Appendix B. Level Four Subject Areas and Texts 209

Appendix C. Siyam Nikāya Temple Manuscript Collections 213

Appendix D. List of Manuscripts Brought from Siam in 1756 217

Glossary 219

References 223

Index 235

Author's Note

UNLESS otherwise noted, all translations are my own.

I have chosen to use "Lanka" rather than "Sri Lanka" when referring to events on the island before the twentieth century. This is an effort to retard anachronistic nationalist appropriations of this study.

Acknowledgments

I HAVE HAD the good fortune to receive generous support at all stages of this project, and express my appreciation to the following institutions: the American Academy of Religion, the Fulbright-Hays Fellowship Program, Harvard University's Center for the Study of World Religions, Mellon Fellowships in the Humanities, NEH Summer Stipends, the Title VI Fellowship Program, the University of Chicago's Committee on Southern Asian Studies, the University of Chicago's Divinity School, and the University of South Carolina. Tissa Jayatilleke and his staff at the United States Educational Foundation in Colombo offered considerable support during several visits. I am grateful to the Inter-Library Loan staff at the University of South Carolina's Thomas Cooper Library, and to the University of Chicago's Regenstein Library, Harvard University's Widener Library, the British Library, and Peradeniya University's Main Library for permission to use those collections. Graduate student assistants at the University of South Carolina helped me a great deal by cheerfully chasing books and xeroxing rare articles. In particular I would like to thank Jennifer Holcombe, Michael King, Heather Langdale, Mardi McCabe, and Amy Suessle.

The roots of this project lie in a dissertation completed for the University of Chicago's Divinity School. I thank all of my teachers for their kindness and careful guidance over many years. Special thanks are due, however, to Frank Reynolds, who advised the project with compassion and insight, as well as to Steven Collins and Charles Hallisey, whose support for my research was, and continues to be, unstinting and inspiring. At Cornell University, Jim Gair made special provision for me to study literary Sinhala; without his generosity this work would have been greatly delayed. In Sri Lanka I owe a debt of gratitude to P. B. Mīgaskumbura, who guided my early readings in Sinhala and continues to share with me his rich knowledge of Sri Lankan history and culture.

Laura Ahearn, Seth Fleisher, Charles Hallisey, Frank Reynolds, and Mark Whitaker all read an early draft of this manuscript and collectively gave me the courage to continue. I am particularly grateful to Laura and Mark, who read the whole thing in one weekend before providing acute suggestions for revision. Although I received stimulating questions and suggestions from several audiences during the last four years, colleagues present at Harvard's Buddhist Studies Forum and the Workshop in Buddhist Studies at Princeton proved especially helpful. José Cabezón, Charles Hallisey, and Steven Teiser all read the last draft but one for Princeton University Press with characteristic care and rigor. I would like to thank Mark Allon for his support of the project over many years, and his special kindness during the last phase of editing. Deborah Winslow was kind enough to share hard-to-find maps from Sri Lanka. Eric Stevens at the University of South Carolina's Cartography Laboratory saved me much worry with respect to map production. I am grateful to the Royal Library, Copenhagen, for permission to reproduce two plates. At Princeton University Press it has been a pleasure to work with Brigitta van Rheinberg and her assistant, Mark Spencer, as well as with Margaret Case and Ellen Foos.

In Sri Lanka I have been fortunate enough to receive gracious hospitality and generous assistance at Buddhist temples and educational centers in many parts of the island. I offer special and respectful thanks, however, to Malvatu Vihārayē Anunāyaka Sumaṅgala Mahāthero, to Nātha Dēvālayē Pansalē Varakavē Dhammaloka Thero, and to Malvatu Vihārayē Saṃgharāja Pansalē K. Dhammakitti Thero.

I would like to thank several other people who read bits of the manuscript with thoughtfulness, responded helpfully to questions, offered generous hospitality, and/or listened to my ravings with good humor: Gayle Baldwin, Anne and Maurice Blackburn, Celia Brickman, Joanna Casey, John Clayton, Suneel and Chandra de Silva, Carl Evans, Julie Gifford, Sarah Heimann, Louise Jennings, Elise LaRose, Cécile Lomer, Anne Lucht, Visaka and Somnath Parua, Shantanu Phukan, H. L. Seneviratne, Godwin Samararatne, Nayan Shah, K. D. Somadasa, Don Swearer, M. and H. J. Thamotharan, G. Vijayavardhana, and Suzan Tiemroth Zavala. To Dom Lopes I offer this small token of affection and respect, with thanks and all good wishes.

Columbia, South Carolina, August 2000

Abbreviations

EZ	*Epigraphia Zeylanica*
MV	*Mahāvaṃsa*
SD	*Sārārthadīpanī*
SS	*Sāratthasamuccaya*
SSC	*Saṃgharājasādhucariyāva*
SV	*Saṃgharājavata*
Vibh-a	*Vibhaṅga-aṭṭhakathā*
Vm	*Visuddhimagga*
V.O.C.	Vereenigde Oost-Indische Compagnie

BUDDHIST LEARNING AND TEXTUAL PRACTICE IN EIGHTEENTH-CENTURY LANKAN MONASTIC CULTURE

A comic stance knows there is, in actuality, no ending (happy or otherwise) — that doing history is, for the historian, telling a story that could be told another way.

Caroline Walker Bynum
Fragmentation and Redemption

CHAPTER ONE

"Destroying the Thick Darkness of Wrong Beliefs"

TOWARD the end of the 1770s, a poet writing at the request of a powerful Buddhist monk on the island we now know as Sri Lanka juxtaposed four images of Lankan Buddhist life.[1] The first, with which he described the time before his patron's monastic order came into being, was an image of darkness, hypocrisy, and delusion. It described a time in which, according to the poet, Buddhist monks betrayed the ideals of monasticism.

> Not bearing [proper] qualities in [their] minds,
> bearing [only] the form of the monastic community with [their] bodies,
> distant from the sun of the teaching,
> [they were] in darkness for the period so described.

With the second, the poet alluded to his patron's teacher, the monk responsible for founding a new monastic order—the Siyam Nikāya (Siamese Order)[2]—to which the patron belonged. Crafting his verse, the poet emphasized a transformation of Lankan monasticism by playing images of darkness and light against each other. At the poet's hands his patron's teacher was depicted as the agent of an illumination vast enough to embrace all of Lanka.

> Like a person staying away from kaduru poison,[3]
> he left the layman's home that offers suffering.
> He illuminated this Lankan isle.
> What had been like a darkened home,
> [came to seem] like a tree full of lights.

Our poet understood this broadly transformative illumination as the result, above all else, of heroic Buddhist learning. Two heroes stood out in his imagination: the leader of the monastic community and the king of the royal court. According to the poet, King

[1] His poem, *Saṃgharājavata*, is discussed at length in Chapter Four. The quotation in the title is from SV v. 194.

[2] A *nikāya*, in this context, is a group of monks who accept each other's higher ordination as valid and who perform monastic rituals together. See further Chapter Two.

[3] The poison of the kaduru tree, contained in the tree's inviting blossoms.

Kīrti Śrī Rājasiṃha took the sovereignty of Lanka.
Like the sun bringing light to Buddhist teachings and institutions,
destroying the thick darkness of wrong beliefs,
he had *Butsaraṇa* learned and Buddhist teachings spread everywhere.

The extended enlightenment of Lanka was only possible, however, because royal support for Buddhist instruction was matched by the preparation of monks as teachers and scholars. This preparation was assured by the leader of the monastic community, or *saṃgha.*

[His students] lived near the Lord [lit. king] of the Monastic Community,
who possessed infinite knowledge.
They descended into the ocean of advanced learning, investigating.
With the eye of wisdom they saw grammar and logic [related to]
Sanskrit, Pāli and Sinhala.[4]
The lordly Buddhist teachings and institutions of Lanka existed everywhere.[5]

These images, taken from the hagiographic poem called *Saṃgharājavata* (The Activities of the Lord of the Monastic Community), take us to the heart of an eighteenth century transformation of Lankan Buddhism. The events to which these images allude, and the manner in which the images themselves are constructed, point to a moment of significant change in the dominant understandings of what it meant to be Buddhist, a monk, and learned in Lanka. The form and focus of the poem demands our attention for reasons extending well beyond the history of Lankan Buddhism, however. Taken seriously as a culturally located articulation of aesthetic and religious ideals, the poet's creative labor brings to light dimensions of South Asian history hidden by Orientalist and post-Orientalist historiography. The poet's vision—elite, public, patronized, and preoccupied with the relationships between monasticism, religious learning, and religious transformation—crystallizes the key arguments of this study. His verses invite a new historiographic perspective on pre- and early-colonial South Asian histories. This perspective brings into view the dynamic processes through which South Asians created and contested local understandings of "tradition" and claims to authority. In other words, it highlights the fact that a politics of representation and knowledge characterized South Asian societies both prior to and simultaneously with its better-known colonial counterpart.

Three arguments are central to this study. First, I challenge the con-

[4] Sanskrit, Pāli, and Sinhala were the literary languages most important to Lankan Buddhism. See Chapter Three.

[5] These verses are, respectively, SV vv. 70, 205, 194, and 191. "Buddhist teachings and institutions" translates *sāsana*. *Butsaraṇa* is an important devotional text, composed in the thirteenth century.

ventional view that an essentially stable and monolithic "traditional" Theravādin Buddhism existed in South and Southeast Asia prior to the intensification of colonialism that occurred in the nineteenth century.[6] In doing so I underscore a historiographic irony and show that post-Orientalist emphases on colonial "constructions" of South and Southeast Asian cultural traditions have diminished rather than enhanced our understanding of precolonial and colonial histories. Second, developing a methodological tool appropriate to my challenge, I argue that the idea of "textual communities" provides a useful concept with which to analyze processes that encourage the continuity and the transformation of cultural forms within South and Southeast Asian religious communities at different times, and for varied reasons. At the same time, however, I also suggest modifications to the way that textual communities are described in recent scholarship. These modifications are relevant to the European contexts for which the concept of textual communities was first developed, as well as to those outside England and the continent. Third, providing a sustained example of transformation to counter claims for a stable "traditional" Buddhism in South and Southeast Asia, I show that a reformulation of the social organization and the intellectual practices of Lankan Buddhist monasticism took place during the eighteenth century. This reformulation transformed the character of Buddhism in Lanka by altering the way that lay and monastic Buddhists understood the texts and practices most deserving of their attention. It was crucially influenced by three factors: the formation of a new Buddhist monastic order, the systematization of monastic education, and the development of a commentarial genre called the *sūtra sannaya* (an explanatory commentary written in Sinhala for Pāli *suttas*) for use within the new educational system.

THE PROBLEM OF "TRADITIONAL" BUDDHISM

Studies of Buddhism in Lanka and Southeast Asia tend to emphasize substantial continuities in religious thought and practice from the time the Theravāda was established in a specific cultural area[7] until the ad-

[6] Theravādin Buddhism is the form of Buddhism that now dominates Sri Lanka and Southeast Asia. For a more detailed account of its beginnings, see Chapter Two. Unless otherwise indicated, in this study "Buddhist" means "Theravādin Buddhist."

[7] The pace of the introduction of the Theravāda varied throughout the region. The following dates are commonly accepted for the beginnings of Theravādin communities: in Lanka, the third century B.C.E.; in Thailand, the twelfth-thirteenth centuries C.E.; in Burma, the eleventh-twelfth centuries C.E.; in Laos, the fourteenth century C.E.; in Cam-

vent of intensive colonial influence during the nineteenth century.[8] The most articulate English-language spokesman for this perspective on Buddhism in pre-nineteenth-century Lanka is Richard Gombrich, whose studies consistently emphasize the conservatism of Theravādin Buddhism from at least the fifth century C.E. until the nineteenth century.[9] In Gombrich's view, "The confrontation with Christianity is the one great and sudden break in Sinhalese Buddhist history, far more significant than the vicissitudes which affected the fortunes of the Sangha during the previous two thousand years" (1988, 23).

The idea of thirteen centuries of conservative "traditional" Buddhism followed by a nineteenth-century "watershed" (Gombrich 1988, 172) has had a deleterious effect on the study of Buddhist history in Lanka, as have the closely related views on the history of Buddhism in Southeast Asia that stress persistent structural tensions in Buddhist societies from the third century B.C.E. into the nineteenth century C.E.[10] Although those scholars who emphasize the singularity and continuity of "traditional" Buddhism have made very significant contributions to the study of Buddhist South and Southeast Asia, the very authority they command has allowed historians to shirk the task of investigating the pre-nineteenth-century history of Buddhism in Lanka and other regions identified with the Theravāda. Our tendency to accept our own "traditional" authorities has been compounded by several factors. First, to write histories of Buddhist communities in periods before the nineteenth century is a daunting task. The sources for such historical accounts are largely literary or commentarial, written in an array of translocal and local languages and structured tropologically according to the demands

bodia, the eleventh-twelfth centuries C.E. (Swearer 1995). It is important to realize that the rise of monastic orders affiliated with the Theravāda did not mean a quick or complete transformation in the religious ideas and rituals of any region. See, for instance, Bizot (1976) and Strong (1992).

[8] Discussions of Buddhism from the nineteenth century onward typically emphasize Buddhist responses to Christian missionary activities and to the demands of rationalist, scientific visions of the world articulated by European scholars. These studies of what is often described as "modern" or "modernist" Buddhism often stress the growing importance of lay Buddhist practice and lay autonomy from monastic communities, as well as monastic debates on the proper role of Buddhist monks. See, for instance, Bechert (1988), Gombrich and Obeyesekere (1988), Malalgoda (1976), Obeyesekere (1970) and Swearer (1995).

[9] Heinz Bechert, to whose work Gombrich's formulations are in part indebted, also assumes a relatively consistent "traditionelle Theravāda-Buddhismus" lasting at least from the third century B.C.E. to the nineteenth century C.E. and defined in part by a pattern of monastic degeneration and reform (1988). See also Gombrich (1971).

[10] The most influential of the latter has been Tambiah (1976). On Gombrich's historical analysis, see also Malalgoda (1972, esp. 160).

of politics and aesthetics. More than historians of Buddhist (and non-Buddhist!) South and Southeast Asia would like to admit, our historical scholarship has been limited by the languages we fail to engage.[11] Second, historians of Buddhism remain deeply influenced by the double legacy of Weberian historico-sociological and text-critical approaches to the study of Buddhism. Whether entranced by the drama of "early Buddhism's" dramatic claims for an "other-worldly asceticism" or drawn by the text-critical invitation to work backward toward what the Buddha "really" taught, many historians of Buddhism have focused their attention on the early formative period "witnessed" by canonical texts.[12] It is perhaps not unreasonable to think that such a focus is at times sustained by the lingering traces of an Orientalist tendency to see the "natives" as ill-equipped (and mercifully temporary) custodians of Buddhist texts rather than as the makers and users of such texts.[13] As Lopez notes, "with rare exception, there was little interest in the ways in which such texts were understood by the Buddhists of Asia" (Lopez 1995, 7).

It is not only the complexity of the evidence for Theravādin Buddhism as lived and organized prior to the nineteenth century that makes studies of the later colonial period attractive, however. The urgent ideological commands of postcolonial (sometimes nationalist) and post-Orientalist scholarship have made it instinctive, and often nearly unavoidable, to deconstruct the impact of colonial conditions on religion, ethnicity, caste, class, gender, and so on. Such studies are often sophisticated and provocative.[14] We must recognize, however, that the claims made by such studies are often greatly weakened precisely because we do not know enough about Buddhist communities prior to the latter portion of the nineteenth century to make secure arguments about changing or continuous modes of religious practice, or about the interaction between religious identities and political institutions.[15] As Carol

[11] There are, of course, important exceptions such as Hallisey (1995) and Pollock (1995).

[12] For arguments against the transparent authority of such texts see Schopen (1997) and Strenski (1983).

[13] "However, there are two underlying strategies that characterize the orientalist way of looking at things. One is the tendency to constitute a particular space as inherently timeless (or confined to its past, which is much the same thing)" (Breckenridge and van der Veer 1993, 17). For a useful discussion of Orientalist forms of knowledge, see Ludden (1993). On the "ideologies of empire" that shaped the Euro-American academic study of Buddhism, see Lopez (1995).

[14] On Lanka see, for instance, Jeganathan and Ismail, eds. (1995), Malalgoda (1976), Roberts (1982, 1997), Rogers (1987), Spencer, ed. (1990), and Whitaker (1999).

[15] I construe this last term broadly enough to include the informal institutions that sustain communal and regional interests.

Breckenridge and Peter van der Veer have observed, "Part of the difficulty with the 'colonial discourse' mode of entry into the politics of 'otherness' is that it locates the otherness of the other wholly (and even solely) in the colonial moment, thus eliding the question of pre- or noncolonial differences of consequence" (1993, 10).

We still know far too little about what it meant to be "Buddhist" in Lanka in any period before the late nineteenth century, about the religious institutions that shaped an understanding of identity and "tradition," and about the social and political activities that embraced and constrained all forms of Buddhist practice. Arguments that assume the existence of a relatively stable "traditional" Buddhism in Lanka and other parts of South and Southeast Asia make it harder, not easier, to write histories of these Buddhist communities before, during, and after the advent of colonialism. Sheldon Pollock's incisive comments are apposite here: "What troubles me is, first, the strong formulation of this [post-Orientalist] interpretation, whose logical extension is that colonialism in South Asia produced certain forms of domination *tout court*; and second, the thinness of the history of precolonial domination on which, ironically, this new historicism is based, and, moreover, its potential for precluding such an analysis. . . . If we want to argue that colonialism reconstituted tradition, should we not do a careful reading of the earlier tradition (or rather, traditions) that was the object of transformation?"[16]

Yet the roots of the "traditional" commonplace are still more complicated. Indeed, conventional understandings of "traditional" Buddhism in South and Southeast Asia are strikingly overdetermined. Scholarly understandings of the "traditional" monolith emerge in significant part from a naiveté on the part of historians who read indigenous Buddhist historical narratives. Contemporary historians of Buddhism, time and again, draw the rhetorical structure of these indigenous narratives into their own scholarly work without attending to their rhetorical character. By this I mean that historians of Buddhism appropriate tropes such as decline-and-revival and degeneration-and-reform, coming to see these tropes as straightforward descriptions of recurrent trends in Buddhist societies. In doing so, historians fail to recognize the conventional motifs through which what might be called a "dominant discourse" effaces the processes of change that have allowed it to assume this position of dominance.[17] I am arguing, in other words, that historians of Buddhism

[16] Pollock (1993), 97, 99–100. See also Hallisey (1995, 49–50).

[17] See, for instance, Carrithers (1979a, 1979b), Gombrich (1988), Dewaraja (1988), Malalgoda (1976), and Tambiah (1976). For an economic analysis of royal participation in the reorganizations of monasticism often referred to as evidence of "revival," see Aung Thwin (1979; 1985).

in South and Southeast Asia have failed to see that indigenous voices of recurrence and repetition construct the history of Buddhism as, essentially, the history of the constant movement between decline and revival or, as our poet would have it, between darkness and light. These voices do not simply describe. Oddly, historians of Buddhism (and historians of South and Southeast Asia generally) have rarely applied the critical insights of post-Orientalist scholarship when writing histories of pre- and early-colonial contexts. Scholars are increasingly sensitive to the way that colonial scholars and administrators shaped the essential traditions of the colonized by writing privileged representations of these traditions (such as "Buddhism") into "official" history. However, historians of Buddhism, for instance, have not recognized that the Buddhists whose texts they read were led by equally powerful understandings of natural dominance, and equally powerful conventions of representation, to depict the history of Buddhism as one of periodic returns to essential purity. Historians of South and Southeast Asia have rarely noticed that, long before the British East India Company and the Dutch Vereenigde Oost-Indische Compagnie (V.O.C.) controlled Asian lands and waters, Asian participants in religious and political communities used written representations to construct "tradition" and to efface change in the interests of an accepted (or emerging) hierarchy.[18]

TEXTUAL COMMUNITIES

It is one thing to declare that one's elders and betters are mistaken in some important respects, and quite another to offer an alternative. In the ensuing chapters I offer an alternative to the conventional view of stable, "traditional," Buddhism by focusing on one period in the history of the Lankan Theravāda that I believe is better described as a moment of reformulation than as a period of reformation. Taking my cue from the eighteenth-century poet who linked the illumination of Lanka to the spread of Buddhist teachings, I begin to ask questions about the nature and place of Buddhist learning in eighteenth century Lanka. And, curious to probe beyond the poet's heroic vision, I explore the degree to which the two leaders—of the court and of the monastic community—might be seen as responsible for key aspects of the reformulative process. Since most of the evidence available for writing histories of South and Southeast Asian Buddhism before the nineteenth century is textual (in a narrow sense), any effort to dislodge the "traditional" monolith

[18] For a discussion of some of the problems involved in applying Said's perspectives to Buddhist Studies, see Lopez (1995a, esp. 11–12).

must provide a new approach to the interpretation of these texts.[19] In developing such an approach, I take up the following subjects: the textual forms that shaped lay and monastic understandings of proper Buddhist action during the latter two-thirds of the eighteenth century; how these textual emphases differed from those that characterized other periods; how the contents of texts influenced those who encountered them in oral or written form; and the role that changing patterns of textual composition, redaction and reception played in the definition of new religious groups.

I have found the idea of textual communities, a term first used to analyze literacy and textuality in Europe, helpful to an exploration of these themes. Writing a history of eighteenth-century Lankan Buddhism from the perspective of textual communities provides a way to examine the Theravāda as "a tradition dependent on local conditions for the production of meaning" (Hallisey 1995, 51). Thus I speak of the emergence of a new textual community in Lanka during the latter two-thirds of the eighteenth century. In my use of the term "textual community," I differ somewhat from scholars who have developed the concept for work on European contexts. The modifications I introduce are rooted in my attempt to apply the concept of textual communities to a single Asian context, yet I believe that these modifications are relevant to those who study textual practices in areas distant from eighteenth-century Lanka.

The idea of textual communities was first broached by Brian Stock in his study of rising literacy rates in Europe during the eleventh and twelfth centuries. Stock analyzes the development of an unprecedented degree of literate influence on society, due in substantial part to the appearance of textualized vernacular languages. As literacy "penetrated medieval life and thought," Stock claims, it "brought about a transformation of the basic skills of reading and writing into instruments of analysis and interpretation" (1983, 11). Thus a text-based rationality emerged in Europe, and this affected the way that men and women understood their own experience as individuals and as members of social groups. Building on these basic assumptions, Stock uses the idea of textual communities to describe dissenting religious groups in eleventh-century Europe. He argues that authoritative texts and literate interpreters of them helped to constitute these new religious groups distinguished by their dismissal of beliefs and practices not legitimized through texts. Certain characteristics identified these groups as textual

[19] That textual evidence dominates the record does not mean that archaeological and art historical evidence should be ignored. For useful examples of its application see Schopen (1991; 1997) and Holt (1996).

communities, according to Stock. First, they included an individual who mastered the written version of a text before using it to reform the community's thought and action (90). Second, their members were not necessarily all literate but were bound by their acquiescence to the authority of a literate interpreter of the authoritative text or texts. Third, the community's members formed a voluntary association in which community activities took "place around an agreed meaning for the text" (522). Fourth, the group was defined by the adoption of "a type of rationality inseparable from the text" as a norm for behavior, with the effect that activities not authorized by the text were dismissed as popular and inappropriate and there was a "turning away from ritual and symbol and towards an intellectualism inseparable from the study of texts" (523–524). Because texts formed the central point of orientation in these communities, they shaped the experience of literate and nonliterate members of these communities; "as texts informed experience, so men and women began to live texts" (4).[20]

When adopting the term "textual community" to analyze the Lankan Buddhist context, we find that Stock's characteristics do not map perfectly onto the Asian evidence. For instance, although there is evidence that at least some literate leaders of the Siyam Nikāya understood encounters with particular textual forms as useful tools with which to reorient monastic practice—in a manner somewhat akin to the "reformative" characteristic of textual communities as discussed by Stock—there was no single text or set of texts identified as the distinctive doctrinal point of orientation for the monks who participated in the Siyam Nikāya's educational institutions. Nor are there good grounds for emphasizing either a strong sense of voluntary association as characteristic of the new Lankan textual community or consistent levels of self-conscious reflection on the communal nature of the interpretive stances adopted toward particular texts. Given a slightly looser defini-

[20] Several aspects of Stock's argument have been criticized. Clanchy (1983) queries Stock's assertion that the eleventh and twelfth centuries saw a radical increase in actual literacy rates, whereas Graham (1987) provides convincing evidence of the coexistence of orality and literacy. This diminishes the argument that the rise of literacy brought about dramatic changes in individuals' experiences of communication and cultural authority. Finally, the claim that rising literacy led to substantially new levels of standardization and systematic rational thought have been weakened by revisions to the early work on orality and literacy (e.g., Goody 1968; 1977) on which Stock relies (esp. notes 14–16). In this regard see, for instance, Graham (1987, 17–18; 176 nn. 4, 6). Street (1984) provides an incisive discussion of two opposed approaches to the study of literacy (sometimes discussed as "literacies" or "literary practices"). The central debate concerns the propriety of discussing literacy as an autonomous variable that operates independently of specific social contexts. Fabian (1993) suggests that attention to reading as an activity may offer a corrective to dematerialized studies of literacy.

tion, however, the term "textual community" remains a useful tool with which to think about the lives of texts in relation to the lives of men and women. I use the term to describe a group of individuals who think of themselves to at least some degree as a collective, who understand the world and their appropriate place within it in terms significantly influenced by their encounter with a shared set of written texts or oral teachings based on written texts, and who grant special social status to literate interpreters of authoritative written texts. Although members of a given textual community are oriented by and toward shared texts, their interpretations of these texts are not homogeneous.

In thinking about the processes through which texts came to influence the way eighteenth-century Buddhists understood their place in the world and the actions they should undertake, as well as the connection between interpretive command and social status, I am drawing on certain refinements to Stock's work suggested by Martin Irvine. Most important for my purposes are two elements. The first is Irvine's attention to the circumstances that sustain accepted interpretive strategies within a textual community. A second is his insistence that relationships of hierarchy and inequality are created when particular individuals and groups are identified as custodians of authoritative interpretation. In Irvine's words, "A textual community is formed by the two dimensions of the social function of texts, which are as inseparable as the two sides of a sheet of parchment—a received canon of texts and an interpretive methodology articulated in a body of commentary which accompanied the texts and instituted their authority. . . . The apparatus of interpretive discourse was formalized in the methodology of the arts of discourse and articulated in a body of commentary and criticism that authorized the received texts as objects of serious study and as expressions of a collective cultural memory" (1994, 15). This interpretive methodology not only defines specific "texts as repositories of authority and value"; the ability to interpret according to this authoritative method also defines the interpreter as a powerful member of the larger society in which the textual community participated, by creating a particular identity and social position (2).

The Lankan context suggests new questions appropriate to the study of textual communities in Asia and elsewhere. First, I argue that it is important to look closely at the social conditions that promote a stable and self-replicating interpretive authority within a single textual community and at those that allow for interpretive shifts and challenges. Whereas, for instance, Irvine makes a strong case for the comprehensiveness and stability of *grammatica*[21] over four centuries, the Lankan

[21] The "whole discipline concerned with literacy, the study of literary languages and texts, and the principles for interpretation and criticism" (Irvine 1994, 5).

monastic elites whom I discuss found room to develop substantially new understandings of textual authority and interpretive propriety. In the course of time, however, with the systematization of education, these new views on authority and interpretation reached a position of dominance stable enough to affect Lankan Buddhist culture for at least two centuries. Thus, social and institutional factors that affect the stability of an "interpretive methodology" deserve sustained attention. Second, the Lankan case underscores the importance of exploring the ways that a textual community's dominant interpretive strategies are sustained and challenged by the institutional location of those who engage these strategies. Where Irvine sees a textual community's authoritative strategies of interpretation as stable, pervasive, and bound to subtly normalizing social hierarchies, I suggest that we remain alert to the possibility that these strategies will have varying degrees of impact on individual acts of interpretation. Individual and collective practices of discipline and devotion, for instance, affect the degree to which authoritative trajectories of interpretation are accessible, compelling, and internalized. Similarly, as the social status of a textual community's members varies, so may their degree of openness to the dominant interpretations of the community. The Lankan context strongly suggests that there is more room for variation and resistance in interpretation than current models of textual community allow for.

TRANSFORMING LANKAN BUDDHISM

I understand the reformulation of Lankan Buddhism during the eighteenth century as a transformation caused by the intersection of three shifts that took place within the island's Buddhist community: a change in the social organization of Buddhist monasticism, the emergence of new ways of conceiving the intellectual practices appropriate to monasticism, and the introduction of a particular textual form into these practices. A claim as far-reaching as my claim for "transformation" demands extensive evidence, which I find by examining Lankan Buddhist monastic institutions and practices from several perspectives. I look closely at the transmission and standardization of elite religious education in a context dominated by manuscripts rather than by printed texts, and explore the links between monastic reading, interpretation, and the constitution of monastic identities suitable to the new Siyam Nikāya. Since the education of monks was a socially organized phenomenon that brought monks and lay Buddhists into specific relationships, I also write about the way that the shared needs of royal and monastic leaders led to the systematization of educational advancement and patronage, and about the impact of the newly organized monastic education on the nature of other lay-monastic interactions on the island. In doing so, I explain that the use of *sūtra sannaya*s to train monks as preachers created a new textual community that encompassed lay and monastic Buddhists in Lanka. This textual community was defined in part by a new view of proper learning and authoritative textuality, a view that had considerable impact on Buddhist activities in Lanka during the nineteenth century and beyond. In fact, the character of nineteenth- and early twentieth-century Lankan Buddhism was caused in part by the changes in the organization and focus of monastic education that took place between the 1730s and the 1780s.[22]

By examining the eighteenth-century reformulation of Lankan Buddhism from the perspective of textual communities, I bring into view important aspects of Lankan history prior to the intensification of colonialism in the late nineteenth century. The educational institutions and textual practices of this new community of lay and monastic Buddhists were significantly untouched by the slowly encroaching powers of the Dutch, French, and British colonial establishments. By offering a new reading of indigenous Lankan histories that emphasizes their importance to the emergence of this new textual community, and by drawing attention to the diverse acts of interpretation engaged in by the community's participants, my work provides a new way to think about "the invention of tradition" (Hobsbawm and Ranger 1983) and the limits to it in pre- and early-colonial contexts. Further, because I argue that the new textual community that arose in the eighteenth century influenced the nature of Buddhist practice and self-understanding during subsequent centuries, this study complicates the usual post-Orientalist view of the construction of knowledge and tradition. The evidence for an eighteenth-century reformulation of Lankan Buddhism shows clearly that Asians not only reconfigured "traditional" practices in response to colonial definitions of desirable knowledge. In addition, local definitions of desirable knowledge clearly helped to set the terms for the colonial construction of Asian "tradition" as well as for local responses to that which was newly defined as "traditional."

MEDIEVAL TEXTUAL COMMUNITIES?

The discussions of textual communities on which I draw, as well as analyses of other textual practices (such as reading and memorization),

[22] I focus on this period, which I identify with the "early" Siyam Nikāya. This period begins with the emergence of a distinctive group of monks under the leadership of the monk who became the Siyam Nikāya's founder—Väliviṭa Saraṇaṃkara. It concludes with the deaths of Saraṇaṃkara and his chief patron (Kīrti Śrī Rājasiṃha) in 1778 and 1782, respectively.

were developed on the basis of the history of textual production, transmission, and reception in Christian Europe between the fourth and fourteenth centuries. Questions naturally arise about how I understand the application of these analytical perspectives across time and space, and how I justify the analogical application of a twelfth century French case, for instance, to an eighteenth-century Lankan one. To answer such questions, I first examine some of the conventional periodization schemes used in studies of Europe and in studies of Theravādin South and Southeast Asia.

The primary scholars of textual practices in European Christendom on whose work I draw in this study—Mary Carruthers, Rita Copeland, John Dagenais, Martin Irvine, and Brian Stock—all use the terms "medieval" or "middle ages" to describe the temporal focus of their work. However, as one would expect, there is no uniformly accepted approach to periodizing European histories. Although a threefold periodization of the Middle Ages is quite common, according to which the Early Middle Ages fall between 300 and 1050 C.E., the High Middle Ages between 1050 and 1300 C.E., and the Late Middle Ages between 1300 and 1500 C.E., Norman Cantor argues against 1500 as the dividing line between the late Middle Ages and modernity. According to Cantor, the start of "our modern industrial mass society" and "the start of the long withdrawal from the Christian faith" makes the early eighteenth century a turning point between the Middle Ages and modernity (1973, 6–8). Jacques Le Goff pushes the chronological boundaries of the medieval still further with his argument for an "extended Middle Ages" characterized by "a set of slowly evolving structures" that lasted from the third century until the middle of the nineteenth century. Le Goff prefers the nineteenth century to the eighteenth as the cusp of modernity, since it is only in the nineteenth century that the experience of industrialized society and mass education became characteristic of European society (1985, 21).

Historians of South and Southeast Asia have recently begun to address the problems involved in writing historical studies that use terms and periodization schemes developed in relation to European religious, educational, and industrial changes. One result of this has been a move to apply the methods of the Annales school to study history over the *longue durée* in specific Asian regions. An excellent example of this approach is Anthony Reid's work on Southeast Asia between 1450 and 1680, which contends that societies across Southeast Asia shared important developments during this period.[23] These included increased com-

[23] Reid notes that the fourteenth century is arguably a better starting point for the early-modern period but that the paucity of evidence from this period discourages its use (1993b, 16).

mercial and urban activity, the appearance of new military technology, a movement toward more centralized states, and an unprecedented stress on orthodox, textually oriented religious tradition (1988, 1993a, 1993b). Reid is one of several historians (often using quite different methods) who argue against the view that precolonial civilizations were "extraordinarily conservative, if not static" (Lieberman 1997, 449).

The movement to define an early modern period spanning the years between 1450 and 1670 or 1800 is seen by some as a helpful departure from the "Orientalist encapsulation of the study of indigenous precolonial Southeast Asia" (Lieberman 1997, 450). However, many questions remain about what is involved in identifying "early modern" contexts within Asia or over still larger regions.[24] In particular, historians debate the importance of using materialist criteria (such as demography, monetary flows, or climate changes) in relation to nonmaterialist ones (such as shifts in indigenous self-representation (Wyatt 1997) or the "vocabularies that cut across local religious traditions" (Subramanyam 1997).[25] There is also little consensus about the usefulness of projecting contemporary nation-state boundaries backward in historical analyses. These arguments about whether and how it is appropriate to speak of early modernity are closely related to arguments about nationalism and protonationalism.[26]

The regional and temporal focus of this study (Lanka roughly between the years 1730 and 1780) and the primary object of inquiry (a transformation of Buddhism rooted in changing monastic organization, education and textual practices) pose significant challenges to periodization. Although the years with which I am concerned fall within the most generous chronological range assigned to early modernity, the fit between this context and definitions of early modernity is poor. For instance, although coastal cities grew as they became centers for colonial administration as well as shipping and fortification, this growth was by no means matched in the capital of the highland Kandyan Kingdom where the Siyam Nikāya first developed. Moreover, we have no clear indications of the impact that greater urbanization on the coast had on

[24] In this regard see the special issue edited by Lieberman (1997).

[25] Subramanyam's work identifies the following characteristics of early modernity: the definition of "a new sense of the limits of the inhabited world," an exacerbation of long-term structural conflict between settled and nomadic societies, the rise of a slave trade to new levels, the beginning of new cash crops, changes in "political theology," the emergence of notions of universalism and humanism, a change in "the nature and scale of elite movements across political boundaries, effective fluidity between 'cultural zones,' and pan-religious vocabularies for organizing experience."

[26] See, for instance, the tensions between the views set out by Lieberman (1997) and Anderson (1991).

the development of monastic institutions during this period.[27] Political organization in Lanka at this time was in considerable flux. Colonial powers backed by some local elites drew the island into the embrace of empire, while the central Kandyan Kingdom attempted to maintain independence but remained highly vulnerable to the colonial powers and to threats from within local elite communities. Finally, there is no clear evidence of an unusually strong interest in religious orthodoxy or religious textuality. No political or religious community was in the position to define orthodoxy; more important, the very idea of orthodoxy seems to have been quite foreign to the Buddhist communities of the time. We see a continuation of debates about proper disciplinary practices for monastic Buddhists, and perhaps about proper devotional activities for all Buddhists, but not yet any attempt to codify the beliefs appropriately Buddhist to any greater degree than was customary from at least the twelfth century onward.[28] Although I will show that specific Buddhist communities developed new ideas about what sorts of religious texts were most desirable and efficacious, there is no sign that Lankan Buddhists in the middle of the eighteenth century were more concerned with textually oriented forms of Buddhist practice and identity than they had been since at least the twelfth and perhaps the fifth century. Finally, there is no clear evidence that the technologies of textual production, transmission, and reception changed significantly before the nineteenth century.

By 1730, however, many inhabitants of Lanka were undoubtedly aware of their participation in activities often now theorized as characteristic of modernity (e.g., Collins 1998). For instance, it was increasingly clear that they were (perhaps reluctant) participants in a new form of global economy driven by the demands of growing capitalist economies in colonial homelands. It is certainly the case that these demands altered the constraints on political organization, and on social and economic advancement. The presence of Christian missionaries (Catholic and Protestant) undoubtedly posed certain challenges to the existing pluralism of beliefs and devotional practices oriented toward the Buddha, a range of Indian deities, and the prophetic monotheism of Islam. We know very little about how such pluralisms were conceived by local

[27] The sources are richer, however, by the time we turn to the middle of the nineteenth century, on which see Roberts (1982). For studies of pre-nineteenth-century commercial activity and their effects on the island's social institutions, see C. R. de Silva (1992), K. M. de Silva (1981), and Dewaraja (1988).

[28] The twelfth century is a useful marker for these purposes for reasons discussed in the first section of Chapter Two. Although Reid argues for a "retreat of the 'scriptural trend'" in insular Southeast Asia in the late seventeenth century (1993, 16–17), Lieberman (1993) and Ishii (1993) assume its continuity for mainland Southeast Asia.

populations before or after the advent of assertive Christian activity. It does seem clear, however, that the Christian presence did not yet constitute a powerful influence toward scripturalism or reformism, two -isms often connected to the experience of modernization.[29] Nor is it likely that the presence of European strangers and certain technological innovations had created a dramatic rupture in the understanding of the world set out in earlier Buddhist cosmologies.[30]

The imperfect fit between the Lankan context and discussions of Asian early modernity should come as no surprise, since any attempt to develop a periodization scheme necessarily privileges some cultural variables over others and analyzes them with the greatest accuracy. I try to keep several interpretive trajectories in view at the same time, and for this reason have decided to forsake the use of terms like "medieval," "early modern," and "modern" altogether, in favor of an approach that describes the phenomena in question and assigns them only a date. Doing so makes it easier to examine several different types of social process and institution simultaneously without allowing interpretive emphases from one form of analysis to bleed into another. For instance, subsequent chapters examine a range of social events and contexts: translocal political and economic structures; local and regional forms of political organization and patronage; shifts in the organization of, and activities undertaken by, local religious institutions; and the text-oriented activities characteristic of a new Buddhist textual community. I emphasize different variables and causal patterns, and different rates of change, when analyzing particular aspects of Lankan culture that have bearing on my argument for an eighteenth-century reformulation of Buddhism. Even as translocal political and economic contexts continued to shift throughout the period of focus, for instance, aspects of royal patronage remained consistent with that characteristic of earlier periods, and when inconsistent were often determined more by pressures at the local level than at the translocal level. Changes in monastic organization during this period have less to do with colonial experience than with the power of individual personalities in conjunction with local political interests. The nature of textual practice shows continuities in technology, moderate continuities in motivation and discontinuities in content that are difficult to explain but are probably due to the convergence of dominant monastic personalities and local shifts in devotional emphasis.

We might say, then, that an uneven rate of change characterized the social activities that touch on the object of this study. Thus, any attempt

[29] See, for instance, Geertz (1971) and Seneviratne (1999).

[30] On which see Collins (1998) and Reynolds and Reynolds (1982).

to analyze these activities in the Lankan case by developing a comparative perspective on them will proceed most effectively not by comparing Lankan and non-Lankan materials on the basis of a broad periodization scheme (matching up the Middle Ages on two continents, for instance), but by looking closely at separate social activities to see where broadly analogous situations might be found in other cultural settings. In this study I draw on studies of European Christian cultures only in the analysis of royal-monastic patronage relations that sustained the growth of new educational systems, in examinations of the technologies of learning and discipline related to monastic life, and in discussions of textually oriented community identities within and beyond the monastic world. Studies of learning, and especially monastic learning, in European Christian settings between the fourth and fourteenth centuries are appropriate because the dominant understanding of monastic and clerical learning, the patronage institutions that supported it, and the technologies used to sustain it were all closely similar to their counterparts in eighteenth-century Lanka. They are therefore a useful basis for the attempt to to gain a new purchase on the Lankan case and to make the Lankan case accessible to other scholars. The similarities I isolate to defend this view are the following: the use of manuscripts rather than printed books;[31] the characterization of learning as a religiously significant activity understood as an act of devotion, as a responsibility to the life of the larger religious community, and as part of ethical inculcation;[32] the importance of commentarial genres in the transmission and standardization of clerical and monastic understandings of religious teaching;[33] the role of royalty and court elites as key patrons of monastic and clerical learning;[34] and the relationship between monastic and clerical self-definition and the development of educational institutions.[35] Literacy rates may not be comparable, though there is some disagreement about the rate and regional effects of rising literacy in Europe. Holt (1996) and Seneviratne (1999) note low literacy rates in Lanka before the nineteenth century, whereas Carruthers (1990) and d'Avray (1985) note evidence for considerable levels of lay literacy in Europe from an

[31] For Europe see Carruthers (1990), Clanchy (1983), Dagenais (1994), Petrucci (1995), and Rouse and Rouse (1979). For Lanka see Malalgoda (1976), Perera (1962), and Somadasa (1987).

[32] For Europe, see Carruthers (1990) and Leclercq (1982). For Lanka see subsequent chapters of this study.

[33] For Europe, see d'Avray (1985), Irvine (1994), and Rouse and Rouse (1979). For Lanka, see subsequent chapters of this study.

[34] For Europe, see Irvine (1994) and Nardi (1992). For Lanka, see subsequent chapters of this study.

[35] For Europe, see d'Avray (1985), Irvine (1994), and Nardi (1992). For Lanka, see subsequent chapters of this study.

early period, though perhaps especially in urban areas after the twelfth century.[36]

Despite these comparisons to European contexts, my analysis should not be understood either as the pursuit of a lowest common denominator able to support arguments for similarity between European and Asian cultural spheres or as an argument in support of an Orientalist view of Asian laggardliness on the continuum toward modern self-realization. Rather, by developing a more explicitly comparative conversation about the history of textual production, transmission and reception in relation to religious institutions, this study begins to provide the tools with which to make more subtle arguments about the conditions of possibility for, as well as the meanings attributed to, these forms of textual practice. My study allows scholars of the Theravāda to reconsider the relevance of textual production, transmission, and reception in a particular cultural setting. It also alerts scholars of many textual communities linked to and shaped by religious institutions that the interpretive models drawn from European Christendom are part of the beginning, but not the end, of an analytical journey. In putting the matter thus, the study is quintessentially anti-Orientalist. Rather than arguing that eighteenth-century Lanka is to be understood in terms of "medieval" Europe because Asia languishes behind the West in a humid stupor and because "real" history is made up of structures and events that follow a particular trajectory discernible in Europe, this study argues for and exemplifies forms of analysis that assume the usefulness of a dialogical, rather than monological, analysis of cultural contexts in terms of one another.

THE STUDY

The remainder of this study develops over six chapters. In chapter 2, "Contextualizing Monasticism," I offer a brief sketch of eighteenth-century Lankan religious and political organization as a backdrop to subsequent discussions of monasticism, education, and textual practice. This chapter indicates the key players in Lankan religious and political life—Dutch colonials, Kandyan kings, Lankan aristocrats, Southeast Asian polities, brahmins, monks, and Muslim teachers. Chapter 3, "Marks of Distinction," contains an overview of the Siyam Nikāya's formative period with special attention to three stages in the development of the new order's educational institutions. Providing the first de-

[36] But compare the views of Carruthers and d'Avray with Clanchy's comments on the variable levels and meanings of literacy (1983).

tailed discussion of pre-nineteenth-century Buddhist education in South and Southeast Asia, I describe the creation of a widespread monastic educational system. In doing so, I discuss the possibilities for the standardized transmission of religious learning in a pre-print era, and emphasize the centrality of education to the collective identity of the Siyam Nikāya.

Chapter 4, "'They Were Scholars and Contemplatives,'" elaborates the claim that scholarly acceptance of the "traditional" commonplace stems in part from a misreading of indigenous Buddhist histories. By looking closely at the way five eighteenth-century Buddhist histories develop a long-standing trope of decline-and-revival I am able to identify the emergence of an innovative discourse on monasticism in Lanka. This discourse was first articulated at the same time as the Siyam Nikāya began to command authority, and was sustained in large part by written representations made by authors connected to the Siyam Nikāya. In that chapter I argue that the impact of the new discourse on monasticism was considerable.

With chapters 5 and 6 I argue for the rise of a new Buddhist textual community in more detail by looking at the place of a single commentarial genre in the life of the early Siyam Nikāya. I argue that *sūtra sannaya* commentaries had a substantial impact on Lankan Buddhism. Chapter 5, "'He Benefited the World and the *Sāsana*,'" shows this with respect to the second stage of the Siyam Nikāya's formation. I discuss the rising popularity of the *sūtra sannaya* genre, showing that it became a prestigious one for Siyam Nikāya monks, and develop a close reading of the first *sūtra sannaya* composed during the eighteenth century—*Sārārthadīpanī* (Illuminator of Excellent Meaning). I explain that the composition of this text by the Siyam Nikāya's founder distinguished this monk as learned and worthy of respect. Here my analysis explores the links between language and prestige, explaining that favorable "linguistic pedigrees" were created when the Siyam Nikāya's founder composed *Sārārthadīpanī.* Turning to an analysis of the rhetorical possibilities of bilingual commentary, I make yet another argument for the effect of the *sūtra sannaya*s during the second stage of the Siyam Nikāya's development. There I explain that *Sārārthadīpanī* provided a point of disciplinary orientation for the first monks connected to the Siyam Nikāya, and that it also served as a subtle criticism of the Siyam Nikāya's monastic competitors.

Chapter 6, "Readers, Preachers, and Listeners," continues to elaborate evidence for the rise of a new Buddhist textual community in eighteenth-century Lanka. Looking this time at the third stage of the Siyam Nikāya's formation, I examine two related processes of reception by developing a close reading of *Sārārthadīpanī* from the perspective of monastic readers and by exploring more and less constrained instances of monastic reading. Finally, I argue for the impact of the *sūtra sannaya* commentaries well beyond a narrow circle of literate monastics by showing that the images and arguments contained in these commentaries entered the life of a larger Buddhist community that responded to *sūtra sannaya*-based preaching.

A brief concluding chapter, "'Let Us Serve Wisdom,'" argues for the impact of the Siyam Nikāya, its educational system, and the eighteenth-century popularity of the *sūtra sannaya*s well into the nineteenth and early twentieth centuries. Criticizing discussions of "Protestant Buddhism" for too great a preoccupation with the Euro-American impact on Lankan Buddhism, I show that the roots of Protestant Buddhism's "fundamentalism" lie in the eighteenth-century activities of the Siyam Nikāya. As this discussion unfolds, I explain that early Orientalist understandings of Buddhist textual authority were made possible by the educational developments that took place in the early Siyam Nikāya.

CHAPTER TWO

Contextualizing Monasticism

THE TRANSFORMATION of Lankan Buddhism that occurred during the latter two-thirds of the eighteenth century took place as a result of three intersecting changes in the Lankan context: a change in the social organization of monasticism, alterations in monastic intellectual practice, and the use of a new textual form in monastic education. My argument for this transformation or "reformulation," as I sometimes call it, and the related claim that the idea of textual communities provides a subtle and powerful tool with which to reveal the dynamism of Buddhist cultures, cannot be understood properly without at least a glimpse of the larger social context in which the emerging Siyam Nikāya participated. New developments in Buddhist learning and the formation of a new monastic order were made possible not only by particular aspects of this larger social context; external events also shaped it in important ways.

A VERY BRIEF HISTORY OF BUDDHISM IN LANKA

The exact dates of the "historical" Buddha's life remain contested, but there are good reasons to think that the Enlightenment of Sakyamuni Buddha can be dated to the period between 550 and 450 B.C.E.[1] The monastic community (Pāli *saṃgha*), including male and female renouncers, was formed during his lifetime. A substantial number of lay men and women showed their interest in and respect for the Buddha's teachings by offering material support to the *saṃgha*. In all likelihood, many of these lay people did not identify themselves solely with the Buddhist community but, instead, supported a range of religious figures, including the brahmins (who were the ritual specialists in the tradition now known as Hinduism) and renouncers of various sorts called *samaṇas*, who included followers of the Buddha and of his contemporary, the Jain leader Mahāvīra.[2]

[1] See Bechert (1991). Following Buddhist views on the nature of Buddhahood one would speak of Sakyamuni Buddha as "the buddha of our era," since he is preceded and followed by other buddhas who achieve enlightenment alone before founding a community of followers.

[2] See further Carrithers (1983a), Gombrich (1988), and Gomez (1989).

In the years following the Buddha's death, members of the monastic community struggled with problems of community regulation and the interpretation of oral teachings given by the Buddha during his life. These struggles, and the "councils" or communal recitation sessions held in the attempt to resolve them, eventually yielded a range of Buddhist schools distinguished by different understandings of what constituted authoritative teachings, of the proper approach to their interpretation, and of the degree of interpretive authority allowed to other monastic teachers in the Buddha's absence. The formation of multiple schools was also encouraged by the emergence of regional differences within the larger Buddhist community. Simultaneously, a rich array of devotional rituals developed as tools for the liberating recollection of the Buddha and his teachings, and as strategies for the attainment of superhuman powers aimed to offset the immediate problems of human life.[3]

From some of these schools developed the Theravādin tradition of Buddhism, identified by its acceptance of a particular form of the Buddhist monastic code and its self-representation as part of the Vibhajjavādin school. Scholars differ on when the Theravāda tradition was established as a clearly separate tradition. Most scholars ascribe the origin of the Theravāda (Sanskrit *Sthaviravāda*) to the second century after the Buddha's death, though most Theravādins have attributed their "canon" to the first communal recitation of Buddhist teachings held after the Buddha's death.[4] Jonathan Walters has recently argued on the basis of literary and inscriptional evidence, however, that it is impossible to identify the clear presence of the Theravāda before the second century C.E. and that the Theravāda was not defined as a non-Mahāyāna Buddhist tradition before the tenth century C.E. (Walters 1997, 119). In any event the arrival of the first Buddhist devotees in Lanka is typically dated to the third century B.C.E.. Histories of the Buddhist community in Lanka from that time onward are often organized around shifts between civilizational centers on the island. The result of this is that kings, monks, and religious texts are identified by their place in the following scheme: the Anurādhapura period (543 B.C.E.-1000 C.E.), the Poḷonnaruva period (1058–1234), the Daṁbadeṇi period (1220–1293), the Kuruṇägala period (1293–1347), the Gampola period (1347–1412), the Kōṭṭe period (1412–1580), the Sītāvaka period (1530–1592), the Senkaḍagala (or early Kandyan) period (1480–1706), and the Mahanuvara or Kandyan period (1706–1815).[5] In sources written

[3] See further Gombrich (1988), Gomez (1989), and Reynolds and Hallisey (1989).

[4] On defining Theravāda, see, for instance, Gombrich (1988, 110–12).

[5] These dates follow Sannasgala (1964).

in English and European languages (and even in Sinhala, the language used by some contemporary Sri Lankan scholars writing on Buddhism) there are few detailed accounts of devotional trends, shifts in the political patronage of Buddhist institutions, monastic organization, or literary production during these periods.[6] One major disadvantage of this dating scheme is its inattention to local communities in the island's north, west, and east. These were often of considerable cultural, economic, political, and military importance (de Silva 1992). From the thirteenth century until the early seventeenth century, for instance, the Jaffna Kingdom remained independent from other Lankan political centers and from polities based on the Indian subcontinent. After the fall of the Jaffna Kingdom to the Portuguese, a portion of nonpeninsular north and north-central Lanka called the Vanniar became increasingly autonomous and influential (Arasaratnam 1996, esp. chapter 9). Despite the use of royal capitals and civilizational centers to orient chronology, one should not assume the existence of stable and thorough central control throughout the island. The situation on the ground is better described as a galactic polity (Tambiah 1976, 70) in which centers and peripheral powers continually redefined their relations with each other.

It is generally accepted that the authoritative texts of the Theravāda, the Pāli *tipiṭaka* ("three baskets"), was codified in the fifth century C.E. by monks connected with a monastic group called the Mahāvihāra. A Pāli commentarial tradition developed at roughly the same time, just after the composition of a normative compendium of Buddhist teachings called the *Visuddhimagga,* which has served as a crucial point of reference for Buddhist scholars throughout subsequent centuries (Collins 1990; Gombrich 1988, 153–154).[7] The royal capital at Anurādhapura became a trading entrepôt and an important center for Buddhist learning inhabited by Buddhists from several parts of the Indian subcontinent and Southeast Asia, who espoused a wide range of views on Buddhist teachings and devotional practice. At the same time, monastic communities (and especially those close to the royal capital) gained power and land. Early monastic communities contained male and female monastics, but formally institutionalized female monasticism diminished after the tenth century. This suggests that Buddhist nuns never attained the levels of landed autonomy characteristic of male monasticism (Gunawardana 1979, 37–39; 1988, 37–39).

The threat of invasions from the southern part of the Indian subcontinent and the wish to control the southern region of Lanka better are

[6] The best in Sinhala is Sannasgala (1964). In English see inter alia Dewaraja (1988), Gombrich (1988), Gunawardana (1979), Hallisey (1988), Mahinda (1995), Malalgoda (1976), Mirando (1985), and Walters (1997, 1998, 1999).

[7] The *tipiṭaka* contains three sections: the *Suttas*, the *Vinaya*, and the *Abhidhamma*.

probable causes for the decline of Anurādhapura and the rise of Poḷonnaruva as a royal capital and civilizational center some sixty miles to the southeast (see map in figure 2.1). By the twelfth century, it appears that a homogenization of authoritative teachings and devotional practices took place (at least in elite circles close to the royal court) that favored non-Mahāyāna Buddhist teachings and Mahāvihārin monks (Gunawardana 1979, 313–337; Walters 1997). A learned literate culture flourished in elite monastic and court circles (Gunawardana 1979, esp. 137–169). In the thirteenth century, the impact on the island of political and military force initiated in the southern part of the Indian subcontinent led to the shift of the royal capital to Daṁbadeṇi approximately ninety miles to the southwest. The royal capital was moved several more times thereafter through the southwestern and central highland regions of the island. Such movements were responses to multiple causes, including changing constraints on trade and competition between regional political leaders.[8]

We know remarkably little about the nature of religious institutions and practices from the Daṁbadeṇi period until the Mahanuvara period. However, good arguments have been made for the rise of newly intense and personal forms of devotion between the ninth and twelfth centuries (Hallisey 1988, esp. chapters 2–3). Such devotion focused on the figure of the Buddha and was perhaps influenced in part by the emerging popularity of Śaiva *bhakti* (devotionalism focused on the god Śiva) among non-Buddhist communities in Lanka and southern India. There are also indications that the twelfth and thirteenth centuries marked the beginning of a growing preoccupation with preaching and writing in Sinhala rather than in Pāli, the language of the *tipiṭaka* and the fifth-century commentaries (Godakumbura 1955, 56–66, 73–76, 81–97; Mahinda 1995, chapter 5). This can be considered part of a movement throughout the Buddhist world to develop locally focused Buddhist communities, in part because of changes in regional military and trading organization that made a translocal Buddhist world much less secure (Reynolds and Hallisey 1989, 15–22).

The beginnings of European colonial presence on the island can be dated to the early sixteenth century with the arrival of the Portuguese who worked from their base on the southwestern coast of the Indian subcontinent. Although the direct impact of the Portuguese was felt primarily in the coastal regions in the north, south, and southwest, Buddhist communities further inland were also affected because of alterations in trading patterns that affected the availability of food, the need

[8] See Sannasgala 1964, 119–122, 188–189, 215–218, 237–243, 290–294, 309–314, 383–383; de Silva 1992, 89–144.

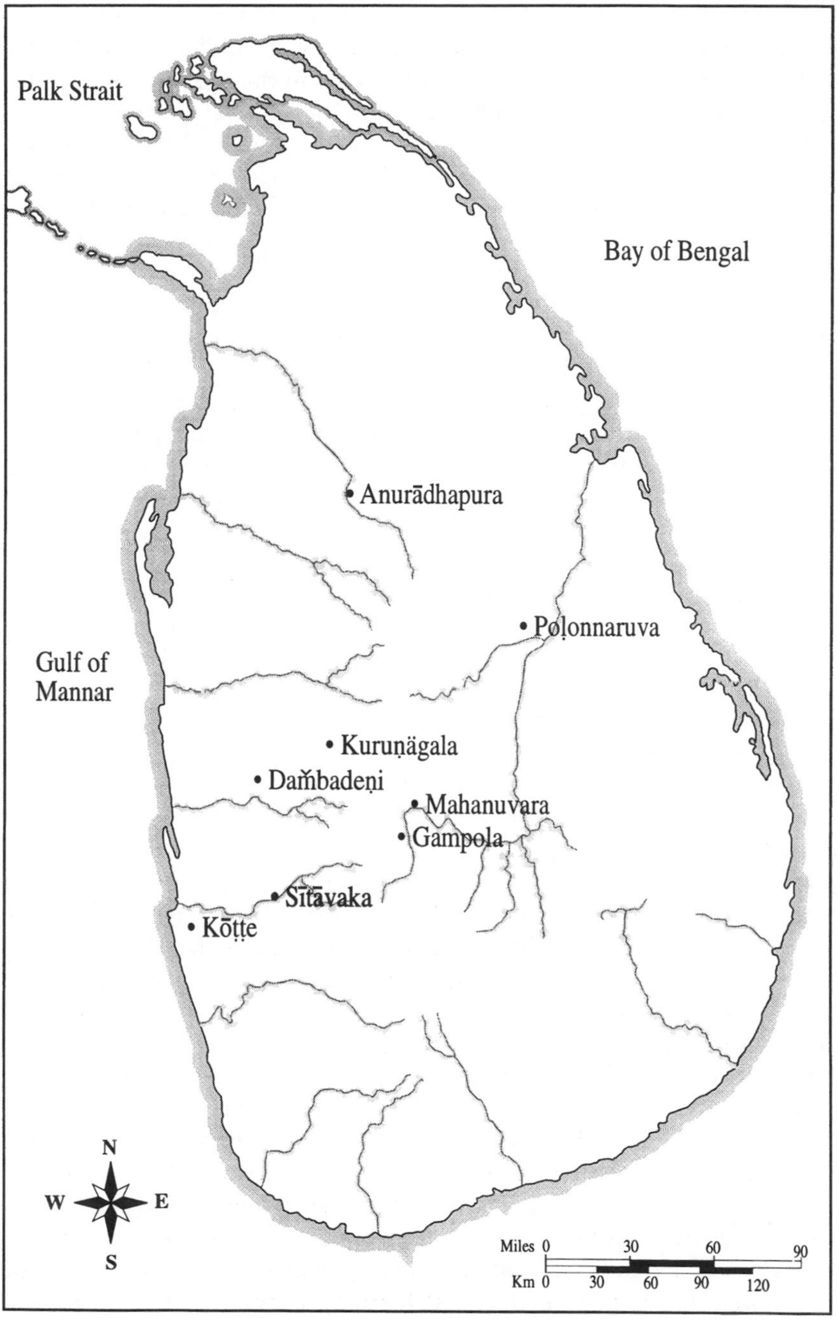

Figure 1. Map of Civilizational Centers

to reduce the Portuguese threat in part by negotiating with other colonial powers, and the arrival of lay and monastic Buddhists who fled the coastal areas. Some sectors of the population in the southern and southwestern maritime areas converted to Catholicism, and shifting alliances between local Buddhist and Christian communities and the Portuguese enhanced political instability from the end of the Kōṭṭe period into the Kandyan period. The simultaneous development of competing ruling centers in Kōṭṭe, Sītāvaka, and Senkaḍagala is one sign of this instability (de Silva 1992, 107–144). In the early years of the Kōṭṭe period, however, large and powerful Buddhist monastic institutions formed once again on the island. Centers of monastic higher education with ties to political elites provided environments conducive to an efflorescence of literature and debates about monastic life and Buddhist devotion. There is evidence of a growing cultural influence from the southern region of the Indian subcontinent that affected Lankan religious practice. An increasing interest in Sanskritic aesthetic forms for the articulation of Buddhist devotionalism is also visible (de Silva 1992, 102–106; Sannasgala 1964, 246–248).

With the rise of Dutch power in the region and greater stability in Senkaḍagala in the middle years of the seventeenth century, the Portuguese began to lose their position of dominance. The elimination of the last Portuguese base on the island took place in 1663. The Portuguese were rapidly replaced by the administrators of the V.O.C. Although the direct control of the Dutch on the island was once again largely limited to the coastal regions (including what was previously the Jaffna Kingdom) and another area just slightly inland from the southern coast, in which cinnamon harvesting took place, the effects of the Dutch presence were felt much more widely. Dutch officials embarked on a long process of intimidation and negotiation aimed at reducing the power of the central highland Kandyan Kingdom that had emerged from the chaos of the Kōṭṭe and Sītāvaka periods as the sole serious contender to Dutch authority. Kandyan rulers continued to demand control of areas seized from the Portuguese and the Dutch officials continued to contest these claims (Arasaratnam 1996, esp. chapters 2–3; Dewaraja 1988, esp. chapter 8). The period on which this study focuses, the latter two-thirds of the eighteenth century, was characterized by the continued oscillation between negotiation and military threat.

Although the focus of my attention in the following chapters is monastic education and Buddhist textual practices, it is important not to lose sight of the political and economic processes that helped to shape the form and meaning of Buddhist learning during the period. For instance, the fact that the Siyam Nikāya's higher ordination was initiated by monks from what is now Thailand (then the Siamese kingdom of

Ayutthaya) rather than by those from what is now Burma, had much to do with relations between Kandyan rulers and V.O.C. officials, and with specific Dutch concerns about trade with the kingdom of Ayutthaya. Or, to take another example, the importance of monastic learning to a hierarchy of prestige in the Kandyan Kingdom makes little sense until one realizes the degree of monastic competitiveness characteristic of the time (and not just *that* time).

KANDYAN-V.O.C. RELATIONS

The primary goals of the V.O.C. in relation to Lanka were to extract as many valuable resources as possible from the island (with a special interest in cinnamon, areca nuts, and elephants) and to interrupt other trading patterns in which the island's residents participated.[9] This was part of an attempt to create a trade monopoly and to orchestrate trading prices throughout the entire market in which the company played a dominant role. Such goals were often quite antithetical to those of the Kandyan Kingdom's rulers and traders, who sought to maximize low-cost, high-profit trade with South, Southeast, and East Asia. Such trade was sought not only to raise revenues for the kingdom and its traders but in order to assure that the population of the inland kingdom had access to key commodities such as salt and cloth. From the 1660s until the 1690s, the V.O.C. attempted to gain control of all the island's ports and eventually declared a company monopoly on key export articles and all major imports except rice. Because this tactic backfired by diminishing local traders' interest in supplying export commodities, and because of the damage done to V.O.C. interests by local smuggling, the company liberalized trade somewhat in 1694. However, it continued attempts to interrupt trade between Lanka and the southern part of the Indian subcontinent, which they saw as a major threat to regional trade prices.

In the period with which I am concerned, after about 1730, the Kandyan Kingdom was for a time assured of its most important commodities and of some trade revenues, although these were lower than in the period prior to company control of the ports. This situation continued until the 1750s and made it possible for the kingdom to send political and religious embassies to the southern part of the Indian subcontinent and to parts of Southeast Asia. The V.O.C.'s willingness to put its ships at the service of the kingdom's rulers was due in part to the view (often

[9] This section draws primarily on Arasaratnam (1996), de Silva (1992, 129–144), Goonewardena (1980), and Malalgoda (1976, 28–49).

substantiated by subsequent events) that this predisposed the kingdom to negotiate with the company more favorably. At times, as in the case of embassies to Ayutthaya in search of Buddhist monks prepared to bring higher ordination to Lanka, these embassies were orchestrated to serve company interests in the region.

In the latter part of the 1750s, however, anti-V.O.C. sentiment began to grow in the southern region of the island and, when the kingdom provided support to some of these resistant groups, tensions grew between the company and the kingdom, leading to the invasion of Kandy in 1765.[10] Although this expedition was unsuccessful, a subsequent one was not, and resulted in a 1766 treaty between the V.O.C. and the Kandyan Kingdom. The terms of this treaty were far from advantageous to the Kandyans, since the treaty acknowledged Dutch sovereignty throughout the maritime regions of the island. Because of this, all licit foreign trade passed through Dutch control, and access to other foreign powers was severely limited. Despite disputes between the kingdom and the company, the V.O.C. refused to negotiate. Although the Dutch officially controlled the island's maritime regions, however, many residents of the southern and southwestern areas continued to identify more with the Kandyan Kingdom than with the Dutch colonial regime. This manifested itself in several ways: continued Kandyan influence over the flow of southern products to the Dutch for export; the temporary and permanent movement of local maritime residents to the kingdom; the kingdom's frequent willingness to serve as a safe haven for Catholic priests working in the maritimes; and the willingness of many maritime inhabitants to accept the rule of the Kandyan kings in matters concerning the administration and occupation of Buddhist temples. Malalgoda notes that effective Portuguese and Dutch power rarely extended beyond twenty miles inland (1976, 29) and notes that ties between the maritimes and the Kandyan Kingdom were partly due to the fact that some maritime leaders from the highest (*goyigama* or *govikula*) caste were connected by kinship ties to the kingdom (47).

REGIONAL NETWORKS

Despite the unavoidable presence of the V.O.C., it would be a mistake to think of Lanka as defined primarily by that relationship.[11] During the latter two-thirds of the eighteenth century, the island was still enmeshed in a variety of ties with other parts of South Asia and with Southeast

[10] This date is Arasaratnam's; de Silva uses 1764.

[11] In this section I draw primarily on Arasaratnam (1996), Godakumbura (1966), Goonewardena (1980), Reid (1993a, Chap. 1) and Wickremasinghe (1960).

Asia. These ties often affected the unfolding of political and religious events. Despite Dutch attempts to control trade between Lankan inhabitants and merchants from the ports in the south of the Indian subcontinent, the combined effects of smuggling and corruption assured that such ties continued. Much of the transport and internal trade of goods from these ports were undertaken by Hindu and Muslim merchants, working from ports in the north, northwest, and east of the island. Trade from Bengal and the northwest coast of the Indian subcontinent was encouraged rather than impeded by the Dutch. It is not clear to what extent independent Lankan trade developed with merchants from those regions.

After an absence of ties between Siam and Lanka from the sixteenth until the middle of the eighteenth century, connections began again through the Dutch, to whom Ayutthaya had opened its ports in the seventeenth century. As Goonewardena notes, a "triangular relationship arose between Ayutthia, the Dutch and the Sinhalese in the last two decades of king Boromakot's reign" (1980, 2).[12] However, the intensity of contact between Ayutthaya and Lanka varied with relations between Ayutthaya and the V.O.C. After a period of diminished V.O.C. interest in the 1740s, the company attempted to court Ayutthaya again in the 1750s. This contributed to the successful arrival of monks from Siam to initiate higher ordination for the Siyam Nikāya. Since Lankan embassies to Ayutthaya included a stopover in the Dutch administrative center of Batavia (now Jakarta), it is reasonable to assume that there were some contacts between Lankan officials and inhabitants of Dutch-held Southeast Asia, but their nature remains unclear. After the Burmese conquest of Ayutthaya in 1766, there were no formal political contacts between Lanka and Siam for the remainder of the eighteenth century.

Because of prior contacts between Lanka and various Southeast Asian kingdoms, it is not surprising that the Kandyan court communicated with Pegu (north-central Burma) and Arakan (western coastal Burma) between 1739 and 1749. This occurred in the attempt to have monks brought to Lanka who could confer higher ordination, since the quorum of monks with higher ordination (Pāli *upasampadā*) required to conduct the higher ordination ritual no longer existed in Lanka. These requests were unsuccessful for several reasons. Ties between the Kandyan Kingdom and the various Burmese polities were apparently quite weak. At the time these requests for visiting monks were initiated, the Kandyan king had to ask the Dutch about the conditions of Buddhism in Arakan and Pegu. One embassy to Pegu was thwarted by a shipwreck.

[12] Boromkot is also known as King Mahā Dhammarāja II, r. 1733–1758.

ADMINISTRATION OF THE KANDYAN KINGDOM

The administration of the Kandyan Kingdom was formally organized under centralized royal authority.[13] In fact, power relations between the royal court and its administrative appointees were quite unstable. This instability created considerable room for elite monastics to involve themselves in local politics. The formative period of the Siyam Nikāya overlapped with the reign of three kings: Śrī Vīraparākrama Narēndrasiṃha (r. 1706–1739), Śrī Vijayarājasiṃha (r. 1739–1747), and Kīrti Śrī Rājasiṃha (r. 1747–1780). The reign of Śrī Vijayarājasiṃha is said to mark the start of the Nāyakkar dynasty in Lanka; this continued until the Kandyan Kingdom lost its independence to the English in 1815. Śrī Vijayarājasiṃha was the brother of Narēndrasiṃha's wife. Their family was associated with a group of regional military leaders and administrators called Nāyaks, who served the Vijayanagar Empire in the south of the Indian subcontinent from the fourteenth century onward. Some historians of Lanka have emphasized the "outsider" nature of the Nāyakkar rule, and resulting tensions between members of the royal family and the Kandyan aristocracy. According to K.N.O. Dharmadasa, for instance, a rebellion against Kīrti Śrī Rājasiṃha in 1760 "was planned by a section of the elite who had come to resent the fact that an ethnically and culturally alien dynasty had entrenched itself" in the center of local political autonomy (1976, 17).[14]

The problems besetting this sort of analysis are many and, as Dharmadasa's subsequent caveat indicates, it may be "that as far as some sections of the Kandyan populace were concerned the Nāyakkar presence on the throne had become an accepted fact. The ardent espousal of the Buddhist cause by the Nāyakkar kings and the skillful integration of the Nāyakkar personality with the Sinhalese traditions, especially under Kīrti Śrī and Rājādhi [Kīrti Śrī's successor], might have made them acceptable as any ruler of Sinhalese ethnicity could be" (21). As H.L. Seneviratne has noted,

> The view that Nayakkar kings were "aliens" ignores important facts: (1) All Nayakkars subsequently to become kings of Kandy grew up in Kandy; (2) cultural and revivalist enthusiasm on the part of the kings and in society was under way well before the advent of the Nayakkars in 1739; (3) the Tamil language and other "alien" cultural forms were prestigious, and socially and culturally mobile sections of the people were anxious to copy

[13] This section is based primarily on Dewaraja (1988, chap. 10–11), Dharmadasa (1976), and Seneviratne (1976).

[14] See also Dewaraja (1988, 26).

> them. . . . Indeed on close observation the accession of Nayakkars does not appear to be the shocking violation of tradition, calling for immediate reconciliation between king and subject by resort to revivalist means.[15]

Moreover, "The elevation of the queen's brother to the throne as Śrī Vijaya Rajasingha was the logical outcome of a pragmatically dictated set of practices, that had grown in the Kandyan court for over one and a half centuries" (58).

At all events, the kingdom was administered in a manner that gave royal and aristocratic interests considerable scope for expansion and collision. Below the king the greatest administrative authority was held in the hands of two men known as *adigār*s, each with responsibility to oversee one-half of the kingdom's territory. These *adigār*s were appointed by the king, who typically tried to minimize dangerous collusion between the *adigār*s by making appointments from two aristocratic families who were not close allies. Below the *adigār*s was a network of "chiefs" (de Silva 1992, 133) who commanded significant hereditary and nonhereditary lands that added to their income, status, and level of influence. The least powerful of these, according to Dewaraja, were the *raṭērāla*s, administrators in charge of the nine districts closest to the royal capital in the city of Kandy (or Mahānuvara, the Great City).[16] It was the duty of the *raṭērāla*s to collect a grain tax owed to the king. Because they administered lands relatively close to the capital city, they were under close scrutiny and acted with less autonomy than chiefs of more distant lands. Administrative units in the outlying areas were led by a *disāva*, and their numbers varied according to the strength of the kingdom in relation to the V.O.C.[17] *Disāva*s were expected to collect revenues from the district for use by the king, oversee certain sorts of labor claimed by the royal court, administer justice in the district, and carry out other orders communicated by the *adigār*s. Because of their greater distance from the kingdom's center, *disāva*s were able to exercise considerable autonomy. At times they were called upon to serve the king in negotiations with foreign powers; sometimes they used these opportunities to their own benefit. Beneath the *raṭērāla*s and the *disāva*s stood a further chain of local administrators.

[15] Seneviratne's analysis is supported by Gunawardana (1993), whose analysis of eighteenth- and nineteenth-century texts concludes that Nāyakkars were considered to be Sinhala (that is, locals rather than outsiders).

[16] These were: Uḍunuvara, Yaṭinuwara, Tumpanē, Hārispattuva, Hevāhäṭa, Dumbara, Kotmale, Uḍa Bulatgama, and Pāta Bulatgama.

[17] In 1815 these numbered twelve, including: Satara Kōralēs, Sat Kōralēs, Ūva, Mātale, Sabaragamuva, Tis Kōralēs, Valapane, Uḍapalāta, Nuvarakalāviya, Vellassa, Bintänna, and Tamankaḍuva. It appears that, at least as early as the reign of Kīrti Śrī Rājasiṃha, six additional districts were included, all bordering on sea coasts important for trade.

It is difficult to evaluate the relative strength of the royal family and the aristocracy led by the administrators just described. Dewaraja's classic analysis of Kandyan politics during the eighteenth century betrays this difficulty when she writes that "the court officials and provincial governors had a free hand in the administration and also in deciding issues both domestic and foreign" before continuing to say that "the Nāyakkar kings as we shall see maintained their position by perpetuating existing cleavages and factions among the nobles" (Dewaraja 1988, 91–92). It is most likely that the aristocratic families worked primarily within the constraints of the royal system to further their own ends (and perhaps also out of certain feelings of duty or loyalty), but that occasionally family groups united to oppose what was perceived as a particularly strong threat.

The best-known instance of such unified resistance is "the plot of 1760," which occurred during the reign of Kīrti Śrī Rājasiṃha and shortly after the formal beginnings of the Siyam Nikāya in 1753. One group within the local aristocracy conspired to overthrow the king and to place a Siamese prince on the throne. The leaders are said to have included not only key lay administrators (including one of the *adigār*s, Samanakkoḍi, plus Leuke, his relative) but also some of the leading Siyam Nikāya monks. Välivița Saraṇaṃkara, founder of the Siyam Nikāya, and his chief student, Tibboṭuvāvē Buddharakkhita, were named among the conspirators. The plot was discovered, the Siamese prince deported (with the reluctant assistance of the Dutch), and the lay administrators executed. After spending a period at some distance (according to some, in formal exile) from the court, Saraṇaṃkara and Buddharakkhita were pardoned and reinstated as, respectively, Leader of the Monastic Community and Chief Monk of the Malvatu Temple (an important monastic center).[18] Dewaraja writes: "There is no evidence to say when, exactly, the traitors were pardoned, but certainly by 1768 Saraṇaṃkara was functioning as Saṅgharāja once again, and later in his reign the king invited Tibboṭūvāvē to bring the Cūlavaṃsa [a royal-monastic history] up to date. Whether this was due to the king's realization of his weakness or to his natural clemency it is difficult to decide" (1988, 126).

Although the plot of 1760 is sometimes depicted, following a nineteenth-century account, as an attempt by local Buddhists to oust an unwanted non-Buddhist ruler, most historians now agree that this interpretation is incorrect. According to Dewaraja, "it is clear that this was no organized attempt by the Buddhists of the Kandyan kingdom to overthrow the Nāyakkar domination. Only a few chiefs of consequence joined in it. The reason for this treachery seems to be a personal one

[18] In addition to Dewaraja's work, see Kotelawele (1977) and Suraweera (1968).

[related to the waning court influence of the *adigār* involved] . . . the bhikkhus of the Malvatte [= Malvatu] vihāra were in no way united against the king. One of the king's informants who revealed the plot was [another Siyam Nikāya monk] Hulaṃgamuve" (122–123).

Seneviratne has suggested that resentments against the royal family were sometimes the result of perceived threats to the economic security of the local aristocracy (1976, 60). This makes sense in view of the fact that, because of their ongoing contacts with the southern part of the Indian subcontinent, members of the Nāyakkar family were well placed to participate in, or at least to influence, regional trade (sometimes licit, and sometimes illicit). With regard to the events of 1760 in particular, John Holt concludes that "[t]he attempt to assassinate [the king] was based primarily on economic motives and rationalized by appealing to sentiments generated by considerations of the king's alleged religious otherness" (1996, 29). Dewaraja's analysis of monastic participation in terms of connections between Saraṇaṃkara, Buddharakkhita, and the lay administrators also appears reasonable, since Buddharakkhita was a cousin of the *adigār* who apparently played a central role in organizing against the king (1988, 123). The fact that Saraṇaṃkara was formerly a student of Leuke, the *adigār*'s kinsman, may also have played a role.[19] If accounts of Siyam Nikāya participation in the plot are correct, which seems quite likely, the event is a useful reminder of two things: the fissiparousness of elite politics in the Kandyan Kingdom, and the lack of distance between leading monks of the early Siyam Nikāya and the kingdom's political heavyweights.[20] This should come as no surprise: even prior to the Siyam Nikāya leading monks belonged to aristocratic families and thus, of course, to the same caste.[21]

THE ORGANIZATION OF MONASTICISM

In the course of Lankan history, the monastic community was organized according to several structures characterized by strikingly different de-

[19] It should be noted that the *adigār* Samanakkoḍi, Saraṇaṃkara, and Leuke were linked during another contentious political moment: the tribunal held in 1745 that led to the ouster of Catholic priests from the Kandyan Kingdom (Dewaraja 1988, 102–103). See below. Leuke had also offered initial support to Śrī Vijayarājasiṃha's opponent at the time that Narēndrasiṃha's succession was negotiated (Ibid., 85).

[20] Dewaraja notes, for instance, that "[e]ven before the establishment of the Nāyakkar dynasty, the nobles appeared as a threat to the security of the throne. Another potential source of trouble was the sangha or the Order of monks, the upper ranks of which had strong ties of blood with the nobility. The monks had free access to the king and were influential in society at all levels" (1988, 72).

[21] Caste determined labor and marriage practices, as well as land ownership and participation in the administrative elite. See, for instance, Dewaraja (1988, chap. 3).

grees of centralized authority.[22] Throughout much of the Anurādhapura period, for instance, the monastic community was divided into three *nikāya*s. Meaning "group" or "collection," the term *nikāya* is used to classify certain groups of texts considered authoritative by the Theravāda. With respect to monastic organization, however, a *nikāya* is a group of monks who accept the validity of their higher ordination and who therefore perform certain monastic rituals together (Bechert 1977, 362). In the Anurādhapura period, *nikāya*s were composed of a number of monasteries, all of which "accepted the leadership and, in certain instances, the supervisory control of one of the main monasteries at the capital" (Gunawardana 1979, 8). These main monasteries were the Mahāvihāra vihāra, the Abhayagiri vihāra, and the Jetavana vihāra; at times there appear to have been intense rivalries among them. Such rivalries were often presented in terms of adherence to or departure from "orthodoxy," but it is likely that attempts to command property and patronage were most often the primary factor.

There is evidence that, at least within the Abhayagiri and Jetavana Nikāyas, the monastic community was further subdivided into units called *mūla*s (sometimes also called *āyatana*s). A *mūla* was a fraternity of monks led by a *mahāthera*, or senior monk, and was sometimes affiliated with a particular Buddhist temple. Such fraternities also owned property. Gradually, beginning perhaps in the seventh century, the *mūla*s came to dominate the actual administrative structures of the monastic community; this process was complete by the eleventh century. *Nikāya* identities continued to matter in certain formal ways, since *mūla* members often retained a sense of connection to a particular *nikāya*, and since royal injunctions sometimes described the monastic community in *nikāya* terms. However, for all practical purposes, the *mūla*s became the central organizational unit of the Lankan monastic community. There is evidence that certain *mūla*s remained active until the sixteenth century. However, from the later part of the Kōṭṭe Period until the formal beginning of the Siyam Nikāya, a period of approximately 250 years, there was no durable large-scale ecclesiastical structure. Buddhist temples remained, and monks often occupied them but, no centralized monastic community existed. At the same time, the numbers of fully ordained monks diminished, despite the fact that Burmese monks had conferred higher ordination on Lankan monks twice in the sixteenth and seventeenth centuries. There were several reasons for the shrinking number; the most important is political and economic instability that curtailed lay patronage of monastic institutions.

[22] This section draws primarily on Dewaraja (1988, chap. 9), Dharmadasa (1991), Gunawardana (1979, chaps. 1, 8–9) and Malalgoda (1976, 49–69).

By 1730, no fully ordained monks remained in Lanka. Those monks who remained in control of Buddhist temples and their properties were known as *gaṇinnānse*s. A *gaṇinnānse* (lit., "honorable member of a community") was a monk who had become a member of the *saṃgha* without going through the customary procedures for becoming a novice and for receiving higher ordination. Ordination as a novice monk (Pāli *pabbajā*) requires only the presence of one other fully ordained monk. However, higher ordination (Pāli *upasampadā*) must be conferred by at least five fully ordained monks, each of whom has been so for at least ten years. These procedures were impossible owing to the dearth, and subsequent absence, of the fully ordained monks required to officiate at ordinations. The result were the *gaṇinnānse*s, who "represented a new type of monk peculiar to the early Kandyan period, not known before that time or since in the history of Buddhism in Ceylon" (Malalgoda 1976, 54).[23]

The nature of eighteenth-century sources makes it difficult to reconstruct the lifestyle of the *gaṇinnānse*s. There are some indications that they held themselves separate from the larger lay community by observing (at least formally) the ten moral precepts appropriate to a novice monk or a particularly devout lay Buddhist. At the same time, they typically retained their family names rather than taking on a new one, as is customary at the time of Buddhist monastic ordination. In almost all cases they are likely to have participated in a system of monastic succession (Sinhala *ñāti śiṣya paramparā*) that privileged ties of kinship (which earlier was not unheard of but was less formally acknowledged). This helped to preserve close ties between the *gaṇinnānse*s and the aristocracy; most (and perhaps all) monastic incumbents of Buddhist temples were members of aristocratic families. In some cases, there is reason to believe that the relatives whose future they assured were their own children.

In addition to their place as caretakers for temples and temple lands, *gaṇinnānse*s sometimes played a role in the administration of the Kandyan Kingdom. This was the case with Kobbäkaḍuvē Gaṇe Baṇḍāra, for instance, who held a double appointment as *disāva*, in addition to controlling four shrines and one of the two most powerful Buddhist temples in the kingdom. There can be no doubt that, despite the absence of higher ordination and a formal ecclesiastical structure, Buddhist monks were an important force in the Kandyan Kingdom prior to the rise of the Siyam Nikāya. Monastic leaders belonged to local aristocratic families, had considerable access to wealth and property, and par-

[23] He adds that "[i]ndeed, most of the monks in the late sixteenth, seventeenth and early eighteenth centuries belonged to the category of gaṇinnānses" (57).

ticipated in court events and politics. It is therefore no surprise that the emergence of the Siyam Nikāya was often perceived as a serious threat to established monastic groups, a fact that the following two chapters discuss in more detail.

NON-BUDDHIST RELIGIOUS LEADERS

Such monks were not the only religious functionaries in the kingdom, nor in the island at large.[24] Lankan devotional culture was strikingly pluralistic, and this pluralism sometimes affected the activities of Buddhist monks. Brahmins served as ritual officiants at the Kandyan court, where the Nāyakkar kings participated in devotional and protective rituals characteristic of southern Asian Śaivism. Many more must have officiated at temples to the various deities important in the Hindu pantheon, among whom Śiva and his divine relatives had pride of place on the island. These temples were presumably most plentiful in the north and along the western and eastern coasts. Since Muslims played an important role in Lankan trade, in both the coastal and central regions, it is difficult to imagine the absence of preachers, teachers, and Sufi practitioners throughout the island. Goonewardena notes that, at least until the middle of the eighteenth century, "[i]n Kandy, the Muslims enjoyed complete religious freedom, with mosques and priests functioning in many parts of the kingdom including one Muslim priest supported out of the revenues of a Buddhist temple" (1986, 204).

According to Dewaraja, Muslims in the Kandyan region were incorporated into the kingdom's administrative structure and participated in land-based service obligations to Buddhist temples (Dewaraja 1994, Chaps. 3–4). Dutch policy toward the Muslim community was largely antagonistic (chiefly because Muslims were perceived as a threat to Dutch trading interests) but, given the flow of trade between Lanka and parts of the Indian subcontinent, one would assume a certain influx of Muslim teachers and Hindu ritual officiants from outside Lanka, adding to those locals already present on the island.[25]

We know more about the role of Christian priests and ministers, thanks to records kept by the Dutch and the Portuguese. The Portuguese gave special treatment to converted Catholic families with respect to inheritance and taxes. They also supported local-language reli-

[24] My account here draws primarily on Arasaratnam (1996, chaps. 16–19), de Silva (1992, chaps. 10–11), Dewaraja (1988, esp. chaps. 9, 12), Goonewardena (1986), and Kotelawele (1986).

[25] Dewaraja (1994, esp. Chap. 2) makes brief mention of nonlocal Muslim teachers who visited the island during earlier periods.

gious instruction (often by priests born in the Indian subcontinent). As a result, a substantial Catholic community grew up in Lanka during the period of Portuguese control. The activities of various Catholic missionary efforts are well documented, and it appears that the most effective were the Oratorians, who worked out of their center in Goa. The V.O.C. attempted to encourage conversion to their Dutch Reformed Protestant faith by forbidding Catholicism in their territories and by encouraging local participation in schools where Calvinist teachings were part of the curriculum. Although a number of conversions were documented, some company and church officials themselves sometimes noted that they had relatively little substantial impact on the local population.[26] This was presumably in part because Dutch missionaries lagged far behind the Portuguese in making church teachings available in local languages and pursued a policy of Dutch exclusivity in the organization of church leadership. During the period of Dutch control, officials made efforts to quash the continued work of Catholic missionaries on the island. As a result, a growing number of Catholic priests sought refuge in the Kandyan Kingdom, whence they made visits to coastal parishes.

It appears that, from the perspective of the Buddhist monastic community around the time of the Siyam Nikāya's rise, Catholic priests were the most worrying among the various groups of religious teachers and officiants at work in Lanka. For reasons that are still far from clear, the reign of Narēndrasiṃha was a period particularly favorable to Catholic priests in the Kandyan Kingdom. The king apparently paid honor to these visitors and sponsored debates, or perhaps "public discussions," between some of these priests, Calvinist members of the court (who included a French equerry), and Buddhist monks. The priests clearly intended to sustain this favorable position at the court during the reign of the subsequent king, Śrī Vijayarājasiṃha. They met with decreasing success, however, and in 1745 were called to a tribunal in which their presence in the kingdom was questioned. Little is known of the tribunal except that its participants on the Buddhist side included Samanakkoḍi and Leuke as well as the Siyam Nikāya's leader Saraṇaṃkara (all said to be participants in the 1760 plot). The result was the ouster of all Catholic priests from the kingdom, a situation that appears to have continued formally throughout the eighteenth century. That some members of the Catholic community were still considered a threat to at least a section of the Buddhist leadership seems clear from Buddhist sources recounting Catholic attempts to murder Saraṇaṃkara.

[26] See, for instance, the memoirs of the Dutch governors Gollennesse (Reimers 1935), Loten (Reimers 1947), and Schreuder (Reimers 1946).

Reasons for the shift in Catholic-Buddhist feeling are unclear, but it is likely that it had something to do with the composition (in Sinhala) of anti-Buddhist polemics. Catholic priests may have been seen as a threat to patronage of the monastic community, or as a challenge to the position of monastic leaders in and around the court. It may also be the case that some Dutch officials attempted to foment anti-Catholic feeling in order to maximize their advantage in religious and political matters.

CONCLUSION

Even this brief sketch draws attention to several points relevant to subsequent chapters. In the eighteenth century, monastic leaders maintained charged but powerful relations with the royal family and the local aristocracy. Dependent on both groups in certain ways, they retained enough leverage to influence the workings of a political economy strongly influenced by caste and kinship ties. Kings were powerful patrons, but their power was continually restricted from several sides—the V.O.C., local aristocrats, and the monastic community. Placed in an increasingly disadvantageous position vis-à-vis the Dutch, it is certain that participation in Buddhist institutions was an important part of retaining local and regional loyalties and thus leverage against Dutch officials. The king, however, was not the only one whose position was defined in part by competing interests. Buddhist monks sometimes felt themselves to be beleaguered, not as much by Dutchmen as by Catholics. In such a context, the rise of a new monastic community was necessarily an event with profound political implications as well as devotional ones. That the Siyam Nikāya came to command wealth, land, prestige, and elite loyalties attests to several aspects of the new order. Leaders of the emerging Siyam Nikāya were active and astute participants in complex political relations. They were also able to capture the imagination of many of those with whom they came into contact. Without this ability to identify themselves with ideas and symbols that resonated deeply for many within the Lankan Buddhist community, monks of the Siyam Nikāya—like their fellows who received Burmese ordination in the sixteenth and seventeenth centuries—would have faded quickly from view. As we shall see, the success of the Siyam Nikāya depended significantly on the new order's identification with Buddhist learning.

CHAPTER THREE

Marks of Distinction

BUDDHIST monks and their elite patrons were serious, and often self-conscious, participants in the reorganization of Lankan Buddhist monasticism that occurred through the formation of the Siyam Nikāya and the institutional structures and intellectual practices that sustained it. The monks' actions made possible a wider reformulation of Lankan Buddhism, discussed below in chapters 6 and 7.

For the first time in Lanka since the early sixteenth century, a widespread educational system backed by monastic and royal leaders trained Buddhist monks through a common curriculum. This curriculum instructed monks in canonical Buddhist texts and their Pāli-language commentaries as well as in popular Sinhala-language preaching works. It also prepared monks to compete for patronage through prestigious displays of erudition. This educational system was created at the same time as the Siyam Nikāya, and its reach and authority grew in tandem with the new monastic order's power and influence. From its inception, therefore, the life of the Siyam Nikāya was defined primarily in terms of its intellectual practices: Siyam Nikāya monks were educated monks but, more than that, they were monks educated through a centrally guided and standardized curriculum. The process by which the Siyam Nikāya's educational system was created sheds light on the possibilities for the widespread transmission of standardized religious learning in the era of pre-print textuality. In this case, the use of specific textual forms—including grammars and lexicons, monastic regulations, monastic handbooks, and commentaries—made it possible to implement a common curriculum across much of the island. This process of standardization and transmission also depended on a monastic bureaucracy. A system of monastic administration sustained access to the new curricular model and its texts, and encouraged conservatism in the implementation of this curriculum well beyond key monastic centers.

MONASTIC EDUCATIONAL INSTITUTIONS PRIOR TO 1730

There is evidence of large educational institutions (sometimes called *pirivenas* in Sinhala) as part of the major temple complexes constructed in the civilizational centers of the northern central area of the island during the Anurādhapura and Poḷonnaruva periods (Gunawardana 1979, esp. chaps. 2, 4). These educational centers received considerable royal patronage, and their monastic residents produced a rich array of literary, commentarial, and technical works on a variety of subjects in several languages. Of these languages, the most important were Sanskrit, Pāli, and Sinhala. Such centers were also important to religious and political communities outside the island, as we can tell from the records of East Asian pilgrims as well as monks and merchants from the Indian subcontinent and Southeast Asia.

The disintegration of Poḷonnaruva as a civilizational center led to the emergence of subsequent civilizational centers in the central and southwestern regions of Lanka. According to Sannasgala, whose familiarity with print and manuscript sources remains unmatched, *piriveṇa*s were established in Yāpahuva, Daṁbadeṇi, and Kuruṇägala during the Daṁbadeṇi period, and remained inhabited at least through the Kuruṇägala period (1964, 125–126; also Ray 1960, 748–749). With the solid institutional base created by these *piriveṇa*s, the thirteenth and fourteenth centuries were, in Sannasgala's words, a "bright period" for prose literature and commentary written in Pāli, Sanskrit, and Sinhala (126, 191).[1] Despite the movement slightly south and center into the low highlands of Gampola, there was a significant degree of continuity within the monastic community. The monastic lineages created in the Daṁbadeṇi and Kuruṇägala periods continued into the Gampola period. Sannasgala notes a substantial amount of literary production during these years, as well as the beginning of a rising interest in poetic forms to express Buddhist and non-Buddhist subjects (215–219).[2] The Kōṭṭe period saw the creation of new and well-endowed educational centers (such as those led by the monks Toṭagamuva Śrī Rāhula and Vīdāgama Maitreya (Godakumbura 1955, 191–200; Sannasgala 1964, 244–245; Ray 1960, 776) along with substantial innovations in literary production.[3] Monastic institutions received great support during the reign of Parākramabāhu VI (1412–1467), in particular. With the arrival

[1] Well-known works composed during this period include *Dhammapada Sannaya, Butsaraṇa, Saṅghasaraṇa, Saddharmaratnāvaliya, Pūjāvāliya, Kavsilūmiṇa, Visuddhimārga Mahāsannaya,* and *Sidat Saṅgarā.* On shifting forms of devotional expression in literature, see Hallisey (1988).

[2] The literature of the period included works such as *Eḷu Attanagalu Vaṃsaya, Mayūra Sandēśaya, Nikāyasaṃgraha, Bālāvatāra Sannaya* and *Saddharmālaṅkāraya.*

[3] Sannasgala notes a shift from the highly developed Sinhala prose traditions of the eleventh-fourteenth centuries to Sinhala and Sanskrit poetry. Buddhist preaching still relied on the earlier prose texts, a sign of continuity between the monastic educational institutions of the Daṁbadeṇi, Kuruṇägala, and Gampola periods and those of the Kōṭṭe period (1964, 245–248). See also Hēvāvasam (1966, 7).

of the Portuguese in 1505, however, the vitality of monastic institutions diminished. This created discontinuities in education and a related deterioration in the pace and level of literary production. At Portuguese hands there was destruction of Buddhist temples, shrines to popular deities, and *piriveṇa*s. The eventual conversion of King Dharmapāla to Catholicism in 1551, which negatively affected the level of patronage and security granted to Buddhist institutions, gave further impetus to monastic movements inland toward the Kandyan region (Sannasgala 1964, 245). Shortly thereafter, in Kōṭṭe's neighboring kingdom of Sītāvaka, it appears that Buddhist institutions (including temples, *piriveṇa*s and libraries) suffered damage. This destruction is typically attributed to the hostility of King Rājasiṃha I (1581–1592) to Buddhist teachings (Sannasgala 1964, 293; Hēvāvasam 1966, 295).[4] Whatever the reasons, the deterioration of Buddhist institutions and diminished patronage of them were further cause for the departure of monks from the monastic life and the movement of monks into the central highlands of the island (Hēvāvasam 1966, 7). P.B.J. Hēvāvasam argues that the decline in the numbers and prosperity of monastic centers in the later Kōṭṭe and Sītāvaka periods accounts for the diminished level of textual production at this time and the growing role of lay people as authors and scribes (1966, 294–295).[5] The movement of monks inland from the civilizational centers of Kōṭṭe and Sītāvaka coincided with the rise of a new center in the Kandyan region in the late fifteenth and sixteenth centuries, which marks the start of the Senkaḍagala period. Conditions in the highland regions, however, were initially unfavorable to the growth of strong monastic institutions. Political instability meant that political leaders had little time and few economic resources to spare for the support of Buddhist institutions. Moreover, Hēvāvasam notes conditions of food shortage that reduced the level of lay support for monks. It is unclear whether such shortages were the result of political instability, drought, diminished trade, or a combination of all three (12).

From the beginning of the sixteenth century until the middle of the eighteenth century, no durable centralized Buddhist ecclesiastical structure existed in Lanka. There were no large monastic educational institutions and, importantly, there was no centrally regulated monastic curriculum. *Gaṇinnānse* monasticism was clearly structured, but this structure was local and familial rather than island-wide and suprafamilial. This does not mean that there was a total absence of monastic

[4] Mirando (1985, 27), however, argues that this view is mistaken and cites evidence of Rājasiṃha I's support for Buddhist rituals and literary production. In his view, the Portuguese were the primary threat to Buddhist institutions.

[5] Hēvāvasam also argues that the growth of village poetic traditions from the seventeenth century onward has its roots in these changes in textual practice.

educational practice in Sri Lanka during this period, however. Abhayaratna Adikāri notes that the chief Kandyan temples, the Asgiriya and Malvatu Vihārayas, existed as centers for learning, but that they were not centers in which technical subjects (Sinhala *śāstra*), including the technical aspects of language, were taught (1991, 232). This is at odds with T. Silakkhandha's analysis, which cites a history of the Asgiri Vihāraya (the *Asgiri Talpata*) to support the view that the technical aspects of language were studied at both the Malvatu and Asgiri Vihārayas from the late 1670s into the 1740s (1995, 291–294).[6]

A number of eighteenth-century sources suggest that the level and availability of monastic education in the central region of the island varied greatly from temple to temple and teacher to teacher. Accounts of Saraṇaṃkara's search for Buddhist texts and teachers portray a situation in which monks who had received higher ordination in the seventeenth century (at the hands of Burmese monks) handed down some knowledge of Pāli language and texts to their students who either did not receive higher ordination and lived as *gaṇinnānse*s, or who received it but later left that status to reside in temples as novice monks. (I refer to both sets of monks as *gaṇinnānse*s, since the difference between them was slight, and the number of novices quite small.) The situation in southern Lanka appears to have been similar to that in the central, Kandyan, region. According to a southern monastic tradition, Siṭināmaluvē Dhammajoti, a monk from Tangalle who became one of Saraṇaṃkara's first students, is reported to have traveled from temple to temple in the southern region, collecting available works in both Pāli and Sinhala before going to the Kandyan Kingdom to study with Saraṇaṃkara, the Siyam Nikāya's founder (Hēvāvasam 1966, 33).

Despite the inconsistency that appears to have characterized monastic educational resources and experiences during this period, there is substantial evidence that a rich textual legacy from earlier periods was pro-

[6] For instance, according to Silakkhandha, the *Asgiri Talpata* and the *Asgiri Upata* report that king Narēndrasiṃha (r. 1739–1747) was educated by the head monk at Asgiriya, Gaṇanāyaka Golahänvattē Dharmakīrti, and that King Kīrtī Śrī Rājasiṃha received his early education at the hands of Dharmakīrti's student Golahänvattē Dhammadassi. Moreover, he claims that monks at the Asgiri Vihāraya studied Pāli, Sanskrit, grammar, prosody, and preaching during Narēndrasiṃha's reign (1995, 298–299). It is worth noting the existence of a certain degree of rivalry between some monks affiliated with the Asgiri and Malvatu Vihārayas, and that those accounts of the late seventeenth and early eighteenth centuries which paint the bleakest picture of educational practice are influenced by the somewhat pro-Malvatu orientation of the eighteenth-century sources discussed in Chapter 4. Silakkhanda's view, which depicts pre-Siyam Nikāya educational practice in slightly more enthusiastic terms, may be influenced by his own affiliation with the Asgiri Vihāraya.

tected. Monastic traditions support the idea that a range of Buddhist texts were preserved, probably in temple collections, from which only a few of the texts preferred for preaching were copied or used.[7] Moreover, a careful look at the first texts composed by Saraṇaṃkara between 1718 and 1747 confirms that many important Buddhist texts were preserved despite the absence of major monastic educational centers after the Kōṭṭe period. *Sārārthasaṅgrahaya*, for instance, draws on commentaries to the *tipiṭaka* and *Visuddhimagga* (composed in the fifth century C.E.), as well as the *Milindapañha* (composed between the second century B.C.E. and the fifth century C.E.). Another of Saraṇaṃkara's works, *Sārārthadīpanī,* overtly draws on Pāli commentaries (dating to the fifth or thirteenth century) written for parts of the *tipiṭaka* as well as on a range of story literature written in Sinhala and Pāli (Blackburn 1996, 37–39; Mirando 1985, 92–100). In addition, many of the texts included in the monastic curriculum initiated by Saraṇaṃkara clearly belong to a long Lankan tradition of literary writing in Sanskrit and Sinhala.

Thus, although by 1730 there were no large monastic educational centers on the island, nor was there a clearly standardized monastic curriculum, it is likely that monks taught younger monks and laymen at temples scattered throughout the island. Many texts not regularly used were still preserved, including canonical and commentarial texts in Pāli, works on grammar and poetics (in Pāli, Sanskrit, and Sinhala), and an array of earlier verse and prose texts (in Sinhala and Pāli) suitable for preaching. Prior to the rise of new monastic educational institutions associated with the Siyam Nikāya, the possibilities for monastic education depended greatly on local circumstances: the student's commitment to seeking learning; the knowledge of nearby teachers; the texts that those teachers had obtained through their own monastic lineages; and the texts that were favored for preaching and ritual purposes. They were, to use a distinction suggested by Charles Hallisey, following an apprenticeship model rather than a curricular model of Buddhist education.[8] The result was the absence of any sizable and significantly homogeneous Buddhist textual community in Lanka between the sixteenth century and the middle of the eighteenth century.

[7] See Adikāri (1991, 231) and Sannasgala (1964, passim). Varakavē Dhammaloka, senior lecturer at the Department of Sinhala, Peradeniya University, says that between the sixteenth and the first third of the eighteenth century very few of the available texts were used on a daily basis, but that all existing manuscripts were protected by temple residents. Personal communication, 3 July 1997.

[8] Personal communication, 30 September 1998.

THREE STAGES IN THE FORMATION OF MONASTIC EDUCATIONAL INSTITUTIONS

I identify three stages in the development of the Siyam Nikāya and the educational institutions that emerged in tandem with it. These distinctions are based on the changes I perceive in the degree to which monastic education was institutionalized and transmittable, and linked to a single clearly defined monastic order. The first stage was characterized by the emergence of a new group of peripatetic monastic teachers and students, called the Silvat Samāgama (the Disciplined Community). The second was marked by the start of a monastic educational center, called Niyamakanda, near the city of Kandy, and by the growing popularity of the Silvat Samāgama at the Kandyan royal court. A third and final stage began with the formal start of the Siyam Nikāya as an independent monastic order in 1753. During this stage, monastic educational centers were established throughout much of the island for Siyam Nikāya monks. These centers followed a similar curriculum and were part of a formal monastic administrative system.

Stage One

The Lankan monk most actively involved in the establishment of the Siyam Nikāya as a new and influential monastic order was Välivița Saraṇaṃkara. Born in 1698, Saraṇaṃkara belonged to an elite family from the central highland region of the island. This family, the Kulatungas, were members of the highest caste—the *govikula*, or *goyigama*—and exercised considerable influence in Kandyan politics. Kulatunga Mudali, for instance, possessed high administrative rank, and during the reign of King Vimala Dharma Sūriya II (1687–1707) served both as the *disāvā* of Vellassa and as the *rațerāla* of the Tumpanē district near the Kandyan capital (Dewaraja 1988, 116).

As a boy, Saraṇaṃkara received novitiate monastic ordination from a *gaṇinnānse* named Suriyagoḍa Unnansē. Although Suriyagoḍa at that time no longer retained his *upasampadā* status, he had earlier received higher ordination from visiting Burmese monks who came to Lanka during Vimala Dharma Sūriya's reign. Saraṇaṃkara was unable to receive higher ordination since, by the early part of the eighteenth century, Lanka lacked the requisite number of *upasampadā* monks to perform the ceremony. Saraṇaṃkara is said to have studied with two men (one layman and one novice monk) who had, in their turn, studied under one of the last monks with higher ordination on the island (Dhammarakkhita 1995, 143–145). Saraṇaṃkara gained a reputation as a serious student and as a diligent monk. In time, this reputation attracted a following of *gaṇinnānse*s from the central, southern, and western regions of the island.

The group of monks who first gathered around Saraṇaṃkara attempted to differentiate themselves sharply from their *gaṇinnānse* fellows. This they did through public displays of disciplined monasticism. In addition, they showed disdain for the monastic practices of monks outside the Silvat Samāgama by refusing to pay customary honor to senior *gaṇinnānse* monks (Vācissara 1964, 160; SSC, 16). Tensions developed in the island's monastic community (most clearly in the Kandyan Kingdom) between the Silvat Samāgama and members of the *gaṇinnānse*s hostile to Saraṇaṃkara and his followers. As some monks from the main *gaṇinnānse*-led temples of the Kandyan Kingdom joined the Silvat Samāgama, conflict between the two groups intensified. Influential *gaṇinnānse* monks sought a royal judgment against the Silvat Samāgama in the attempt to diminish the new group's threat. They received support from King Narēndrasiṃha, who required the Silvat Samāgama to show normal deference to their senior monks and to distance themselves from the royal capital. This situation did not last long, however, and for reasons explained later, Saraṇaṃkara gained Narēndrasiṃha's favor.

Even at this early stage, the monks associated with Saraṇaṃkara (and who were to become early members of the Siyam Nikāya) participated in distinctive forms of education. It is difficult to reconstruct the first stage of the Siyam Nikāya's educational institutions with confidence because nearly all of our evidence for this period comes from the enthusiastic biography of Saraṇaṃkara, *Saṃgharājasādhucariyāva* (The Excellent Deeds of the Lord of the Monastic Community). Because this text was clearly written in part to extol the merits of Saraṇaṃkara and his early students, it would be unwise to accept it unquestioningly. However, although its portrayal of the radical break between Saraṇaṃkara's commitment to learning and the ignorance of his monastic predecessors may be overstated in the interests of strategic representation, it seems likely that the less rhetorically powerful details about monastic education largely reflect actual practice.

Saṃgharājasādhucariyāva recounts that Saraṇaṃkara traveled from region to region with the first members of the Silvat Samāgama. These monks studied together, with those better educated instructing those less well read, and preached to the lay people. Monks studied the training rules for monks, the daily duties of monks, and foundational monastic discipline in accord with the *Vinaya* (a section of the *tipiṭaka*), as well as the technical aspects of language, including grammar. A letter known as *Anuśāsanā Vaṭṭōruva* dated to 1730 supports *Saṃgharājasādhucariyāva*'s account of the way monks studied training rules and daily monastic duties, but does not comment directly on the study of language: "[A monk] should make much of the teachings, including *dinacariyāva* [an account of a monk's daily duties], *sekhiyāva* [minor rules for monastic conduct], etc. . . . He should be diligent with regard to [action, doing things] such as making offerings and showing homage to the Triple Gem, learning the Dharma and the [way to] recite the required *paritta* [protective verses]" (Somadasa 1987, Vol. 2, 303–304). In addition to their own education, traveling members of the Silvat Samāgama taught lay people to write the alphabet. According to *Saṃgharājasādhucariyāva* itself,

> From Udapola Kōralē a large group called the Silvat Samāgama went throughout the districts of the Four and Seven Kōralēs, preaching to many good [lay]people. For those who were old enough and wanted to become monks—whether or not they were educated—they had them dress in saffron robes [standard monastic dress], and gave the ten precepts [appropriate to a novice monk]. Separately from the two *vihārayas* [the Asgiri and Malvatu Vihārayas, then the center of the *gaṇinnānse* "establishment"], the honorable Välivița [Saraṇaṃkara]'s community emerged. They taught reading and writing: from the *Hōdiya* [an alphabet text for Eḷu Sinhala script] to youngsters who didn't know their letters, and from the *Äṇavum* [a text containing favorite *paritta*] and *Sakaskaḍaya* [a biography of Buddha] to virtuous people who knew the alphabet already, and from the *śataka pot* [collections of Sanskrit poems] to some people" (SSC 17–8).

At the same time the monks learned "all-night preaching, vocabulary, verbal roots, and grammar while practicing the *dhūtāṅga*s [ascetic practices] including [those outlined in] *Heraṇasikha* [Training for a Novice] [as well as in those passages known as] *dinacariyāva*, *satarasaṃvara sīlē* [four types of restraint through virtue], *sil ōlo gannā sūtis yodhayo* [thirty-four forces that destroy virtue], and *sekhiyāva*" (SSC, 18).

The available evidence suggests that even at the start of the Siyam Nikāya's formation, long before the order was formally established in 1753, Saraṇaṃkara sought to shape a sense of collective identity among the monks who followed him. This identity stressed the importance of study and teaching in monastic life. *Anuśāsanā Vaṭṭōruva* is important in this regard because it shows that Saraṇaṃkara envisioned the monastic community developing around him as one identified with disciplined and educated monasticism. He appears to have had an appreciation for the valuable role played by shared educational experiences focused on set textual units. It is also possible that Saraṇaṃkara understood that traveling teacher-monks who exhibited strict discipline were well placed to develop support within the lay community. This, at any rate, appears to be what happened.

Stage Two

The establishment of a royally supported monastic education center called Niyamakanda, probably in the mid to late 1730s (near the end of the reign of Narēndrasiṃha) marks the shift to the second stage in the development of educational institutions connected to the Siyam Nikāya. This would not have been possible without changes in the level of royal recognition accorded to Saraṇaṃkara and his followers. After the setback caused by complaints made to the king by monks of the Asgiri and Malvatu Vihārayas, which resulted in the temporary distancing of the Silvat Samāgama from court circles, Saraṇaṃkara and his followers entered a period in which they received considerable support from King Narēndrasiṃha (r. 1706–1739) (Hēvāvasam 1966, 22–24). Accounts of royal-monastic interactions given by *Saṃgharājasādhucariyāva* suggest that Narēndrasiṃha's support was motivated in part by the importance of educated monks to a cosmopolitan court where linguistic skills and the exhibition of erudition were valued for convenience and prestige (SSC 19–21). Whatever the reason, Narēndrasiṃha ordered the establishment of an educational center not far from the Āmbäkkē Dēvālaya outside the city of Kandy. Niyamakanda was sometimes also called a *śāstrāyatana* (a place for the study of technical subjects—meaning subjects like grammar, prosody, medical science, and astrology) and sometimes a *sāmaṇera piriveṇa* (an educational center for novice monks) (Adikāri 1991, 232). The king provided the land for this center, as well as food and other supplies for the students and teachers living there (Dewaraja 1988, 167). *Saṃgharājasādhucariyāva* recounts that "a group of students was living in the temple which had been set up well with a great hall and various living spaces" (SSC 24).

There was no set curriculum at Niyamakanda. Rather, this was the site at which the elements of the subsequent Siyam Nikāya curriculum were put together. According to the manuscripts and monastic histories surveyed by Hēvāvasam, Niyamakanda residents sought to gather and correct existing texts, and to compose commentarial guides and lexicons for these texts. He also mentions that efforts were made to teach students how to use preaching texts (1966, 25–26). *Saṃgharājasādhucariyāva* states that "Saraṇaṃkara taught the students . . . instructing them in the protection of the precepts and making them engage the appropriate path. Zealously teaching many students to read and write, essential Buddhist teachings and the technical aspects of language, etc., day and night he was also able to compose new verses, including verses with eight syllables [Pāli *aṣṭakas*], etc." (SSC 24).

During the second stage, which lasted from the establishment of Niyamakanda until 1753, Saraṇaṃkara's position with respect to his royal patrons was quite secure. This is clear from the fact that he served as royal tutor to the next two kings, Śrī Vijayarājasiṃha and Kīrtī Śrī Rājasīmha, prior to their accession to the throne (Dewaraja 1988, 173). He also received royal invitations to compose works on Buddhist themes (Sannasgala 1964, 406, 669) and was given royal support for attempts to bring monks from Southeast Asia to Lanka in order to perform higher ordination ceremonies (de Silva 1992, 137). Although it is certain that Saraṇaṃkara's position was received with disfavor by some within court and monastic circles, there is no evidence of serious threats to his status. This is important in the context of educational developments because these circumstances assured those connected with Saraṇaṃkara the stable patronage needed to develop a curriculum and to educate the first generation of the Siyam Nikāya leaders.

Stage Three

The major institutional developments characteristic of the third and final stage did not occur until the reign of the next king, Kīrti Śrī Rājasiṃha (r. 1747–1787). I date the start of the third stage in the formation of the Siyam Nikāya and its educational institutions to 1753. At this time, the new monastic order was formally established when Lankan monks (including Saraṇaṃkara and other members of the Silvat Samāgama) received higher ordination from a group of Siamese monks brought to Lanka at Saraṇaṃkara's request and with royal support. As I shall explain later in more detail, the formal establishment of the Siyam Nikāya created conditions that made participation in the order attractive even to those "establishment" monks who had criticized Saraṇaṃkara and his early followers. The introduction of higher ordination from Siam coincided with a movement from Niyamakanda to major monastic educational centers at Buddhist temples throughout the Kandyan region, the central and southwest region of the island, and the southern maritimes. Most of these centers were established after 1753. The construction or restoration of the temple educational centers in question typically coincided with the establishment or reestablishment of monastic boundaries (Pāli *sīmā*), which made temples ready for the performance of certain monastic rituals, and with the appointment of newly ordained *upasampadā* monks as temple incumbents.

Nine temple centers in the Kandyan region became the most important sites for monastic higher education during this period, and Niyamakanda ceased to function as these sites became active. These were: Gaḍalādeṇiyē Saddharmatilaka Vihāraya, Asgiri Vihāraya, Degaldoru Vihāraya, Dambulu Vihāraya, Malvatu Vihāraya, Gaṃgārāmaya Vihāraya, Ampiṭiya Vihāraya, Nittavela Vihāraya, and Sūduhumpola Vihāraya (Adikāri 1991, 232–233; Hēvāvasam 1966, 29; Silakkhanda 1995, 303). Further from Kandy, Ridī Vihāraya to the west, Pälmadullē Vihāraya in the southwest, Atmahāsthāna Vihāraya at Anurādhapura to the north, as well as the Kurumburē Vihāraya and the Mātara Kalugala Ārāmaya in the southern coastal region, all became active centers for all levels of education (Dhammaratana 1995, 46). In addition to those most famous temple centers, Adikāri notes that many other temples became centers for organized education in the Satkōralē (Seven Kōralē), Satarakōralē (Four Kōralē), and Sabaragamuva districts, as well as in the Dutch-controlled southern maritimes known in Sinhala as Ruhūnu (1991, 232–233). It is not clear, however, whether all of these temples offered instruction at the most advanced level of the curriculum. Hēvāvasam argues in favor of consistent high-level education in the southern maritimes, noting that by the 1790s nearly all temples in Ruhūnu provided education in the technical aspects of language (1966, 16–17).

The establishment of these temple-based educational centers was initiated with the combined support of Saraṇaṃkara and King Kīrti Śrī Rājasiṃha, after which they were handed over to monks chosen by the Asgiri or Malvatu Vihāraya leadership as Incumbents and educational directors. These centers were not called *piriveṇa*s, the term used earlier to designate large centers for monastic education, but were instead called places for advanced study (Sinhala *usas vidyā-sthāna*s) or centers (Sinhala *madhya-sthāna*s) because they were smaller, more numerous, and more autonomous than the earlier *piriveṇa* institutions (Adikāri 1991, 232–233). Monks living in temples other than the central Asgiri and Malvatu Vihārayas sometimes acquired all of their education at their home temple or at a nearby temple center, whereas others received some schooling at these locations before going on to one of the Kandyan educational centers for more advanced studies. The oral histories recounted to me by monastic incumbents in temples connected to the Siyam Nikāya strongly suggest that only the "best and the brightest" monastic students went on to study in Kandy. To do so was to have a chance to capture the attention of court and monastic elites and to rise in the monastic administrative system. According to the incumbent at Mulkirigala Rajamahavihāraya, for instance, among the monks trained at that temple by one of the first generation of Siyam Nikāya monks, only two went to Kandy for advanced studies.[9] At Mädavela Rajamahavihāraya, even though this temple was much closer to Kandy than the southern Mulkirigala Rajamahavihāraya, only the cleverest monks remained in Kandy (in this case at Malvatu Vihāraya) longer than the customary few months surrounding the higher ordination rituals.[10]

ROYAL PATRONAGE OF THE NEW EDUCATIONAL INSTITUTIONS

The king provided support for monastic education undertaken by the Siyam Nikāya in several ways. In addition to the construction and reconstruction of temple buildings that became sites for monastic education, the king supervised the appointment of incumbents to these temples and sometimes made appointments directly. He also made gifts to monks and lay people who participated in these educational institutions, encouraged promising monastic scholars, put royal authority behind monastic regulations that set forth guidelines for education, and supported visits by foreign monks who participated in the new educational institutions.

Architectural and inscriptional evidence from the eighteenth century makes clear the king's important role in the construction or renovation of many of the temples identified as centers for monastic education. Such work included the establishment or rehabilitation of basic structures, as well as the fabrication of images and the decoration of spaces within which preaching and monastic rituals took place and in which manuscripts were stored.[11] In addition, once temples were habitable, it was necessary to provide food, medicine, clothes, and manuscript materials for the resident monks and lay men or boys who resided at the temple and performed various tasks. *Mahāvaṃsa* (The Great Lineage) provides an account of royal involvement in Buddhist institutions that indicates the many ways in which the king became involved in the (re-)construction of temple centers and their support. Such accounts are supported by official deeds (called *sannasa*s) which accompanied royal grants of lands for the support of temples. For example, *Mahāvaṃsa* described the renovation undertaken at the Gaṃgārāmaya Vihāraya, one of the educational centers listed in the previous section, thus:

[9] Personal communication, 6 July 1997.
[10] Personal communication, 15 July 1997.
[11] See Gatellier (1991, vol. 1) and Lawrie (1896/1898, passim).

> The large, beautiful eye-catching temple, in delightful proximity to the Mahavulaka River [Pāli *gaṃgā*], was known as Gaṃgārāma on account of its construction in that location. It was designated by the king [as] a Rājamahavihāra [Great Royal Temple]. And then enemies who had arrived in the city destroyed the temple, in its beauty and splendor, which had been well made in this way. The king properly restored it, holding a great festival just as [it was done in] the previous eye[-opening ceremony, for an image] festival. Having had a large festival and having had a delightful monastic residence made for the [monastic] community near [the temple's image hall], the king made many offerings, giving clothes and ornaments to the painters. He settled the monastic community there, which, as always, was respectful and devoted to study and meditation, and often did it service [by bringing] the things the monks required. He, who was respectful of the Triple Gem, conducted an offering [Pāli *pūjā*] to the Buddha exactly as it had been described in the past, made an offering to the *dhamma* and the monastic community together, and developed a heap of merit for himself and the rest of the world. (MV 100: 201–209)

The provision of what was necessary most often occurred through grants of land and labor that guaranteed a supply of foodstuffs for the temple. Such instructions are clearly articulated in the donative reports collected by Lawrie. In a rock inscription made in 1752 at Gaṃgārāma Vihāraya, for instance, Kīrti Śrī Rājasiṃha's reconstruction of the temple is described, followed by a list of the lands selected by the king for the temple's support:

> "[T]he king caused to be appointed men for different grades of service; and considering that fields and gardens are also necessary, he dedicated from [various villages] lands, comprising 83 amunu and 3 pelas sowing extent, together with all the appurtenant high lands, low lands, houses, trees, and plantations, inclusive, to be perpetuated forever; [these] were inscribed on the rock by the command of the king, who sat on the throne of Siriwardhanapura in Senkadagala [the Kandyan area], like Indra [the king of the gods] in stately grandeur.
>
> A man who takes either grass or firewood, or a flower, or a fruit from what is dedicated to Buddha, shall become a pretaya [hungry ghost] in the world to come. (Lawrie 1898, 817).

Royal support was given to laymen and monks who participated in educational pursuits. *Mahāvaṃsa* recounts that Kīrti Śrī patronized the scribes who provided the manuscripts that were used in education, and that were also copied as acts of devotion which brought the patron religious merit: "Out of faith he had many other manuscripts copied, such as the *Saṃyutta Nikāya* [part of the Pāli *tipiṭaka*]; he gave wealth for writing. In seeing for himself the others who had gone forth [as monks], the good lay people and the manuscripts which had been written, his mind was pleased" (MV 99: 33–34). Moreover, the king and his successors offered support to particular groups of novice monks who were prepared to participate in the new educational institutions of the Siyam Nikāya.

> Having investigated [to see who were] the smart, beautiful, and well-behaved novices, they [the two men appointed as the king's seconds] had the eightfold requisites given to those novices in an offering worthy of a king. [They also had them given] higher ordination. Having [them] trained properly in the teachings of the *Vinaya* and the *Sutta*s they had residences made which were of great benefit, and settled the monks there, serving [them] with respect and honor, considering the various duties [they had] toward the people and the *sāsana* [Buddhist teachings and the institutions that sustain them]. (MV 99: 89–91).

> From that time [1753] onward, [Kīrti Śrī Rājasiṃha] had novices and others brought who were clever at grammar and Buddhist teachings, and had them given higher ordination. Thus, gradually, properly discerning those worthy of novitiate and higher ordination in the supreme *sāsana* of the Buddha, he had them given novitiate and higher ordination in the proper way. Discerning those monks, among the monastic groups which had become numerous in Lanka, who were worthy of teaching positions, who were competent, and who were always respectful of the protection of study and meditation, he ordered them to study in the group [of monks] who had come from Ayutthaya. (MV 100: 97–101).

Once monks were ordained, the king played a significant role in determining monastic appointments and movement through the administrative system. By promulgating monastic regulations under his own name, Kīrti Śrī Rājasiṃha helped grant authority to the Siyam Nikāya and its new educational institutions for which the monastic regulations (Sinhala *katikāvata*s] provided a guide to practice. These regulations addressed the pace and content of monastic education, specifying, for instance, the texts appropriate to monks at different levels of seniority. They also instituted a set of controls for monastic participation in scribal activity, in the attempt to make certain that no monk received private payment for copying work and that all texts composed or copied had their place in the larger institutional strategies of the monastic community. Finally, royal patronage extended to the expensive and time-consuming embassies needed to bring monks to Lanka from abroad as part of the steps taken to found and institutionalize the Siyam Nikāya. Three embassies arrived in Lanka from Siam. The first, in 1753 under the leadership of the Siamese monk Upāli, performed the *upasampadā* ritual that marked the formal start of the Siyam Nikāya, and then went on to establish monastic ritual boundaries at many of the main temples. A second embassy arrived in 1756, under the leadership of the monks Visuddhācāriya and Varañāna, and remained until 1764. The third embassy arrived in 1759 and was drawn into the 1760 plot against Kīrti Śrī Rājasiṃha.

THE EIGHTEENTH-CENTURY CURRICULUM

Four Levels of Study

Hēvāvasam suggests, primarily on the basis of *Saṃgharājasādhucariyāva* and accounts of monastic education at southern temples, that the curriculum used in the educational institutions affiliated with the Siyam Nikāya assumed four levels of study (1966, 20–21). Here I adopt his four-level framework to discuss this curriculum but draw on other sources as well when describing the texts studied by students at each level.[12]

At the first level students were introduced to the Sinhala script. The text used at this level was called a *Hōḍiya pota*, after the Sinhala word for alphabet (*hōḍiya*). The *Hōḍiya pota* provided examples of each letter, which students were able to practice by copying the shapes in the sand (Hēvāvasam 1966, 20–21).[13]

Those at the second level had some facility with the script but needed practice reading the letters and pronouncing them (Hēvāvasam 1966, 20). To this end, they worked with a text called *Äṇavum* (Sorata 1970, sv; Vijayaśirivardhana 1989, 140). From there they turned to *Sakaskaḍaya*, a biography of the Buddha composed in a somewhat Sanskritized Sinhala during the eighteenth century by Saraṇaṃkara's student Attaragama Rājaguru Baṇḍāra. They read this biography aloud from a manuscript, or *pus kola pota*. Following that they learned a set of texts orally, listening to the teacher and repeating the sounds with the aim of memorizing these texts. Developing memorization skill was as important as learning the content of the texts. This set of texts comprised *Nampota* (a Sinhala list of major temple and pilgrimage sites), *Magul*

[12] In a study of education during the Mahanūvara Period, Vijayaśirivardhana uses a three-level model to discuss progress through the curriculum (1989). I prefer Hēvāvasam's framework because it accommodates a more nuanced discussion of student progress through a large collection of texts.

[13] For an example, see Reynolds (1981, 62). The script used for writing Sanskrit and Pāli words includes more letters than are included in the *hōḍiya*. Students learned this more extensive *miśra* ("mixed") script at the more advanced levels.

Lakuṇa (a Sinhala list of Prince Siddhartha's auspicious characteristics), *Gaṇadevi Hälla* (a set of Sinhala verses about the god Ganeśa), *Vadankavi Pota* (a set of Sinhala devotional verses), and *Buddha Gadya* (a Sanskrit poem in thirty-four *ślokas*, or couplets, used to teach intonation and attributed to Rājaguru Baṇḍāra. Students spent between one and two years working through this stage of the curriculum (Vijayaśirivardhana 1989, 130, 144, 165–169, 211–214).[14]

The third level introduced students to the technical aspects of Sanskrit, Pāli, and Sinhala as well as to basic Buddhist teachings, rules for monastic discipline, and meditative techniques. Important at this stage were a set of texts called *śatakas*, which are Sanskrit poems one hundred verses long. Students first learned to pronounce the poems by following their teacher, and then learned the meaning of the poems by studying eighteenth-century commentaries written in Sinhala. These commentaries provided Sinhala synonyms for each Sanskrit word and sometimes gave additional details about the text. The *śatakas* studied at this stage were: *Nāmāṣṭa Śatakaya* (eighteen *ślokas* on the 108 names of the Buddha), *Navaratnaya* ("nine gems" of verse in composed in *śloka* form), *Vyāsa Śatakaya/Vyāsakāraya* (101 *ślokas* on various aspects of morality), *Bauddha Śatakaya/Bhakti Śatakaya* (a devotional poem to the Buddha), *Sūrya Śātakaya* (*ślokas* on the sun's characteristics), and *Vṛttamālākhyāva* (*ślokas* about the incumbent of Rammungoḍa Vihāraya, also composed in the fifteenth century).[15] The training in Sanskrit provided by study of these works prepared students to study more advanced works on astrology and poetics. Several works on Sanskrit grammar were composed by Rājaguru Baṇḍāra for student use. These included *Saṃskṛta Nāmavaranägilla*, which explains nominal declensions (Sannasgala 1964, 486). By the time students had completed studying these works, they were usually close to thirteen years old (Vijayaśirivardhana 1989, 145–146).

Students developed their memorization skills, but also became more adept at reading manuscripts, in part by consulting commentaries with their teacher (Hēvāvasam 1966, 20). Their reading abilities were also enhanced by consulting monastic handbooks, called *baṇa daham pot* (sing. *pota*) or sometimes simply *baṇa pot*, which contained essential sections from Buddhist *suttas*, rules for monastic discipline, and short discussions of meditative techniques. The practice of making monastic

[14] This list of texts is confirmed by a brief history of monastic education written in Sinhala for contemporary Sri Lankan monks (Maṅgala n.d., 112).

[15] According to Adikāri (1991, 242–244), the following *śataka pot* were also used: *Anuruddha Śatakaya* (a series of devotional verses on Sakyamuni Buddha and previous buddhas, attributed to a monk named Anuruddha) and *Pratya Śatakaya* (*ślokas* on mental discipline).

handbooks, though related to earlier compositions of essential monastic rules (Sannasgala 1964, 476), began in the eighteenth century as a result of Saraṇaṃkara's attempt to train the members of the Silvat Samāgama. In a letter written to his first group of students, Saraṇaṃkara set out a model for student use of monastic handbooks. There, in the *Anuśāsanā Vaṭṭōruva*, Saraṇaṃkara instructed each person studying to become a novice monk to write out the *Anuśāsanā* and to keep it with him. The student was told to consult the written copy during the week between collective monastic observances and to say it aloud. Included in the *Anuśāsanā* are references to basic Buddhist texts, or sections of text, that the student was supposed to study, including those on a monk's daily duties, on monastic rules, and on the obligatory *pirit* (Pāli *paritta*), or protective, texts for recitation within the temple (Dhammānanda 1969, 143). According to Sannasgala, Saraṇaṃkara composed a monastic handbook that accompanied the *Anuśāsanā* and provided a detailed list of study texts. Students listened to their teacher recite the texts on the list, which they repeated orally. Thereafter, using the handbook, students reviewed the material morning and evening until they had completed all of the study texts contained in it (1964, 476–477). This monastic handbook provides valuable evidence of what was considered fundamental by the founder of the Siyam Nikāya, and underscores the importance of compendia-based study to the educational practices of the time. Students still at an early stage of their monastic careers were not expected to work their way through the entire body of authoritative literature contained in the *tipiṭaka*. Rather, they engaged Buddhist teachings set before them in the form of extracts from larger texts. The contents of this monastic handbook are listed in Appendix A. The handbook, which touches nearly every aspect of monastic life, aims to create a condensed but comprehensive framework for monastic conduct in which mental and physical action are equally controlled.

Grammars were used to help students read Pāli selections contained in the handbooks. The most important were probably Saraṇaṃkara's *Rūpamālāva* and Rājaguru Baṇḍāra's *Varanägilla* and *Saddhavinicchayapakaraṇa*. The first is a Sinhala commentary for Pāli stanzas that set out Pāli declensions (Hēvāvasam 1966, 21–22; Vijayaśirivardhana 1989, 381–382). *Varanägilla* is an analysis of Pāli nominal declensions arranged to complement *Rūpamalāvā*. *Saddavinicchayapakaraṇa* is a discussion of Pāli prefixes, particles, and verbs by the same author (Sannasgala 1964, 479–80, 485–486).

At the fourth level, students deepened their knowledge of Buddhist teachings by working with more difficult texts, a step that also prepared them to compose works of their own and to preach for lay and monastic audiences. At the same time, they studied more advanced texts on the technical aspects of language (Sinhala *śabda śāstra*), and explored the traditional body of knowledge on poetics (Sinhala *chandas-alaṃkāra-kāvyaśāstra*). This was also the stage at which students could learn other technical subjects such as medicine (Sinhala *vaidya*), astrology (Sinhala *jyotiśāstra*), and law (Sinhala *artha-/nīti-śāstra*). As at earlier stages, learning took place in a close student-teacher relationship. Teachers provided interpretive guidance and students were expected to draw this guidance into their memory or record it, if they were provided with writing implements (Vijayaśirivardhana 1989, 147–149, 381, 557).[16] Although we do not have a single text containing the list of works to be studied at the final stage of the curriculum, it is possible to suggest areas of study and popular texts on the basis of eighteenth-century intertextual references and manuscript traditions. It is clear that students were typically trained in the areas of preaching, poetic theory and composition, prose composition, protective techniques and meditation, Pāli *tipiṭaka* and commentaries, medicine and sometimes in the visual arts.[17]

Siamese Additions to the Curriculum

Monks who arrived from Ayutthaya in the second embassy brought with them a large collection of books for use in Lankan educational institutions. There is insufficient evidence to conclude whether the majority of the texts brought from Siam were then unavailable in Lanka; some of the works selected may have been chosen simply because they were appropriate gifts. However, it is clear that some of the texts brought from Siam came to play a role in the Siyam Nikāya's educational centers. This is reflected by Saraṇaṃkara's instruction to Dhammapāla, one of his students, in a letter. He advises Dhammapāla on his

[16] From the extant evidence it is not clear whether students compiled notes in written form. Given the inscription technology of the time that would have been a costly and time-consuming process. See also Chapter 6 below.

[17] Since most of the evidence for texts used in these areas is available only in Sinhala sources, I have compiled it in Appendix B for interested readers. I do not provide information on preaching there, since monastic preacher training is discussed in Chapter 6. In addition, in order to give a fuller idea of the texts likely to have been studied by advanced students, in Appendix C I provide a list of manuscripts held in several key temples that were educational centers for Siyam Nikāya monks. Because these manuscripts have been little used in the twentieth century, and because nineteenth-century use was closely similar to that of the period with which I am concerned (as I explain in the following section), they provide a reasonably good but by no means perfect indicator of the texts available to monks for study. Appendix C does not list texts mentioned earlier for study at lower levels of the curriculum.

choice of texts from which to prepare lessons on monastic discipline, instructing him to use local works and those brought from outside the country (Dhammānanda 1969, 148). The fact that texts brought from Siam entered the manuscript holdings at major temples connected to the Siyam Nikāya is clear from the extant texts, which include carefully bound manuscripts with gilded leaves written in Mūl script. These are often labeled *Siyāmika pota*, meaning "Siamese manuscript" (Blackburn 2001).[18]

Monastic Examinations

Monastic regulations indicate that monks were expected to have memorized, and sometimes command, certain texts in order to qualify for higher status such as higher ordination, freedom from *nissaya* (close proximity to a monk's preceptor), or that of a *thera* (monastic elder). Candidates for higher ordination were evaluated by their teachers prior to the beginning of higher ordination rituals, in order to assure an appropriate competence and the ability to perform satisfactorily at the *upasampadā* itself. However, there is no evidence that a formal examination system was established for the Siyam Nikāya during the eighteenth century.[19] Indeed, such a system does not appear before the establishment of Vidyōdaya Piriveṇa in the 1860s by Hikkaḍuvē Sumaṇgala (Blackburn n.d.a, 14); the examination and degree system characteristic of the Ayutthayan monastic community (Tambiah 1976, 203–204) was not adopted by the Siyam Nikāya along with the Siamese *upasampadā*.[20]

THE WIDESPREAD AND CONSISTENT IMPLEMENTATION OF THE CURRICULUM

Stage three in the Siyam Nikāya's formation and the development of its educational institutions provides a useful illustration of textual transmission and standardized textual practices in South Asia prior to the widespread use of print technologies. We have several types of evidence to support the view that the Siyam Nikāya's formation led to quite consistent patterns of monastic education, and historians of Sinhala litera-

[18] Since the list of works brought to Lanka in 1756 is of some interest, I have reproduced it (from Vijayavardhana and Mīgaskumbura 1993) in Appendix D.

[19] This view is supported by personal communication by Varakavē Dhammaloka Thero and P. B. Mīgaskumbura on 24 June 1999.

[20] Such selectivity appears to have been characteristic of the Siyam Nikāya. See, for instance, Vijayavardhana and Mīgaskumbura (1993), and Blackburn (n.d.b.).

ture familiar with manuscript traditions throughout the island are in agreement on this point (Hēvāvasam 1966, Sannasgala 1964). Hēvāvasam states, for instance, that "those who studied with Saraṇaṃkara's students rather than with Saraṇaṃkara himself also used the books which Saraṇaṃkara had discovered" (1966, 32). Moreover, histories of monastic education written for contemporary monastic audiences in Sri Lanka make this point repeatedly, even when they are not written by monks closely connected to Saraṇaṃkara through their teacher-student lineage (Amaravaṃśa 1995; Maṅgala n.d., 119; Silakkhanda 1995, esp. 317–330). Further, evidence from the late nineteenth century is helpful: the print record shows the popularity of the *sūtra sannaya* genre I discuss below, which originated with Saraṇaṃkara's educational program. Adikāri's important account of the nineteenth-century *piriveṇa*s emphasizes that the origins of the *piriveṇa* curriculum may be found in the Siyam Nikāya's eighteenth-century educational practices (Adikāri 1991, esp. 238–250).

Reasons for the widespread and consistent implementation of the curriculum include organizational centralization, educational conservatism, and the form of texts used.

Centralized Ordination and Monastic Administration

Higher ordination was only conferred on Siyam Nikāya monks at the two temples—Asgiri Vihāraya and Malvatu Vihāraya—which served as the joint administrative headquarters for the order after its formal beginning in 1753. This meant that any monk with a serious career in the monastic community paid at least one visit to Kandy. The length of the monks' stay in the capital city undoubtedly varied. There are reports that some monks stayed for quite some time before and/or after *upasampadā* was given. Malalgoda writes that those who had been looking after temples in different parts of the country came to Kandy in large numbers to receive ordination. "After being ordained and instructed in the doctrine and the monastic rules for some time, they returned to their own temples" (Malalgoda 1976, 65). The centralization of higher ordination ceremonies in Kandy guaranteed that most monks and their teachers (even those arriving from areas under Dutch control) spent time in temples of the Kandyan area, where they met teachers and other students and had opportunities to collect manuscripts or at least to study them. Public demonstrations of advanced learning by the candidates for higher ordination also created a common orientation to monastic learning and its display.[21] Given the limited resources characteris-

[21] See, for instance, Buddhadatta (1950, 2), and Blackburn (n.d.a.).

tic of temples more distant from Kandy and the considerable constraints on communication across long distances, time spent in Kandy was an important opportunity for formal and informal study sessions and attempts to gather texts, whether oral or written (as well as for gossip and networking, of course).

Those involved in the higher ordination events were not the only monks with occasion to visit Kandy and to take away with them manuscripts and ideas about desirable education when they departed from the city. Monks with leadership positions in the Siyam Nikāya did so, as well. A new administrative hierarchy was established in 1753 along with the reintroduction of higher ordination from Ayutthaya. This hierarchy provided a substantial amount of centralized control and required certain monks to spend periods of time in Kandy, the capital city.[22] Beginning in 1753, Kīrti Śrī Rājasiṃha reestablished the position of *saṃgharāja* (leader of the monastic community) and the appointee, Saraṇaṃkara, was given the greatest authority within the Siyam Nikāya. Beneath the *saṃgharāja*, was an *upa-saṃgharāja* (deputy leader of the monastic community), below which the Siyam Nikāya was divided into two administrative divisions; one was identified with the Malvatu Vihāraya and the other with the Asgiri Vihāraya. Each division was headed by a *mahānāyaka* (supreme chief monk), assisted by two deputies called *anunāyaka*s (deputy supreme chief monks). Beneath this top tier was a committee made up of *nāyaka*s (district chief monks), who were appointed as the district heads for the Malvatu or Asgiri Vihāraya (Bechert 1988, 213; Malalgoda 1976, 67–68). All of these monastic leaders received appointments from the king. They came to Kandy to accept them and then spent further time in Kandy on monastic business, which included participation in ecclesiastical courts formed to consider matters relating to land, pupillary succession, and monastic discipline (Malalgoda 1976, 67–68; Tambiah 1962, 92–93). The incumbents (*vihārādhipati*s) of existing temples were usually appointed through a system of succession internal to the temples whereby the deceased incumbent's chief student took over the leadership of the temple. When disputes arose over succession to the position of incumbent, an appeal process allowed monks involved in the dispute to make their case to the administrators within their monastic division and, ultimately, to the king. In the case of new or restored temples, however, it was common for the king to appoint incumbents, stipulating the continuation of

[22] On earlier systems of monastic administration see Gunawardana (1979, chapters 1, 8–9), Ratnapala (1971) and Sannasgala (1964). It is possible, but by no means certain, that the system of monastic administration developed for the Siyam Nikāya was influenced by reports of centralized monastic organization in Ayutthaya. See Tambiah (1976, 179–183).

the incumbency through pupillary succession (Dewaraja 1988, 171). The large number of temples built and restored during the reign of Kīrti Śrī Rājasiṃha gave the king considerable influence over monastic administration.

This administrative system affected the spread of the Siyam Nikāya curriculum in several ways. First, monastic administrators moved back and forth between the temples in which they resided and the Kandyan administrative center. This guaranteed a continual exposure to the educational models developed in Kandy and transmission of these models—and manuscripts—to more distant monastic centers. Second, those holding the position of chief monk were in a position to influence monastic education in their district significantly on the basis of their experiences in Kandy. Precisely because the district chief monks controlled affairs at the individual temples within their district, they were well placed to shape the development of educational centers in those areas and to influence monastic attitudes toward education in less formal ways, as well. Also, because higher ordination practices and the nature of monastic administration encouraged the inflow of monks to Kandy, it was easier than it otherwise would have been for texts and ideas to be transmitted from Kandy throughout large parts of Lanka. This was inevitably not entirely a one-way process, nor were the texts and ideas brought from Kandy received with uniform responses across the island. The evidence we have of higher education well into the nineteenth century, as well as available manuscript evidence, however, suggests that the Kandyan models had a considerable impact.

Pupillary Lineage, Monastic Administration, and Educational Conservatism

The inclination of monastic administrators at all levels of the hierarchy to maintain the curriculum initiated by Saraṇaṃkara for use in the temples under their supervision was not only the result of time spent in Kandy on monastic business. It also derived from the fact that monks in these positions tended to hold conservative views about the educational practices initiated by Saraṇaṃkara, because they were often monks within his own pupillary lineage. That is, these monks were tied to Saraṇaṃkara through a set of teacher-student relationships. In addition, whether or not they were members of Saraṇaṃkara's lineage, implementation of the curriculum initiated by Saraṇaṃkara helped assure their legitimacy as part of the new order. Further, monks who sought to prepare their student monks to compete for patronage and prestige in court and monastic circles had good reason to use the curriculum established by Saraṇaṃkara.

The monks appointed to the two highest positions and as district chief monks for the Malvatu Vihāraya division of the Siyam Nikāya during the latter two-thirds of the eighteenth century were most often monks who had studied with Saraṇaṃkara or with the first generation of Saraṇaṃkara's students. For instance, the first deputy leader of the monastic community and supreme chief monk of the Malvatu Vihāraya was Tibboṭuvāvē Buddharakkhita, Saraṇaṃkara's "chief student," who retained these posts until 1773 (Bechert 1988, vol. 1, 265; SSC, 32). The second and third supreme chief monks of the Malvatu Vihāraya, Mädavela Siri Ānanda and Däramiṭipala Dhammarakkhita, had also studied with Saraṇaṃkara from an early age (SSC, 31; 46). The fourth was Moratoṭa Dhammakkhanda who, after serving as deputy supreme chief monk, became supreme chief monk in 1787. Dhammakkhanda was the chief student of Tibboṭuvāvē, and his appointments exemplify the importance of pupillary lineage over two generations (Bechert 1988, vol. 1, 265; Malalgoda 1976, 85; SSC 48–49).

At lower levels of the administrative hierarchy, student-teacher relationships continued to influence appointments and to ensure educational conservatism. For instance, Vehällē Dhammadinna (a second-generation member of Saraṇaṃkara's pupillary lineage) held a number of prestigious temple incumbencies, including those for Pälmaḍullē and Kuttāpiṭiya Vihārayas. These put him in control of the hotly contested and valuable Śrī Pāda pilgrimage site. At the same time, he was appointed district chief monk of the Mātoṭa Disāva (Amaravaṃśa 1995, 54; Hēvāvasam 1966, 44). *Saṃgharājasādhucariyāva* recounts other appointments of temple incumbencies linked to pupillary lineage. Although the incumbencies of new and restored temples were determined by the king, membership in a prestigious pupillary lineage like that of Saraṇaṃkara's assured the visibility needed to gain a royal appointment. For instance, Mālimbaḍa, a student of Saraṇaṃkara, was appointed incumbent of Velagama Vihāraya (SSC, 16–17, 34). One generation later, students of Kokunnävē Saṃgharakīrti (one of Saraṇaṃkara's students) were appointed to temple incumbencies in Uva Disāva after receiving advanced education and higher ordination in Kandy (Dhammatilaka 1995, 89–91).

Although appointments at the highest level of the Siyam Nikāya were consistently held by Malvatu Vihāraya monks during the latter years of the eighteenth century, monks connected with Asgiri Vihāraya served as supreme chief monks, deputy supreme chief monks, chief monks, and incumbents within that division. Of these offices, the three highest appointments within the Asgiri division were made by the king, whose decisions were based substantially on the level of erudition shown by monks within the division (Silakkhanda 1995, 193–195). Urulävattē Dhammasiddhi's appointment as supreme chief monk (1753–1778) is exemplary in this regard. Thus, leading monks connected to the Asgiri Vihāraya were those who could demonstrate their literate skills in accordance with the expectations of the new curriculum and who were inclined to assure their pupils' fortune by implementing Saraṇaṃkara's curriculum in the Asgiri Vihāraya's educational program. This, in turn, meant the influence of the new curriculum on incumbents connected with the Asgiri Vihāraya division. As in the Malvatu Vihāraya division, the appointment of incumbents to outlying temples was determined by educational achievements and pupillary lineages (Silakkhanda 1995, 311).

As I show further in chapter 4, monastic learning held an important place in the conversations about monasticism circulating within the Siyam Nikāya and in the representations of the order made by its members for outsiders. In this "discourse on monasticism," learning became an emblem of the Siyam Nikāya, indicating that those monks who did not participate in the new order's educational program rooted in Saraṇaṃkara's early efforts were, essentially, outsiders to the Siyam Nikāya community. The importance of monastic learning as a sign of membership in the Siyam Nikāya, and the identification of Saraṇaṃkara and his early students as the arbiters of proper learning, predisposed the participants in the Siyam Nikāya's new educational institutions (at least during the latter two-thirds of the eighteenth century, when Saraṇaṃkara dominated the community) to do so with a greater conservatism than might otherwise have been the case. In other words, as texts and ideas about curriculum moved through the temple centers of Kandy and into other educational centers as well, monastic students and teachers were likely to accept them either because they understood this as the proper course for monastic practice or because they realized that nonacceptance would define them in ways that would hinder their careers.

It is unlikely that the Siyam Nikāya's system of monastic administration and pupillary lineage was more open than the earlier system of *ñāti śisya paramparā*, which kept temple property and administration within kinship units. In some cases, perhaps, talented students without family connections made their way on the basis of participation in the educational system. There is more evidence to suggest, however, that families made efforts to maintain influence over temple properties by bringing male children into the monastic order who would then participate in the curriculum and administrative position described above.[23] Evidence also

[23] See Lawrie (1896/1898) for temple histories showing patterns of familial control over temple property.

indicates that monks who rose to the highest levels in monastic bureaucracy came from powerful lay families. As I have already noted, Saraṇaṃkara's Kulatunga family participated in court circles and held a high position in the Tumpanē region near Kandy (Vācissara 1964, 155). Similarly, Saraṇaṃkara's chief student, Tibboṭuvāvē Buddharakkhita, came from a family of good standing in the Matale region just north of Kandy, with connections to the highest officials in the Kandyan court administration (Dewaraja 1988, 116; Lawrie 1898, 822). Moraṭota Dhammakkhanda, another Siyam Nikāya leader just mentioned (and patron of the poet discussed in chapter 1), came from a well-known family (Dewaraja 1988, 57). Moreover, the fact that only members of the highest caste within the Sinhala caste system, the *goyigama*, were allowed to receive higher ordination in the Siyam Nikāya meant that the new order functioned as a closed system in which influences from the central Kandyan region predominated. This caste exclusion was not consistently implemented in the first higher ordination rituals of 1753, as a result of which Siṭināmaluvē Dhammajoti (a member of the Durāve caste associated with toddy-tapping)was able to receive higher ordination (Malalgoda 1976, 91).[24] Eventually, however, caste exclusivity became fully entrenched and was legitimized with a decree attributed to Kīrti Śrī Rājasiṃha, though the steps leading up to this decree are not fully known (1976, 88). Such caste consciousness was not unprecedented in Lankan monastic communities and, as Malalgoda suggests, "it may be argued . . . that what had in fact prevailed as the informally established practice was merely formalized during Kīrti Śrī's time" (90; see also Ratnapala 1971, 49). In time, monks educated within the new educational institutions but excluded from higher ordination and control over temple property protested the caste exclusivity of the Siyam Nikāya. When they were unsuccessful in their attempts to have the system altered, these men supported the formation of new monastic orders in the early years of the nineteenth century (Hēvāvasam 1966, 34–90; Malalgoda 1976, 92–100).[25]

Texts Enabling Transmission and Consistent Application

Although administrative procedures enhanced by the prevailing discourse on monasticism aided the spread of the Siyam Nikāya's monastic curriculum and its conservative implementation, they do not adequately explain the relatively rapid transmission of texts and the consistent ap-

[24] According to some sources, Vēhällē Dhammadinna was also a member of a non-*goyigama* community (Malalgoda 1976, 91 n. 51).

[25] I return to this subject in chapter 6.

plication of these texts in monastic educational institutions throughout the island. To account for this, it is necessary to look for particular textual forms, or genres, that made it possible to replicate the educational activities of the Kandyan center throughout areas quite distant from it. Surveying the literary record from the latter two-thirds of the eighteenth century, we find several textual forms that laid out a vision of educational practice, made central topics accessible to students in an easily portable manner, and set forth common interpretive strategies for students studying within these institutions. Without such texts, the ambitious educational plans of Saraṇaṃkara and his early students would have met with only limited success. These texts were advisory letters, monastic regulations, grammars and lexicons, monastic handbooks, and bilingual commentaries.

Copies of several advisory letters written by Saraṇaṃkara to his monastic students have been preserved; they help us to understand how certain aspects of monastic life were regulated for all monks from the Siyam Nikāya centers in Kandy. These letters are important both because of their content and because they set a tone for educational practice. They present Saraṇaṃkara as a caring but watchful leader, self-conscious about his role as the founder of a new company of monks and new educational institutions for them. All of them emphasize the importance of studying works that will help students fulfill expectations for monastic discipline and will allow them to cultivate positive mental states. Although the first letter is relatively brief and relies on monastic handbooks to provide more detailed guidelines, the others are quite detailed. In them Pāli *sutta*s are mentioned by name and instructions are given regarding the use of *Vinaya* commentaries and condensations, as well as certain sections from *Visuddhimagga* and *Milindapañha* that provide information about the forms of asceticism suitable for monks. Provisions are made for advanced students, and for those who are capable of very little intellectual exercise (Dhammānanda 1969, 142–145, 148–149). I have drawn on these advisory letters in previous sections to reconstruct the Siyam Nikāya curriculum.

Monastic regulations, or *katikāvata*s, were promulgated twice during the period with which I am concerned. The first, which contains the most detailed account of monastic education, was set out in 1753 immediately after the introduction of higher ordination from Siam. It was thus contemporary with the introduction of the administrative hierarchy; everyone who sought ordination as a novice was expected to memorize it. Monks were enjoined to recite it at fortnightly monastic gatherings and were held accountable for violations of its rules (Ratnapala 1971, 99–101). Some suggest that these regulations were also included in monastic handbooks (Adikāri 1991, 242).[26] The monastic regulation provided a detailed model for monastic education in *tipiṭaka* and *tipiṭaka*-based texts in which the study of works related to monastic discipline received special emphasis. Thus, although it did not list all elements of the curriculum, it provides valuable evidence of one aspect of monastic education in the eighteenth century, and its references are incorporated in my earlier discussion of curriculum. It also set out rules for the monks' work as scribes or authors in the attempt to control the uses to which monastic education was put. The content of this monastic regulation is consistent with *Saṃgharājasādhucariyāva* and with Saraṇaṃkara's advisory letters, as well as with the collections of eighteenth- and nineteenth-century manuscripts held at major temples connected to the Siyam Nikāya (Blackburn 2001).

Lexicons and works on grammar were also important to the eighteenth-century curriculum since these provided the essential linguistic foundation for reading and composition. It is not surprising that old and new lexicons and grammatical works for Pāli, Sanskrit, and Sinhala were prepared during this period. They were useful in the rapidly growing educational centers, and particularly in centers where the teachers in residence had not yet advanced very far in their own education. Accounts of monastic education written during this period stress the importance of grammar to Saraṇaṃkara and his students, and several monks are singled out for praise as experts in grammar (Sinhala *vyākaraṇa*) (SSC, passim). It is clear from the redaction of lexicons (Sinhala *nighaṇḍu*)—texts containing specialized vocabulary in Pāli, Sinhala, and Sanskrit—that students in Siyam Nikāya educational institutions were expected to develop their composition skills, and that the ability to compose verse compositions was highly regarded.

A new textual form, the monastic handbook or *baṇa* (sometimes *baṇa daham*) *pota* rose to sudden popularity during the period I am discussing and was used regularly in the Siyam Nikāya's educational institutions (Somadasa 1987, ix). These manuscripts contained a collection of smaller texts, or portions of them, which were to be studied by monastic students. The contents of *baṇa pot* were influenced by Saraṇaṃkara's model handbook, described above in the section on curriculum. According to one monastic historian of education, Rājaguru Baṇḍāra also helped to shape expectations about the content appropriate for monastic handbooks (Maṅgala n.d., 112). A study of manuscripts

[26] The monastic handbook manuscripts I have examined, or for which annotated catalogue entries are available, do not support this view. It is possible that monastic regulations were included in some of the first handbooks produced in the eighteenth century. Because monastic handbooks received heavy use they disintegrated rapidly.

shows that the contents of these texts were not completely stable, which suggests that teachers and students at individual temples adjusted the organization of the manuscript to suit their interest.[27] The basic structure of the handbooks, however, remained constant; the texts comprised *Vinaya* condensations, short teachings on different meditative techniques, selected Pāli *sutta*s plus Sinhala commentary, common *paritta* texts, guidelines for daily monastic duties, and devotional verses celebrating the Buddha's virtues. In other words, these monastic handbooks contained the essentials for a monastic life, compiled in a portable form. They were instrumental in the creation of a widespread network of educational institutions, and created considerable common ground among the monks who studied them.

A look at the curriculum outlined earlier in this chapter indicates the importance of texts called *sannaya*s to the education provided for Siyam Nikāya monks. *Sannaya*s, explanatory commentaries written in Sinhala for works originally composed in Pāli and Sanskrit, had a long history of use in Lanka; a number of celebrated *sannaya*s were written during the Poḷonnaruva and Daṁbadeṇi periods. *Sannaya*s varied somewhat in their commentarial style. Usually including both the text on which they commented and Sinhala glosses for its words, they sometimes added more elaborate commentarial passages. At times these explanatory commentaries were composed to display erudition, but they had another function in the classroom, where they allowed students more familiar with Sinhala than with Pāli or Sanskrit to study the contents of important works written in those languages. *Sannaya*s were included in monastic handbooks but also circulated with individual texts such as the *śataka* texts used at the second level of the curriculum and the technical manuals on poetics, astrology and medicine studied by more advanced students.

During the latter half of the eighteenth century, *sannaya*s written between the twelfth and fourteenth centuries were put to use in the Siyam Nikāya educational centers, and new *sannaya*s were written. Among the most important of these was a subgenre called the *sūtra sannaya*, an explanatory commentary written in Sinhala for the *sutta*s of the Pāli *tipiṭaka*. This genre rapidly became popular with students and teachers connected to the Siyam Nikāya, after Saraṇaṃkara composed a new *sūtra sannaya* during what I have called the second stage of the Siyam Nikāya's educational institutional development. The *sūtra sannaya*s be-

[27] See, for instance, *baṇa daham pot* held in the British Library's Nevill Collection and thoroughly catalogued by Somadasa (1987) as well as Reynolds (1981, 101) and Bechert (1997, 117–118). It is quite likely that by the early nineteenth century, when local educational centers had attained a greater degree of autonomy enhanced by the fall of Kandy to the British in 1815, the measure of local creativity in education increased somewhat.

came popular in part because of Saraṇaṃkara's example, but also because they provided a highly efficient way to make selected texts accessible to monastic students. These commentaries were typically written by monks famous for their learning and then copied and distributed throughout various institutions. Judging from extant manuscripts, they sometimes circulated in collections of two or three, but most often circulated independently. A survey of printed and manuscript versions of several of these *sūtra sannayas*, including those for *paritta suttas*, the *Satipaṭṭhāna Sutta*, the *Dhammacakkappavattana Sutta*, and the *Ālavaka Sutta*, shows a striking degree of standardization among these versions, which suggests that the interpretative authority of the *sannaya*'s author was respected. These explanatory commentaries significantly shaped the nature of eighteenth-century monastic education by highlighting certain parts of the *tipiṭaka* as especially worthy of student attention; they thus helped to shape the ways students were to read these *suttas*.

THE PRECEDING discussion, although not exhaustive, helps to explain the success with which the Siyam Nikāya curriculum spread throughout the island and was implemented with considerable consistency at a variety of educational centers. Authoritative models for study laid out in the advisory letters and monastic regulations could be followed in part because monastic handbooks, grammars, lexicons, and bilingual explanatory commentaries allowed students at all levels to gain access to the texts considered most important. The importance of these texts to the educational practices of the time was enhanced by the fact that in many educational centers the teachers themselves were not yet accomplished scholars. They and their students were thus heavily dependent on genres that made important works in Pāli, Sinhala, and Sanskrit accessible through compendia or commentaries.

EDUCATIONAL EXPERIENCE AND MONASTIC IDENTITY

The curriculum developed in Kandy and transmitted to the many local educational centers that were established after 1753 increased the stability of the early Siyam Nikāya by helping to create a clear *nikāya* identity and a shared understanding of monastic practice. The formal start of the Siyam Nikāya, and the introduction of the royally sponsored system of monastic administration, indicated to Lankan monks that no monk could preserve or attain high status and economic security unless he joined the Siyam Nikāya. Thus, although some members of the *gaṇinnānse* "establishment" initially avoided ordination within the new order, their reluctance was short-lived (Vijayavardhana and Mīgaskumbura 1993, xli).

The fact that monks accepted Siyam Nikāya ordination and entered the order's hierarchy offers only a partial explanation, however, of the assimilation of locally variable *gaṇinnānse* monasticism within the newly dominant Siyam Nikāya monastic culture. A fuller explanation must attend to the subtle processes through which the ideals and expectations of Siyam Nikāya monasticism became both normative and deeply influential. Monastic participation in the Siyam Nikāya educational practices played a crucial role in these processes. All monks connected to the Siyam Nikāya participated in the educational practices laid out in this curriculum, whether in Kandy or in an outlying educational center. Members of the Siyam Nikāya therefore experienced a substantially homogeneous educational environment that inevitably shaped their understanding of the monastic life, and of their collective identity. It would be foolish to suggest that participation in common forms of educational practice created monks whose interests and monastic vision mirrored those of their Siyam Nikāya fellows. However, given our understanding of the ways in which institutionalized actions shape human understandings of self and other, as well as the inclination to find certain thoughts and actions natural and unnatural, desirable and undesirable, it is reasonable to claim that the educational experience shared by nearly all monks connected with the Siyam Nikāya had a formative impact on them.

EDUCATION AND LAY-MONASTIC RELATIONS

Although the educational institutions and curriculum were primarily intended to develop a community of learned monks fit to participate in the new monastic order and in the life of the Buddhist *sāsana*, the educational institutions developed during the third stage also had an impact on the lives of lay Buddhists. The temple-based educational centers established at this time served as institutions for lay learning as well as monastic learning (Hēvāvasam 1966). Even in areas without a center for advanced education, many temples connected with the Siyam Nikāya served as smaller schools that offered education through the first two levels of the curriculum (Adikāri 1991, 232–233; Hēvāvasam 1966, 41). We do not yet know enough about the histories of individual temples throughout the island to provide a detailed description of the centers that provided basic and higher education to monks and lay people; nor can we assess changes in literacy rates from the middle of the eighteenth century to the middle of the nineteenth. Hēvāvasam's detailed history of literary developments in the southern maritime region of Rūhunu (though perhaps somewhat overenthusiastic about the accomplishments of Lankan southerners) suggests, however, that the Siyam Nikāya's new educational program did result in the emergence of a sophisticated literate community composed of lay men and women and of monastics. I have already had occasion to note the role played by one layman (and former monk) in particular, Rājaguru Baṇḍāra, in advanced education circles connected with the Siyam Nikāya.

As I show in chapter 6, the impact of the Siyam Nikāya's educational institutions on the lay Buddhist community was not limited to those lay people who studied in these centers. Since the new curriculum prepared monks to serve as preachers and recitors, its effects were felt widely throughout the Buddhist community. For the first time since the early sixteenth century, a widespread educational system using a common curriculum trained large numbers of monks in canonical texts and their Pāli and Sinhala commentaries, as well as in the popular Sinhala preaching works composed in the twelfth and thirteenth centuries. Eighteenth-century sources attest to the importance of trained preaching for the early Siyam Nikāya's conception of desirable monasticism. *Saṃgharājasādhucariyāva*'s monastic biographies, for instance, place a great deal of emphasis on the systematization and success of preacher training. Saraṇaṃkara is described as someone who "had many manuscripts written and expounded, had preaching studied and encouraged preaching to the world" (SSC 55), and even less important figures, such as the monks Maḍabāviṭa and Vīrodha, are identified in part by their attentiveness in preaching to lay Buddhists (SSC 40–41). Moreover, *Mahāvaṃsa's* eighteenth-century chapters are replete with vivid images of monastic preaching and recitation (for example, MV 99: 18–20, 100, 274–277). These attest to the important place held by these activities in the self-understanding of Siyam Nikāya monks. Since textual evidence shows that the benefits of writing, preaching, and listening to Buddhist teachings (*dharmānisaṃsa*) were a point of emphasis in reflections on Buddhist devotion, the popularity of the new monastic order was undoubtedly enhanced by the central place it accorded to training monks as preachers.[28]

The fact that the curriculum created by and for the early Siyam

[28] Mīgaskumbura has noted a new emphasis on *dharmānisaṃsa* in eighteenth-century texts (personal communication, 1994). Mirando agrees, though he asserts that this was true of the seventeenth and eighteenth centuries as a whole (1985, 113–114). In any event, manuscripts dating to the late eighteenth and nineteenth centuries show that *dharmānisaṃsa* texts were popular (Somadasa 1959–1964), as does the composition of Tiboṭuvāvē Buddharakkhita's *Saddharmāvavāda Saṅgrahaya* (Amaramoli 1956), which devotes two chapters to *dharmānisaṃsa*.

Nikāya reached into the lay Buddhist community through temple-based studies and trained preaching helped to create strong ties between the Siyam Nikāya and its lay supporters, and to assure a consistent base of support at the local level.[29] Some idea of local support for Buddhist temples can be gained from a survey of lay donations recorded by A. Lawrie in his documentation on the Central Province (1889–1896). These records show that nonroyal lay donations of land and produce to temples, though not as substantial as those made by the king, were by no means insignificant.

ERUDITION AND PRESTIGE

Texts written during the period of Siyam Nikāya formation make it clear, however, that the order's major patrons were the king and those members of the court closely affiliated with him. I have already shown how important the king's patronage was to the establishment and support of the Siyam Nikāya's educational institutions. These educational centers and the studies that they made possible were crucial to continued royal patronage of the Buddhist community. Advanced education prepared the monks of the new monastic order to vie with their monastic predecessors and opponents for the prestige and patronage acquired through displays of erudition. The importance of learning in this regard is clear from *Saṃgharājasādhucariyāva*'s dramatic account of the events leading up to Saraṇaṃkara's reconciliation with King Narēndrasiṃha and the return of the Silvat Samāgama to the Kandyan court. These events are portrayed as the turning point in Saraṇaṃkara's monastic career. When probed, the narrative logic reveals much about the elite subculture in which the Siyam Nikāya's rise and success was assured.

While the Silvat Samāgama was absent from Kandy, a brahmin from the Indian subcontinent arrived on the island, making his way to the Kandyan court. Once there, he began to recite what appeared to be verses in a language the courtiers could not understand. Puzzled, the king's men sent for the leaders of the monastic "establishment" to interpret at the court. One after the other, Kandy's leading *gaṇinnānse*s failed to understand the visitor, whose versification grew ever more intense. Finally, someone in the court suggested that Saraṇaṃkara be sent for because he was known for his linguistic skill. When brought to the court, Saraṇaṃkara immediately translated the visiting brahmin's Sanskrit verses into Sinhala and Pāli, and then proceeded to lecture the

[29] This became extremely important in the nineteenth century because of the fall of the Kandyan kingdom to the British and the subsequent disestablishment of central support for monastic institutions. For an insightful account see Malalgoda (1976).

brahmin on Buddhist teachings, using three languages. The visiting brahmin was satisfied, ceased his versifying and disappeared. Saraṇaṃkara was feted and allowed back to Kandy with his followers, where he became tutor to the king's heirs and received the grant of Niyamakanda from the king (SSC, 19–21).

That the story is almost certainly apocryphal enhances its value since, as such, it crystallizes the dominant courtly values of the time. It tells us how the ideal monastic success story would go, and in doing so says much about the context in which the Siyam Nikāya's rise and continued existence was assured. Monks were, in part, performers for the royal court because they and other religious leaders (like the brahmins from the Indian subcontinent who were a regular part of the Kandyan court circles) were expected to have a sophisticated command of Lankan literary traditions that would allow them to create new verse compositions for the enjoyment of the king. Those able to satisfy such demands gained prestige in the eyes of the courtly public and (as the stories spread) in the eyes of those more distant from the court. Moreover, they received favors from the king. As Sannasgala notes in his discussion of eighteenth-century poetic compositions, "the composition of verse in Pāli and Sanskrit was greatly esteemed by the inhabitants [of the island] and the king. It was customary to receive gifts of land from the king for such compositions" (1964, 491).[30] Sannasgala's views on prestigious learning are supported by *Saṃgharājasādhucariyāva*. Däramiṭipala Dhammarakkhita, who became the third supreme chief monk of the Malvatu Vihāraya, for instance, is described in *Saṃgharājasādhucariyāva* with detailed attention to his sophisticated grasp of literate traditions. He was "very accomplished at arranging new verses and *aṣṭaka*s [a particularly prestigious type of composition used for poems of praise] and so on, and endowed with a pure and very subtle intelligence [as well as] virtue, merit and potency" (SSC, 46).

The king's lavish appreciation for displays of monastic learning was not limited to the performance of poetic compositions. Vehällē Dhammadinna is known in monastic traditions as a monk who received the much-coveted control of the Śrī Pāda pilgrimage site through a grant from Kīrti Śrī Rājasiṃha after the king became acquainted with the Dhammadinna's scholarly attainments (Amaravaṃśa 1995, 54). Along a similar line, Moraṭota Dhammakkhanda, who officiated at the center for the king's Buddhist devotions—the Daḷada Maligāva—and became the fourth supreme chief monk of the Malvatu Vihāraya, is described

[30] Land was not the only gift received from the king for displays of erudition, as the biographies of Siyam Nikāya monks clearly show. Desirable monastic appointments and ceremonial regalia were frequent gifts.

with explicit attention to his skill before a royal audience. *Saṃgharājasādhucariyāva* relates that he was able to preach elaborate sermons in royal assemblies, drawing on his knowledge of Pāli texts and their commentaries (SSC, 49). The importance of many types of courtly performance to the monks of the new monastic order comes through clearly in another passage from *Saṃgharājasādhucariyāva*. There Saraṇaṃkara's students are celebrated for their ability to "declare the meaning of the Pāli *nikāya*s, commentaries, and so on, and to preach in a royal assembly relying on works like the *Dhammacakkappavattana Sutta* and the *Brahmajāla Sutta* while providing various elaborate and special explanations for three nights running" (SSC 55). Provided by the Siyam Nikāya's new educational institutions and curriculum with the skills needed to participate in a sophisticated literate tradition, students who traversed the entire curriculum sustained the life of the new order. As privileged clients of special patrons, Siyam Nikāya monks were men to be taken seriously.

CONCLUSION

The simultaneous formation of the Siyam Nikāya and its educational institutions, created—for the first time since the early sixteenth century—a centralized educational system that trained monks within a common curriculum. Examination of the literate technologies that made it possible for the Siyam Nikāya to develop a widespread and relatively consistent set of educational practices helps to illuminate aspects of the transmission and standardization of learning in a preprinting era. Foreshadowing arguments made in subsequent chapters, this one began to explore the impact of these new educational practices on the life of the Siyam Nikāya and the lives of its lay patrons from three perspectives: the relationship between monastic education and the inculcation of collective identity, the effects of monastic training on local Buddhist communities, and the way in which advanced education allowed Siyam Nikāya monks to participate in prestigious court displays.

The importance of education to the stable growth of the Siyam Nikāya becomes yet clearer when the eighteenth-century reintroduction of higher ordination from Ayutthaya is compared with the two occasions in sixteenth and seventeenth centuries in which monks arrived from Arakan (in southern Burma) in order to restart the practice of higher ordination in Lanka. These attempts did not produce lasting results: higher ordination did not last more than two monastic generations and no clear collective identity emerged for the Lankan monks ordained by the Arakanese. The reason for this had much to do with the failure to create educational and administrative institutions for the newly ordained Lankan monks. As Kitsiri Malalgoda notes with characteristic perceptiveness, "There is no evidence that the Arakanese monks remained in the island in order to instruct their Sinhalese pupils in the dhamma [Buddhist teachings] and the vinaya [monastic disciplinary rules]. Nor is there evidence that the Sinhalese monks who received higher ordination in 1697 made any serious effort to instruct their own juniors" (1976, 57). The combined efforts of the early Siyam Nikāya leaders and the royal court led by Kīrti Śrī Rājasiṃha shaped a strikingly different course for the Siyam Nikāya. Distinguished clearly from their predecessors and opponents through discourse and educational practice, the stability and longevity of the Siyam Nikāya was assured in large part because of the interwoven processes of education, administration, and patronage.

CHAPTER FOUR

"They Were Scholars and Contemplatives"

I HAVE ARGUED that historians of the Theravāda have failed to recognize the rhetorical and constructive character of indigenous histories of Buddhism.[1] This failure, in conjunction with the other factors explored in chapter 1, sustains the view that "traditional" Theravāda was essentially stable and that its stability was assured by repetitive cycles of degeneration and reform. In other words, as the "traditional" commonplace would have it, the degenerative and reformist "vicissitudes" (Gombrich 1988, 23) described in indigenous histories assured rather than disturbed the stability of Buddhism. This is because the ongoing process of a degeneration from purity and a reformist return to purity is understood in terms of an unchanging point of orientation: namely, disciplined monasticism that follows "early Buddhist" norms. This view is articulated by Michael Carrithers:

> A simplified picture of the history of the Theravāda Sangha is as follows. The order of ascetics, separated from the world, gradually evolves towards the equilibrium state, the domesticated Sangha. Once this is reached, reformers may then arise from within the ranks, and though the majority of the Sangha remain domesticated, there appear groups, necessarily small because necessarily self-referring, of reform monks. As these settle and grow, they evolve towards domestication, and though associated in name with reform, come to entertain in fact the opinions of village literary specialists. Within this overgrown domesticated erstwhile reform groups there then appear further reformers . . . and the process continues (1979a, 297, author's ellipses).

A close look at indigenous histories produced by Lankan Buddhists connected with the Siyam Nikāya during the period of the order's formation clearly shows that modern historians of "traditional" Buddhism have erred in their understanding of these indigenous narratives, and that the decline-and-revival (that is, degeneration-and-reform) perspective that dominates eighteenth-century Buddhist historiography is *not* evidence of essential continuity within the Lankan Theravāda. Rather, this decline-and-revival perspective signals a moment of profound

[1] The quotation in the title is from MV 100: 176–178.

change in Lankan Buddhism. In this moment, monastic and lay elites linked to the Siyam Nikāya altered the terms in which desirable and authoritative Buddhist monasticism was understood.

AN INNOVATIVE DISCOURSE ON MONASTICISM

On the basis of my reading of five indigenous histories of Buddhism composed during the period of the Siyam Nikāya's formation, I argue that an innovative discourse on monasticism emerged simultaneously with the rise of the Siyam Nikāya. This discourse is characterized by an unprecedented self-consciousness about the relationship between learning and proper monasticism, and about learned monasticism as the key to the illumination of the darkened Buddhist *sāsana*. In this discourse, monks connected to the Silvat Samāgama and, subsequently, to the Siyam Nikāya, are portrayed as the saviors of a degenerate Buddhist community in Lanka. Dwelling at length on the Siyam Nikāya's dedication to Buddhist learning and on the order's remarkable ability to develop erudition without sacrificing the standards for monastic discipline and meditative practice, this discourse describes Saraṇaṃkara and other Siyam Nikāya monks as men who draw the Lankan Buddhist community back from the brink of destruction.

Moreover, the innovative discourse on monasticism—which articulated the familiar theme of decline-and-revival in unmistakably new ways—contributed importantly to the reformulation of Lankan Buddhism that occurred during the eighteenth century. The ongoing life of the Siyam Nikāya, and the "natural" authority of the intellectual practices developed within and for the new order, were assured not only by material support and the king's power behind a monastic bureaucracy. The success of the Siyam Nikāya and its educational institutions were crucially sustained by certain ideas that circulated throughout the Lankan Buddhist community through this new discourse on monasticism. The indigenous histories are not empirical accounts of the Siyam Nikāya's formation, nor are they literary flourishes of little importance to the social context in which they were composed. To understand the impact of this innovative discourse, however, one must link historical representations to human action. I do this by adapting aspects of reader response theory first set forth by Stanley Fish (1980). He argued that a shared institutional location makes possible common interpretive responses to a text. I suggest that, in addition, common exposure to textual representations makes possible shared interpretive responses to social institutions.

The five historical narratives that dominate eighteenth-century Lankan historiography are the first *Kīrti Śrī Rājasiṃha Katikāvata*,[2] the final chapters of *Mahāvaṃsa*,[3] *Vimānavastuprakāraṇaya* (Explanation of the [Pāli] Vimānavastu),[4] *Saṃgharājavata*,[5] and *Saṃgharājasādhucariyāva*.[6] These works were composed by laymen or monks connected to the Siyam Nikāya. All of the monastic authors participated in monastic ed-

[2] *Katikāvata*s, or monastic regulations, were promulgated by kings with the support of monastic leaders, usually at a time of monastic reorganization when monastic hierarchies shifted and matters of practice were debated. For further details on their contents, see Chapter 3 and Ratnapala (1971). This monastic regulation was promulgated immediately after monastic higher ordination was reintroduced from Siam in 1753. The regulation was set forth by Kīrti Śrī Rājasiṃha at a convocation of the monks who inhabited the two chief temples in the Kandyan Kingdom, the Malvatu Vihāraya and the Asgiri Vihāraya (Ratnapala 1971, 228). Because of Saraṇaṃkara's close ties to the king as royal tutor and the leading role played by Saraṇaṃkara in the efforts to bring Siamese monks to Lanka, it is likely that Saraṇaṃkara had a significant influence on the regulation's contents. Moreover, the style of the first *Kīrti Śrī Rājasiṃha Katikāvata* closely follows earlier monastic regulations. This suggests a strong monastic hand in the composition of the document, since monks would have been the most familiar with this genre.

[3] These chapters (97–100) are usually referred to as part of the *Cūlavaṃsa*. However, since the term *Cūlavaṃsa* was not used by eighteenth-century authors but was introduced by nineteenth-century European philologists (Kemper 1991, 28 n. 5), I prefer to retain the indigenous title, *Mahāvaṃsa*. These chapters were composed at the invitation of Kīrti Śrī Rājasiṃha some time between 1753 and 1770, when their author, Tibboṭuvāvē Buddharakkhita, was the supreme chief monk of the Malvatu Vihāraya in Kandy and deputy leader of the monastic community under Saraṇaṃkara.

[4] *Vimānavastu* is the Sinhala translation of Pāli *Vimānavatthu*, a collection of stories about Buddhist practitioners whose good deeds led to their rebirth in the Buddhist heavens, where they enjoyed great comfort. On the importance of the Buddhist heavens for the Theravāda, see Collins (1998). *Vimānavastuprakāraṇaya* was written by the monk Gammūllē Ratanapāla in 1770. The author describes himself as a member of Saraṇaṃkara's lineage and as a student of Saraṇaṃkara's earlier student Däramitipala Dammarakhita (Sīlānanda 1901, 206). At that time, Ratanapāla was living in Kandy's Malvatu Vihāraya. According to Sannasgala, Ratanapāla was invited to write the work by another member of Saraṇaṃkara's lineage—Galagedara Indajoti—since Ratanapāla was known for his literary skill. A brief history was appended to the translation of *Vimānavastuprakāraṇaya*; called *Sāsanopakāra Saṃgrahavastuva* (An Abridged Account of Support for the Sāsana), this may have been written at the invitation of Kīrti Śrī Rājasiṃha and with the help of Saraṇaṃkara (Sannasgala 1964, 416–418).

[5] See also chapter 1. *Saṃgharājavata* is somewhat difficult to date, since the text makes no mention of author or date (Sannasgala 1964, 443). It is likely that the work was written shortly after 1778–1779, since the verse biography mentions Saraṇaṃkara's illness and death. According to the text itself, it was written at the invitation of Moratoṭa Dhammakkhanda, who was one of Saraṇaṃkara's students, and who rose to prominence in the Kandyan monastic community and in political circles. Dhammakkhanda was the supreme chief monk of the Malvatu Vihāraya between 1787 and 1811. Prior to that appointment, he served as royal tutor (*rājaguru*) to Rājādhi Rājasiṃha, the king who succeeded Kīrti Śrī Rājasiṃha. He also had responsibilities for the Daḷada Maligāva, the key devotional center of the Kandyan court (Dewaraja 1988, 172). P. B. Sannasgala notes a tradition within Moratoṭa Dhammakkhanda's lineage which says that Muṃkoṭuvē Ab-

ucational centers of the Kandyan Kingdom, and were bound to Saraṇaṃkara through the ties of educational lineage. The lay authors of the two biographical works—*Saṃgharājavata* and *Saṃgharājasādhucariyāva*—voice strongly positive sentiments about Saraṇaṃkara and his students, which shows that they or their patrons were important lay supporters of the Siyam Nikāya's early leadership.

When setting forth ideas related to the past, the present, and the future of Buddhist communities, the five indigenous histories consistently connect the actions of Buddhist monks to the vitality of the *sāsana*. These histories portray the *sāsana* as characterized by alternating moments of worrysome deterioration and triumphant resurgence. Within the framework provided by the decline-and-revival trope, the five histories depict desirable monasticism as learned monasticism. Although they build on earlier Buddhist historiographic conventions, these eighteenth-century works stress the links between monastic learning and the *sāsana*'s vitality to an unprecedented degree. In doing so, they depict monks connected to the Siyam Nikāya in a strikingly favorable light. The consistency among all these histories written over a twenty-five-year period indicates the degree to which these ideas became the natural mode of expression for those who wrote histories of Buddhist monasticism in relation to the newly forming Siyam Nikāya.[7] The fact that these ideas appear in works composed by monks for monks, by monks for the king, and by lay authors for monks and kings shows the degree to which the vision of the early leadership of the Siyam Nikāya as idealized, learned participants in a revival of the Buddhist *sāsana* permeated the literary imagination of lay and monastic literati who celebrated the

---

esiṃha Rāḷa was the author, and argues that this view is supported by the closely similar style of *Saṃgharājavata* and Muṃkoṭūvē's verse biography of Dhammakkhanda (1964, 444).

[6] There is no author mentioned in *Saṃgharājasādhucariyāva*, although a composition date of 1779 is given. In a work no longer extant by Irivinnē Vipassi Himi, the work is attributed to Āyittāliyaddē Muhandiram, and Sannasgala accepts this (1964, 442). Āyittāliyaddē Muhandiram held a mid-level royal appointment in the Kandyan kingdom's administration as a member of the Vedhikkāra Lēkam for Dumbara district, the unit in charge of the king's musketeers. As muhandiram of Dumbara, he was in charge of mobilizing Dumbara's population for military service (Dewaraja 1988, 208). He was also involved with the formal beginnings of the Siyam Nikāya as a member of the embassy sent to Siam in 1750 to procure monks for the reinstitution of higher ordination, and was the likely author of an account of that embassy (Pieris 1903).

[7] These histories echo each other with respect to the following topics, for instance: the ability of Siyam Nikāya monks simultaneously to develop learning, discipline, and asceticism; the involvement of the Siyam Nikāya in a renaissance of Pāli learning and manuscript production; Siyam Nikāya monks' dedication to appropriate learning in contrast to *gaṇinnānse* preoccupations with inappropriate learning; and monastic biographies that stress educational atttainments.

beginnings of the Siyam Nikāya. From 1753, when the Siyam Nikāya was formed under Saraṇaṃkara's leadership, into the 1780s, when the leadership of the Siyam Nikāya shifted after Saraṇaṃkara's death, this vision of monastic practice in relation to the history of the *sāsana* remained a constant. At the same time, with increasingly strong ties between the Siyam Nikāya and the royal court, which resulted in large-scale patronage and royal involvement in monastic administration, the Siyam Nikāya became the dominant monastic community on the island and had significant influence throughout the central and southern regions of Lanka.

INFLUENCES ON THE INNOVATIVE DISCOURSE

Although these five indigenous histories emphasize monastic learning to an unprecedented degree, they should not be seen as radically discontinuous with earlier histories of monastic practice in relation to the Buddhist *sāsana*. Eighteenth-century authors drew on ideas articulated by the fifth-century Buddhist commentator Buddhaghosa, and by other monastic authors writing between the twelfth and the fourteenth centuries who discussed the life of the *sāsana*.[8]

To understand the backdrop of earlier Lankan histories, we must attend to Buddhist discussions of the *sāsana*. As Gombrich notes,

> If Theravāda Buddhists want to refer to Buddhism not just as a doctrine but as a phenomenon in history, a whole religion, they usually call it the Sāsana, the Teaching. For example, where English speakers might talk of the welfare of Buddhism, they would talk of the welfare of the Sāsana. Gotama Buddha founded the present Sāsana. . . . In [Sri Lankan] tradition, Buddhism (the Sāsana) has three constituents: learning, practice and realization. Each depends on the previous one . . . Five thousand years after the Buddha's death, according to tradition, his Sāsana will die out. At this point learning too will disappear. The texts of the Pali Canon will be lost, starting at the end. . . . When that is gone, all is lost: Buddhism has disappeared from the face of the earth. (1988, 3, 150).[9]

The idea that three elements contribute to the continued existence of the *sāsana* is discussed in several commentaries produced in the Theravāda.

[8] Although poetic works composed between the fourteenth and eighteenth centuries may have been known to the eighteenth-century writers, the latter's choice of language and literary style, and the borrowing visible in other works contemporary with them, strongly suggests that the dominant literary influences on eighteenth century authors came from works composed from the twelfth to the fourteenth centuries. See Sannasgala (1964, 391–492) and the account below.

[9] See also Gombrich (1971, 287).

One important passage is found in *Sammohavinodanī*, the Pāli commentary on the *Vibhaṅga* attributed to the fifth-century commentator Buddhaghosa. There the commentary distinguishes between the disappearance of learning (Pāli *pariyatti*), realization/attainment (Pāli *paṭivedha*), and conduct/practice (Pāli *paṭipatti*); learning is glossed as (knowledge of) the *tipiṭaka*, realization as realization of the truth (taught by a Buddha), and *paṭipatti* as the path (taught by a Buddha). Later it states that "learning is the measure for the endurance of the *sāsana*" and that "the endurance of the *sāsana* comes about through the endurance of learning" (Vibh-a 431–432). John Ross Carter notes that in later Sinhala Buddhist literature, the threefold classification became the norm. In the *Saddharmālaṅkāra*, for instance, a fourteenth-century work, Buddhaghosa's formulation is developed:

> *Dharma* that is characterized as the *śāsana* of our Buddha is threefold such as the authoritative teaching, practice and penetration. These are also called the threefold *śāsana*. Of them, *dharma* that is the authoritative teaching is all the words of the Buddha brought together in the three *piṭakas*. *Dharma* that is practice means the thirteen ascetic qualities, the fourteen practices in the *Khandhaka* [of the *Vinaya*], the eighty-two major practices, morality, concentration and insight. Further, the nine *dharmas* that transcend the world, such as the four paths and the four fruits and *nirvāṇa*, that is stream attainment and so forth, are called the *dharma* that is penetration. These [last nine] are also called *saddharma* that is penetration. Further, of this threefold *dharma* only *dharma* that is the authoritative teaching is the basis [*mul*] for the *śāsana* of the Omniscient One. (Quoted in Carter 1978, 133)

A more elaborate discussion of the disappearance of the *sāsana* is found in Buddhaghosa's *Manoratthapūraṇī*, analyzed at length in a study by Jan Nattier. She notes that "whatever the source of their primary inspiration, Buddhist beliefs in the finite duration of Buddhism are quite evident in the canonical scriptures. With relentless consistency, Buddhist writers have predicted the eventual disappearance of their own religion, offering explicit timetables for its extinction" (1991, 28). The *Manoratthapūraṇī* passages describe the gradual disappearance of five aspects of the Buddha's dispensation (56–58). At the end of the first thousand years, followers of Buddhism will no longer be able to achieve the attainments (Pāli *adhigama*) from stream-enterer to enlightened one that mark the final stages of the path to liberation.[10] After an additional

[10] These "final stages" are *sotāpanna* ("stream-enterer," one assured of liberation and free from rebirth in the Buddhist hells), *sakadāgamin* ("once-returner," one who has diminished passion, hatred, and delusion to the degree that he or she will experience only one more birth before liberation), *anāgāmin* ("nonreturner," one who will achieve liberation in his or her current lifetime), and *arahant* ("enlightened one," one who has de-

one thousand years, conduct/practice will disappear. This includes the techniques used to attain meditative trance states and the ability to keep the precepts required of a Buddhist monk. The end of the third thousand-year period will mark the disappearance of learning, after a gradual loss of sections from the *tipiṭaka*, culminating with the *Vinaya*. A fourth one-thousand year period ends with the disappearance of signs (Pāli *nimitta/liṅga*) that are the objects and behaviors (such as robes and celibacy) traditionally associated with monasticism. The deterioration of the *sāsana* is complete when, at the end of five thousand years, the Buddha's relics burst into flame and are completely destroyed. Nattier notes that, although Mahāyāna Buddhist texts often describe non-Buddhist outsiders as the external causes of the *sāsana*'s decline, Nikāya Buddhist works (including the texts of the Theravāda) consistently emphasize the impact of internal causes, which include the admission of women into the monastic community, a lack of respect toward elements of Buddhist tradition, the failure to maintain diligent meditation practice, the absence of care in the transmission of Buddhist teachings, the beginning of divisions within the monastic community, the emergence of false teachings, and an undue level of monastic participation in secular pursuits (120–127, esp. 127 n. 21).

It is clear from these discussions that a belief in the fragility of Buddhist teachings and institutions was part of the foundational conceptual world set forth in the authoritative Pāli texts of Theravādin Buddhism. Texts written later in Lanka, in Pāli and in Sinhala, offer plentiful evidence of continuing interest in the life of the *sāsana* and the place of monastic practice within it. Although the eventual disappearance and reappearance of the *sāsana* was accepted as part of the macrocosmological understanding of the Theravāda, the logic of the predictions of decline provided space for Buddhists to struggle against the internal causes of decline—in rhetoric and in practice—as an effort to slow the deterioration of the *sāsana* as much as possible. The decline-and-revival narratives found in the texts of the Lankan Theravāda reflect the fact that the problem of the *sāsana*'s decline provided a key organizing trope for reflections on the relationship between the life of the *sāsana* and events in monastic communities.

We see this, for instance, in the *Mahāvaṃsa* sections composed in the twelfth and fourteenth centuries that regularly describe kings and leading monks as participants in the life of the *sāsana*.[11] Laudable monks are

---

stroyed all of the defilements and attained liberation). These are labeled the "four paths" in the above quotation from the *Saddharmālaṅkāra*.

[11] It is interesting to note that the decline-and-revival narrative does not characterize the sixth-century section of the *Mahāvaṃsa*, although there are references to the establishment of the *sāsana* and actions that contribute to its brilliance. This may be because the

those who understand the rules of monastic discipline and follow them well; successful kings are those who revive the *sāsana* by finding and supporting disciplined monks. King Parākramabāhu I (1153–1186), for instance, is praised for his ability to revive the monastic community to the level of purity that characterized its origins by removing undisciplined monks from the community and supporting those more disciplined: "he removed the internal stains of the monks by purifying the *sāsana*" (MV 78: 44). Describing a reorganization of the monastic community that occurred approximately one hundred years later (in a section written by a different author), *Mahāvaṃsa* depicts a revival of the *sāsana* under the leadership of Parākramabāhu II (1236–1270). Once again, the renewed success of the *sāsana* is linked to disciplinary purity within the monastic community: "He looked for all the groups [of monks] unembarrassed by impropriety who since [a period of instability following an invasion from southern India in the early thirteenth century] lived only focused on their own wishes, engaged in incorrect activities, with their senses continually ungoverned, had them removed and thus purified the *sāsana* of the perfectly Enlightened One [the Buddha]." . . . Thus the King [endowed] with pure qualities granted it in this way many forms of support and caused the good *sāsana*—(which is like an ocean) of the Omniscient One, the king of the true teaching—to develop properly" (MV 7–9, 84:44).

Another account of the Lankan Buddhist community, written in the late fourteenth century, elaborates the events of Parākramabāhu I's reign in more detail while retaining the decline-and-revival framework and the emphasis on disciplinary purity. According to *Nikāyasaṅgrahāya* (The Nikāya Compilation),[12] King Parākramabāhu I heard about the "stains" on the *sāsana* and wondered whether he should "purify [it], making it spotless." Deciding to do so, he gathered the monastic community of the Mahāvihāra (the Great Monastery) led by Udumbaragiri Āranyavāsī Mahākāśyapa, got rid of the monks who failed to obey the monastic rules, and then united the remaining members of the monastic community. The king's success did not long survive his own death, we are told: "From the year that the king who had thus purified the *sāsana* in this way died, for thirty-six years the *sāsana* existed purely and then . . . again—as before—went into decline" (Samaranāyaka

author of this section sought to emphasize institutional continuities that would strengthen the position of monks connected with the Mahāvihāra (on which see Collins 1990 and Walters 1997, in addition to chapter 2), because Buddhaghosa's account of the *sāsana*'s life history was not yet the site of sustained reflection, or because the author was more preoccupied with meditations on the passage of time in relation to the Buddha than with the lives of *sāsana*s (on which see Collins 1998).

[12] For details on dating, author, and structure see Sannasgala (1964, 224–225).

1966, 79). Monks, as well as kings, are major players in these narratives of decline and revival. *Nikayāsaṅgrahāya* recounts that two leading monks in the thirteenth and fourteenth centuries, Āranyaka Medhaṃkara Mahāsvāmi and Amaragirivāsavāsī Vanaratana Mahāsvāmi, responded to word of the deterioration of the *sāsana* by gathering the monastic community together. Both occasions are described in the following words: "expelling the monks acting improperly, [the leading monk] purified the *sāsana*, exhorted [the others] not to turn away from a life of diligence, and ordered that the *sāsana* should continue in accordance with the [rules of monastic discipline], [and monks] living engaged in study and meditation" (80–82).

Early monastic regulations also elaborated their vision of Buddhist history by linking monastic discipline to the well-being of the Buddhist *sāsana*. Describing Parākramabāhu I, for instance, the *Parākramabāhu Katikāvata* recounts that when

> [he] was consecrated as the sole ruler of all of Lanka [and] was engaged in the pleasant powers of kingship [which were] the manifestations of [his previous] meritorious splendid accomplishments, he witnessed monks in the *sāsana* who were headed for hell, destroyed by the quickly spreading poison of the nonobservance and ill-observance [of proper conduct], rooted [both] in ignorance and in imperfect knowledge. [Then His Majesty reflected thus.] "If a *cakkavatti*-king [a "wheel-turning king"; see Tambiah (1976)] like me were to remain indifferent seeing such a blot on the supremely pure Buddhist-*sāsana*, the Buddha-*sāsana* would perish and many beings would be born in the *apāya* hell. It would be good if I served the Buddha-*sāsana* which lasts five thousand years." (Ratnapala, 1971, 37)

For the most part, these pre-eighteenth-century narratives that describe the Buddhist *sāsana* in relation to monastic life emphasize the importance of monastic discipline (a form of conduct, or *paṭipatti*) to the vitality of the *sāsana* rather than the importance of learning or the realization of attainments through ascetic meditation. We see this in the way that *Mahāvaṃsa* describes Sāriputta, one of the scholarly luminaries of the twelfth century (Gunawardana 1979, 157). Sāriputta's learned qualities were of little interest to the author, who stressed the monk's disciplinary accomplishments. "For the elder named Sāriputta whose discipline was firm, [the king erected] a vast and splendid building with a high upper chamber" (MV 78: 34). Similarly, the monk Mahākassapa, who played a leading role in the monastic reorganization that took place during the reign of Parākramabāhu I, is described very briefly, with some attention to learning but primarily to learning as a guarantor of monastic discipline: "he had long been a part of the community. He was the single [point of] light in the lineage of the *thera*s, confident, a *tipiṭaka* scholar particularly knowledgeable about the *Vinaya*" (MV 78: 6–7).

In several fourteenth-century narratives, however, we see the emergence of a more intense interest in the relationship between monastic learning and the life of the *sāsana*. Although the level of attention devoted to monastic educational attainments, lineages, and so on is not as high as it is in the eighteenth-century histories discussed earlier, these fourteenth-century works begin to emphasize the importance of learning to the life of the *sāsana*. *Saddhammasaṅgaha* (Compendium of the Excellent Teaching), for instance, composed in the fourteenth century by Dhammakitti Mahāsāmi, describes the redaction of the *tipiṭaka* in the first century as an act undertaken to slow a decline of the *sāsana* (Saddhānanda 1890, 48).[13] In his work, the composition of commentarial texts as something done for "the growth of the *sāsana*" (56, 59–61). These formulations, though far from elaborate, assume that the *sāsana*'s vitality is linked to levels of support for the study of authoritative texts. It is this view that impels *Saddhammasaṅgaha's* author to detail the books "compiled by the *theras*" from the time of Buddhaghosa through the thirteenth century (62–64). Dhammakitti Mahāsāmi writes: "For the development of the *sāsana* of the Conqueror [the Bud-

[13] The place of the composition of *Saddhammasaṅgaha* remains unclear. According to Norman, the author was an Indian monk who composed the work after studying in Lanka with Saṃgharāja Dhammakīrti (1983, 179–180). Coedès, however, cites a colophon to the text according to which it was composed in Ayutthaya by a monk who had received higher ordination in Lanka and had studied with Dhammakīrti (1915, 43). His view is supported by the colophon to an eighteenth century manuscript of the text held in the British Library's Nevill Collection (OR.6601 [44]) and by the substantial quotations from *Sotabbamālinī* (a popular Siamese text) that occur within *Saddhammasaṅgaha* (Somadasa 1987, 298). Penth notes the existence of a monastery in Ayutthaya, the name of which supports this view, as well (1977, 264). It is thus not unreasonable to suggest that the work, as the product of a monastic author from Siam who had lived among elite Lankan monastics, reflects discursive trends characteristic of fourteenth-century Lankan monastic culture. The similarities visible between *Saddhammasaṅgaha* and *Nikāyasaṅgrahaya* with respect to monastic learning and the life of the *sāsana* (noted below) offer further support for this view. Whatever its origins, however, *Mahāvaṃsa*'s association of *Saddhammasaṅgaha* with the Siamese monk Upali (MV 100: 117–118) suggests that the text was reintroduced into Lanka during the eighteenth century with other texts brought from Siam, though it does not appear in standard lists of such texts. See Vijayavardhana and Mīgaskumbura (1993, 100), Penth (1977, 268), and von Hinüber (1988, 175–176). Its immediate popularity is visible in *Mahāvaṃsa*'s reference to recitation of the text at the Kandyan court (MV 100: 117–118). Tibboṭuvāvē Buddharakkhita's *Śrī Saddharmāvavāda Saṅgrahaya*, composed in 1773 for the Kandyan court (Sannasgala 1964, 420–421) contains substantial quotations from *Saddhammasaṅgaha*. See Chapter 3, n. 26 above. The widespread presence of eighteenth- and nineteenth-century *Saddhamasaṅgaha* manuscripts in Lankan Buddhist temples testifies to the (re-)localization of the work (Somadasa 1964, sv).

dha], all these works in accord with the *tipiṭaka* were composed by the *theras*" (64) and extols the benefits of inscribing the Buddha's teaching (65–68). He also describes Samgharāja Śīlavaṃsa Dharmakīrti (probably his teacher), in terms far more focused on learning than those found in the twelfth-century sources: "In Sīhala [Lanka], there was a person who, like the moon, shone in the sky of the *sāsana*, enlightening the residents of Lanka with the rays of knowledge. His name was Dhammakitti, and he was virtuous and a mine of merits. Like the moon in the sky, he was visibly present on the Sīhala island. In the *piṭaka*s, and in grammar, etc., he attained complete perfection. Very wise, he brightened the island of Lanka" (90).[14]

Writing slightly later, in 1390 (Sannasgala 1964, 224), another student of Śīlavaṃsa Dharmakīrti, who followed his teacher as Saṃgharāja, composed *Nikāyasaṅgrahāya* in Sinhala. The theme of decline-and-revival is woven throughout the work, which examines the ongoing threat to the *sāsana* posed by monks with "wrong views" on Buddhist teachings as well as by political instability. The councils or communal recitations held on the Indian subcontinent to codify authoritative Buddhist teachings are described as events that establish the *sāsana*, and the subsequent history is written as a series of alternations between decline and efforts to make the *sāsana* "shine."

EFFECTS OF THE INNOVATIVE DISCOURSE

Those who composed histories of the Buddhist *sāsana* during the middle years of the eighteenth century, and who in doing so wrote about monastic practice in general and the activities of the Siyam Nikāya in particular, drew on the earlier works I have just discussed. In several cases (as with *Mahāvaṃsa* and the first *Kīrti Śrī Rājasiṃha Katikāvata*), they understood their compositions as the latest in a series of closely linked narratives. In others the connection was less direct. Even when an eighteenth-century author did not see himself as engaged in the continuation of a serial, however, he drew on the style and contents of earlier works to elaborate his themes. It is almost inconceivable that Gamullē Ratanapāla did not consider sections of *Nikāyasaṅgrahāya* while composing his historical conclusion to *Vimānavastuprakāraṇaya*, or that Tibboṭuvāvē Buddharakkhita composed his descriptions of Saraṇaṃkara without *Nikāyasaṅgrahāya* accounts of the twelfth and thirteenth century monastic communities and *Saddhammasaṅgaha's* com-

[14] On the translation of this passage, see Penth (1977, 270).

ments on Buddhaghosa in mind.[15] Seeking to elaborate the powerful attainments of Saraṇaṃkara and other monks closely affiliated to him, the most natural move for a Lankan Buddhist author was to echo the descriptions of prior monastic luminaries in prose and verse.

The works composed during the latter two-thirds of the eighteenth century, however, do not simply recapitulate the style and contents of previous works with minor adjustments to accommodate a new cast of characters. Rather, their authors develop the theme of monastic learning for the sake of the *sāsana* more insistently and with greater detail than any of those discussed in the previous section. *Mahāvaṃsa*'s description of Saraṇaṃkara, the urgency with which the first *Kīrti Śrī Rājasiṃha Katikāvata* regulates learning for the sake of the *sāsana*, *Saṃgharājasādhucariyāva*'s condemnation of monks who study for personal gain rather than to sustain the *sāsana*, and that work's interlocking educational biographies—all of these evince an unprecedented concern to show that monastic "learning is the measure of the continuation of the *sāsana*" (Vibh-a 431–432). The eighteenth-century histories argue that the monks connected to the Siyam Nikāya pursued learning with an intense awareness of the place of this learning in the life of the Buddhist *sāsana*.

We cannot argue conclusively that the emphases found in the eighteenth-century works have their origin in the self-representation of Saraṇaṃkara and other early participants of the Siyam Nikāya. Nor is it clear that Saraṇaṃkara and subsequent leaders of the Siyam Nikāya made conscious, strategic use of the Theravāda's long-standing decline-and-revival theme in order to develop their authority in the face of competitors' arguments against upstart monastic movements. However, the level of monastic competition at that time and the long tradition in the Lankan Theravāda (as in so many other religious communities) of composing texts in the (perhaps partial) service of local power relations[16] give us good reason to think that at least some of the authors connected to the Siyam Nikāya made conscious use of historical narratives to strengthen their own authority or that of the new monastic order. The consistent and strongly worded dismissal of the Siyam Nikāya's monastic predecessors in the eighteenth-century histories suggests that they were intended, at least in part, to naturalize and sustain the Siyam Nikāya's authority within the Lankan Buddhist community.

Even without the evidence to arrive at definitive conclusions about

[15] The importance of *Nikāyasaṅgrahāya* would have been enhanced by the fact that the temple in which its author had resided (Gaḍaladeṇiyē Saddharmatilaka Rajamahavihāraya) became an important educational center for the Siyam Nikāya. On *Saddhamasaṅgaha*, see note 13.

[16] See, for instance, Blackburn (1999b), Collins (1990), and Walters (1997).

authorial intention, however, it is possible to explore the impact of these narratives on the new Siyam Nikāya. We can ask, in other words, how the ideas contained in the texts helped to sustain or to constrain the order. The consistency of the vision of monasticism found in these texts (and the degree to which it is echoed by other texts and inscriptions described below) is powerful evidence that the texts themselves both reflected and sustained a broader conversation on the nature of appropriate monasticism which may be called, for the sake of convenience, a "discourse on monasticism." In this discourse, religious learning was privileged as crucial to the *sāsana*'s enduring presence but was still linked to disciplinary practice and meditative realization. The discourse continually lauded the monks connected to the Siyam Nikāya while denigrating their predecessors and, by extension, monks contemporary with the Siyam Nikāya's leaders who questioned the new order's emergent command.

The eighteenth-century discourse on monasticism affected the pace and success of the formation of the Siyam Nikāya in four ways. First, by linking the fortunes of monks in Saraṇaṃkara's community closely to the fortunes of the Buddhist *sāsana* and by describing other monks as causes of the *sāsana*'s decline, this discourse on monasticism provided a powerful rationale for the development of the Siyam Nikāya. Participating in a vision of Buddhist history in which learning was linked to desirable monasticism, and the latter to religious revival, individual monastic biographies and the history of the Siyam Nikāya were wedded to the history of the larger Buddhist community. Because of this, members of the Siyam Nikāya were portrayed as particularly devoted and valuable participants in the Buddhist *sāsana*, while those monks not affiliated with Saraṇaṃkara and the emerging Siyam Nikāya were devalued. Second, the combination of the emphasis on Buddhist learning found in these narratives and long-standing ideas in the Theravāda about the power of the Pāli language made it easier to conclude that the monks of Saraṇaṃkara's community were the custodians of true Buddhist teachings and thus appropriate arbiters of Buddhist practice. Third, this discourse identified particular forms of monastic practice—education, composition, and preaching—as desirable. The strong link between monastic learning and the revival of the *sāsana* made in the discourse on monasticism provided a charter for monastic practice in which educational pursuits were highly valued. Fourth, it created a place for royal patrons in its vision of Buddhist history, depicting royal patrons of learned monasticism as participants in the heroic master narrative of religious revival, and thus making royal patronage of the Siyam Nikāya's new institutions appear inviting.

By describing the impact of this discourse on monasticism in these terms, I am arguing that the ideas about monastic life and the *sāsana*'s history that circulated during the middle of the eighteenth century informed the attitude taken by members of the Buddhist community toward the early Siyam Nikāya because they made certain actions appear to be both natural and desirable. This argument can be made with greater clarity by adopting and adapting Richard Davis's understanding of "interpretive communities" (itself an adaptation of work by Stanley Fish [1980]).[17] Davis suggests that

> [v]iewing a stone or bronze sculpted icon is not exactly like reading an arrangement of words on pages of a book, but the idea of interpretive communities—or, as I will prefer, "communities of response"—is just as valuable for considering the plurality of ways viewers approach and encounter a visual subject. Here too, "meaning" emerges through the relationship with the viewer, who brings his or her community's own interpretive strategies to bear within the encounter. Here too, these ways of approaching the object are learned, shared, and susceptible to change. Interpretive strategies for encountering objects, like those for texts, have their own social locations and historical genealogies. (1997, 9)

Davis's discussion of the specific social and historical locations that affect interpretive strategies provides a way to think about the relationship between a discourse on monasticism and the actions undertaken by lay and monastic Buddhists in the eighteenth-century Lankan Theravāda.

Rather than focus on the meaning of written texts (as does Fish) or visual objects (as does Davis), I look at the processes through which meaning is attributed to social institutions. Such social institutions—such as monasticism and kingship—become meaningful in particular ways as individuals encounter strategies for the interpretation of these institutions and come to find these interpretive strategies convincing. Individuals then begin to understand and act toward these institutions in ways naturalized by these interpretive strategies. Seen from this perspective, we might say that the eighteenth-century discourse on monasticism set forth strategies for the interpretation of monasticism and Buddhist history. It thus helped to create a community of monks and lay people prepared to approach the Siyam Nikāya in particular ways. The members of this interpretive community shared attitudes to the Siyam Nikāya and other monastic groups; their actions were shaped in part by these attitudes. Similar to the way that, according to Davis, the poetry of Hindu devotional saints "both reflected and modeled a specific, influential way of looking at images and icons of Viṣṇu and Śiva in their medieval south Indian temples" (38), the eighteenth century discourse

[17] As Fish puts it, for instance, "Interpretive communities are made up of those who share interpretive strategies . . . these strategies exist prior to the act of reading and therefore determine the shape of what is read rather than, as is usually assumed, the other way around" (1980, 319).

on monasticism reflected and modeled a particular, influential way of understanding the institutions of monasticism and kingship, the relationships between them, and the actions appropriate to participants within them. That is, the innovative contents of the broader discourse on monasticism that became audible at the time of the Siyam Nikāya's rise made it possible and natural to think about monasticism and kingship in ways that helped to sustain the Siyam Nikāya.

One of the advantages of this formulation is that it allows us to identify historically distinctive meanings and models at the same time as we allow for the possibility that some participants in these communities were more, and some less, self-conscious about the ways in which interpretive strategies were shaped and about the possibilities for drawing such interpretive strategies into the domain of local power relations. Working with the idea that a distinctive eighteenth-century discourse on monasticism helped to create a coherent and well-integrated community of response to the institutions of monasticism and kingship provides a broad analytical framework, from within which it is possible to broach questions of historical change, consciousness, strategy, and agency. In other words, it is possible to sketch with rather bold strokes the ways in which a new discourse on monasticism created an interpretive community that had a positive impact on the development of the Siyam Nikāya. We can raise separate questions (most of which will remain unanswerable) about the degree to which any one participant in this interpretive community understood his or her participation as strategic. We do not need to think about "religion and the legitimation of power" when writing of the Siyam Nikāya's rise.[18]

INTERPRETING THE SIYAM NIKĀYA

A close look at the eighteenth-century histories shows how their new vision of monasticism shaped positive responses to the Siyam Nikāya.

Linked Histories

The innovative discourse on monasticism identified the beginnings of the Siyam Nikāya under Saraṇaṃkara with the source of new life for

[18] For a time, well represented by two collections of essays edited by Bardwell L. Smith (1978a; 1978b) it was customary to analyze the relations between religious and political institutions in terms of the former's legitimizing relation to the latter. This formulation now seems unsatisfactory, in part because it essentializes "religion" and "politics" in ways that run counter to evidence of historical and contemporary religious communities. It also attributes unduly consistent manipulative intentions to some figures, while at the same time assuming an extraordinarily naive view of those toward whom such intentions are directed.

the Buddhist *sāsana*. As I have shown, the eighteenth-century texts with which I am concerned merged two historical perspectives, describing the life cycle of the *sāsana* as dependent on the life cycle of the Siyam Nikāya. Because the vitality of the *sāsana* was so closely identified with that of the Siyam Nikāya, and especially with the Siyam Nikāya's dedication to learning, this discourse on monasticism provided powerful and articulate reasons for lay and monastic Buddhists to support Saraṇaṃkara and his students. The power of the linked histories also provided a pedigree for the monks most closely connected to Saraṇaṃkara as the Siyam Nikāya became a larger and more complex institution. It is striking that the first lengthy Buddhist biographies composed in the Lankan Theravāda for any figure besides the Buddha—*Saṃgharājasādhucariyāva* and *Saṃgharājavata*—were written during the period in which it was particularly necessary to identify the well-being of the Siyam Nikāya with the vitality of the *sāsana*.[19]

The account of Saraṇaṃkara's deathbed scene in *Saṃgharājasādhucariyāva* describes the monk's realization that he has engaged in "excellent, proper actions for the development and increase of the *sāsana* through meditation, elaborate preaching, [as well as by] speaking to and working with the many skilled and virtuous monks [who were] his students and their students" (57). Here the emphasis on Saraṇaṃkara as the founder of a pupillary lineage is striking, as it is in *Mahāvaṃsa*'s enthusiastic account of Saraṇaṃkara that describes him as "among the monks active in the Conqueror's *sāsana*, [the one] who had long striven to illuminate the Sage's *sāsana* which had come close to destruction for a long time in Lanka, who—energetic day and night—illuminated study and meditation according to [his] strength and wisdom, who had many other students instructed in study and meditation and illuminated the *sāsana* with honor, and who was devoted to the welfare of himself and others (MV 100: 101–5).

Pāli Language

In accounts of the contributions made by Saraṇaṃkara and his students to the life of the *sāsana*, one form of learning stands out sharply and deepens the image of these monks as rightful monastic leaders. The indigenous histories composed during the eighteenth century stress the study of Pāli, the language of the early authoritative texts of Theravādin Buddhism (including the *tipiṭaka* and a set of commentaries on it com-

[19] These works were composed just after Saraṇaṃkara's death and appear intended in part to provide an extended defense of the leadership rights of Saraṇaṃkara's pupillary lineage at a time when the Siyam Nikāya had become large enough for controversies to erupt over leadership of the community (Vācissara 1964, 269–278).

posed in the fifth century). Pāli learning is developed as an emblem of the new monastic community and depicted as the key to the revival of the *sāsana*. This comes through clearly in the heroic accounts of Saraṇaṃkara's struggles to learn Pāli grammar and revive a moribund manuscript culture. It is also signaled by *Mahāvaṃsa*'s account of Saraṇaṃkara as someone with a sophisticated knowledge of "the Buddha's own words" and by the frequency with which *Saṃgharājasādhucariyāva*'s biographical vignettes insist on monks' ability to understand Pāli commentaries, to translate Pāli texts, and to preach on subjects drawn from the Pāli *tipiṭaka*.[20] In order to gain a fuller understanding of Pāli's centrality to the eighteenth-century discourse on monasticism, and the ways in which this discourse shaped the emergence of an interpretive community inclined to accept the Siyam Nikāya as prestigious and authoritative, we must attend to the significance of Pāli within the communities connected to the Theravāda.[21]

Collins notes that in many of the *vaṃsa*s and Pāli commentaries redacted in Lanka and Southeast Asia from the fifth century onward, Pāli language is for the first time privileged as uniquely valuable and described as the root language (Pāli *mūla bhāsā*) of all beings and as "naturally given." By this it was meant that Pāli was the language that "denotes things 'in accordance with the way they really are'" (1998, 49–50).[22] According to one commentary, for instance, in a passage that emphasizes the juxtaposition between Pāli as naturally given and other languages as cultural products, Pāli is the language a child would speak spontaneously if he or she grew up in isolation (1998, 49). Collins explores the implications of the movement to identify Pāli as a naturally given language, as the language appropriate to a Buddha and, therefore, as the most authoritative language for the Theravāda.

> There is, I think, a twofold ideological value in such an attitude [which emerges in the fifth century] to Pali. In the first place, there is the claim to have access to a language, and to states of knowledge and being expressed in it which are exempted from contingency. . . . Linguistic non-contingency . . . is both a representation within transcendentalist ideology, and, when successfully disseminated, part of what creates the autonomy of ideological power and the social position of the clerics who control access to it. . . . Secondly, Pali was a sign of translocality, in both space and time. . . . A text in Pali had *ipso facto* trans-local and trans-temporal reference, linking the here-and-now spatially to the broader world of Buddhism as a contempo-

[20] Detailed examples of this are presented in chapters 5 and 6.

[21] For accounts of the development of Pāli as a language, see Norman (1983) and von Hinüber (1982).

[22] Earlier texts, as Collins notes, did not privilege Pāli absolutely, and recognized "a hierarchy of preferred languages" (1998, 48–49).

rary whole, and temporally to the past of Gotama Buddha, and to the deeper and further temporal horizon of past and future Buddhas. (n.d., 7)

Here Collins suggests that, beginning in the fifth century, Pāli carried a twofold weight of authority within Theravāda Buddhist cultures. First, knowledge of Pāli and the contents of texts composed in Pāli was absolute, unchanging, and unalterable knowledge because of Pāli's linguistic status. This understanding of the link between language and epistemology was forged within the elite literate, and largely monastic, communities of the Theravāda and subsequently helped to sustain their authority and privilege. Second, because Pāli was understood as both "the Buddha's own language" and the "root language," the use of Pāli by a Buddhist writer or reciter provided the verbal or written product with a devotional status and authority it would not have had in a local language or dialect. The use of Pāli also connected Buddhist communities in one region to Buddhist communities in another, which, in turn, added to the status of someone skilled in Pāli. Someone knowledgeable in Pāli was part of a cosmopolitan elite, able to claim a status greater than those confined to merely local knowledge.[23] As Collins notes, "Pali literature was a luxury good in at least two ways . . . it either came from afar or connoted connection with the distant, and the capacity to enjoy and still more create it required arduous training and separation from the economically everyday" (n.d., 66).

The association of Pāli with eternal truth and translocal Buddhist communities, and with a subculture of literate elites, helped to determine the significance of Pāli learning as a theme in the eighteenth-century discourse on monasticism. By describing the early members of the Siyam Nikāya as responsible for the revival of Pāli learning, it wrote them into the history of Buddhism as the only monks on the island with proper access to true Buddhist teachings. Implicit in this narrative was a view that these monks were the only monks with the authority to determine authoritative monastic practice and the only monks able to participate in the larger Southeast Asian Buddhist community.

Valued Learning

The innovative discourse on monasticism did more than influence favorable responses to the monks connected to the early Siyam Nikāya. Its

[23] In using the term "cosmopolitan" here I draw on lectures by R.A.L.H. (Leslie) Gunawardana given at the University of Chicago's Divinity School in 1993. Although it is correct to say that Theravāda cultures gradually became increasingly local cultures from the tenth century onward (Reynolds and Hallisey 1989), it is important to remember that Pāli (to varying degrees according to time and place) retained its place as a sign and constituent of a cosmopolitan, translocal Buddhist identity.

account of the necessary combination of monastic learning and firm discipline also provided a clearly articulated orientation for monastic practice in the Siyam Nikāya. That is, by placing learned monasticism within a narrative of the *sāsana*'s decline and revival, this discourse influenced an interpretive community within monastic circles that accepted the view that religious learning and textual practice were activities of devotional significance and monastic responsibility. This, in turn, enhanced the devotional rationale for monastic participation in the new educational institutions that were established in stage three of the formation of the Siyam Nikāya. To understand the importance of this, it is necessary to explore the ways in which monastic practice was described within the Lankan Theravāda prior to the eighteenth century.

Monasticism was clearly the ideal form of religious practice in Theravāda Buddhism until the late nineteenth century.[24] Buddhist communities understood a monk's lifestyle as the most efficient context for the practice of mental cultivation required on the path to liberation, and the figure of the monk served as an important icon of religious practice. As Gombrich puts it, "we may say that living the life of the monk just as the *vinaya* prescribes it is very close, as close as it is possible to get, to acting out in daily life the spiritual goal of attaining *nibbāna*" (1988, 89). Despite this consistency in the honor accorded to the monastic life (if not always to the monks themselves), Theravādin Buddhist communities held a variety of views—in different periods and different places—on what monastic practice should include. One important marker of this variety was the distinction between *ganthadhura*, or the responsibility to study and preserve texts (whether oral or written), and *vipassanādhura*, the responsibility to meditate.[25] Both forms of monastic practice were defensible with respect to the Pāli teachings considered to be authoritative within the Theravāda, but monks who focused on *ganthadhura* were vulnerable to criticism. The grounds for such criticism were twofold: that scholarly monks paid insufficient attention to the meditative practice needed to complete the path to liberation, and that scholarly work increased their ties to lay (and especially elite) commu-

[24] On changes in the ideal forms of Buddhist practice and the rise of the lay person's authority see, for instance, Bechert (1988), Gombrich and Obeyesekere (1988), and Swearer (1995). Hallisey shows that works written between the eighth and thirteenth centuries promote a greater contiguity between lay and monastic expressions of devotion (1988, esp. 192–207), but there is no evidence that this led to a devaluation of the monk's role.

[25] The distinction is said by some (such as Rahula 1956, 158ff.) to date to a conference of monks held in Lanka during the first century C.E. The terms appear in Lankan inscriptions dating to the Poḷonnaruva Period (EZ, Vol. 2) as well as in monastic regulations composed in the twelfth, thirteenth and eighteenth centuries (Ratnapala 1971). In Sinhala these terms appear as *granthadhura* and *vidarśanadhura*.

nities, thus compromising monastic ideals.[26] Against this background, a new monastic community focused on Buddhist learning was vulnerable to criticism from other monks and from members of the lay community. In the case, of the Siyam Nikāya, however, the innovative discourse on monasticism helped to safeguard the new group of monastics from such criticism. It made participation in the Siyam Nikāya's new educational institutions attractive to monks and acceptable in the eyes of lay patrons.

This was accomplished in two ways. Depictions of Saraṇaṃkara as the founder and exemplar for the early Siyam Nikāya emphasized that his life as a monk was rooted in the twin virtues of monastic practice, *ganthadhura* and *vipassanādhura*. The passage from *Mahāvaṃsa* quoted on p. 98, for instance, describes Saraṇaṃkara as a "forest dweller," and thus connects Saraṇaṃkara to idealized ascetic meditation practice (MV 100: 48–50). Saraṇaṃkara is also described as a scholar committed to both study and meditation and as a teacher who prepared his students to take up this double task (MV 100: 102–104). *Mahāvaṃsa* repeatedly stresses this theme with reference to Saraṇaṃkara's monastic contemporaries in the Siyam Nikāya, describing them as "scholars and contemplatives" (MV 100: 176–178) and as "always respectful and devoted to study and meditation" (MV 100: 207). Along similar lines, the first *Kīrti Śrī Rājasiṃha Katikāvata* includes the following programmatic statement for the monks of the new community: "[the monks] should act according to this monastic regulation, establishing themselves in proper precepts and sustaining the *sāsana* in its pure form. May all members of the monastic community protect the *sāsana*, [by being] endowed with such virtues as contentment, and engaging in *grantha-* and *vidarśanā-dhura*" (Ratnapala 1971, 98).

At the same time, as we have seen, this discourse provided a powerful soteriological perspective on monastic learning. The practice of *ganthadhura* was extolled as crucial to the sustenance of the larger Buddhist community and thus as a highly significant devotional act. This perspective is clearly articulated by the texts from this period in which composition is typically described as a compassionate, pleasing practice.[27] Thus, Saraṇaṃkara's composition of the commentary that forms the focus of Chapter 5 below is described as having "benefited the world and the *sāsana*" (SV, v. 101), and the author of *Vimānavastuprakāra-*

[26] Attempts to stave off such criticism come through clearly in the frequent attempts to identify scholarly monastic leaders with the ascetic and meditative values of forest-dwelling monasticism (Blackburn 1999b).

[27] Such descriptions are by no means unusual within Theravāda textual practice. What *is* unusual is the degree to which monastic learning is extolled in other ways within other, related sources.

ṇaya describes his translation in terms that stress the compassionate nature of the composition:

> This *Vimānavastu* teaching is a teaching as deep as a great ocean. . . . Thus, if [someone] were to think, "I will elucidate the meaning, translating the meaning of the Pāli into Sinhala," it would be like someone trying to empty the water of the ocean with the shell of a mustard seed. . . . However, it is profitable—not useless—to satisfy someone with even a single gem after they've seen a great mine of gems, though it's not possible to empty the entire gem mine. Similarly . . . to preach with even one line and to listen to preaching and so reach *nirvāṇa* are causes of mundane and supramundane benefit. Therefore, for the benefit of good and faithful people who understand only Sinhala . . . I present this explanation of the *Vimānavastu* in brief, translated into the Sinhala language (Sīlānanda 1901, 3–4).

Here Ratnapala affirms the authority of Pāli by admitting that the contents of the Pāli *Vimānavatthu* cannot be fully conveyed by him in the local language of Sinhala, but he continues to insist that it is important to compose a translation. This expression of learning is part of what sustains the greater Buddhist community, including those "good and faithful people" who cannot read the Pāli texts themselves.

Placing Patrons

The discourse on monasticism thus helped to shape positive responses to the early Siyam Nikāya as an authoritative order of monks, and to assure that the educational pursuits of the new order were understood as laudable forms of monastic practice important to the entire Buddhist community. It also played an important role in the formation of the Siyam Nikāya by drawing the royal court into the new interpretive community, encouraging the royal patronage without which the Siyam Nikāya's rise would have been impossible. By linking the Siyam Nikāya to Buddhist learning and to the continued existence of the *sāsana*, this discourse on monasticism made it natural for the king to support the Siyam Nikāya and thus to play his own part in the decline-and-revival history of the *sāsana*. Support by various kings, and especially King Kīrti Śrī Rājasiṃha, was crucial to the formation and continued growth of the monastic community. Temple renovations, land grants, the construction of new educational institutions, the sponsorship of religious festivals, and the authorization of monastic appointments all took place with the assistance of Kīrti Śrī and the two kings who preceded him. In turn, Kīrti Śrī's willingness to patronize the Siyam Nikāya on this very substantial scale was influenced by the discourse on monasticism that interpreted such patronage as an activity of devotional significance, an activity linked to the very life of the Buddhist *sāsana*.

The texts from which I draw my understanding of the discourse on monasticism characteristic of the middle years of the eighteenth century are strikingly consistent in the way they describe the king as a contributor to the life of the Buddhist *sāsana*. According to *Saṃgharājavata*, for instance, "The lord of Sri Lanka, great king endowed with merit, possessing the virtues of a buddha, hoping for the existence of the *sāsana* was pleased [at the prospect of the Siamese ordination that provided the formal start of the Siyam Nikāya]" (v. 146). *Mahāvaṃsa* and *Vimānavastuprakāraṇaya* both include elaborate accounts of the king's careful attention to the royal responsibility for the support of Buddhist institutions and his contributions to the revival of the Buddhist *sāsana*. In the historical account appended to his *Vimānavastuprakāraṇaya*, Ratnapala writes that

> [Kīrti Sri] was living enjoying royal splendor like Sakra, king of the gods, in an excellent city called Senkaḍagal [Kandy] which was ornamented with various decorations such as monastic dwelling places and devotional monuments. . . . He had the Puṣpārama [a residence in the Malvatu Vihāraya] made for the novice Saraṇaṃkara who acted properly according to Buddhist teachings. In doing this he had the great idea of following the line of earlier kings: "Even the meritorious kings such as Dhammasoka and the second Piyatissa[28] shored up the *sāsana* with the help of monks accomplished in [their] conduct, and [the *sāsana*] survived down [to our times]. I should also support the *sāsana* with the help of the Silvat Saṃgha [that is, the Silvat Samāgama]." . . . He purified the *sāsana* by dismissing a group of earlier [monks] with bad conduct from the *sāsana* and administering [moral] precepts to the faithful. He [had ordained] new novice monks, accustoming them to the *dhamma* and *Vinaya*, as well as to the vocabulary, prosody and grammar" (Sīlānanda 1901, 146).

Moreover, Ratnapala writes, "King Kīrti Śrī Rājasiṃha . . . pleased after listening many times to the *Vimānavatthu* teaching itself . . . thought about other ways to support the *sāsana*: 'If a certain monk . . . would teach the Buddha's dhamma to monks and novices, the *sāsana* [that] is the *dhamma* taught by the Buddha will last a long time.'" (Sīlānanda 1901, 120, 202–4). Note that Kīrti Śrī Rājasiṃha is described as an early supporter of Saraṇaṃkara and as a king self-conscious about his contribution to the endurance of the Buddhist *sāsana*. These works por-

[28] These kings are, in order, a third-century B.C.E. Indian monarch lauded as the epitome of Buddhist kingship by Theravādin textual traditions, and his contemporary, the first supporter of Buddhist teachings and monasticism in Lanka. On the importance of Dhammasoka (Asoka) to Kīrti Śrī see below.

tray the king as determined to support Buddhist teachings and institutions, focusing on the patronage of the monastic education of novice monks and the composition of works (like *Vimānavastuprakāraṇaya*) believed to be useful in monastic education.

ROYAL APPROPRIATIONS OF THE INNOVATIVE DISCOURSE ON MONASTICISM

The new discourse on monasticism pervaded the elite court and monastic communities of the Kandyan Kingdom to such an extent that reflections on kingship composed at the king's behest carried on the pattern of representing monks and kings as coparticipants in ongoing efforts to assure the *sāsana*'s vitality. The account in *Mahāvaṃsa* of Kīrti Śrī Rājasiṃha's religious activities is quite elaborate, as befits a work written at the invitation of the king, and occupies most of two long chapters composed in Pāli verse. In these verses, Kīrti Śrī Rājasiṃha is portrayed as a dedicated and powerful participant in the life of the Buddhist *sāsana*. This participation is set forth in ways that emphasize the king's role as a patron of Buddhist learning, as a guarantor of disciplined monasticism, and as someone who recognizes the importance of meditative practice. Referring to Saraṇaṃkara's rise and royal support for his authority in a reorganization of monastic life and discipline, *Mahāvaṃsa* recounts that

> [t]he king heard the news of [ill-disciplined monks] and took stock of the well-disciplined monks, thinking "he's good" [with regard to] that famous novice called Saraṇaṃkara who lived purely, was a forest dweller, was energetic about developing the Conqueror's *sāsana*, virtuous, full of virtues, learned, and skilled in the Buddha's words and in exposition. The ruler of the earth [Kīrti Śrī] investigated [the monastic situation] according to [Buddhist teaching] with [Saraṇaṃkara's] support and rebuked [the poorly disciplined monks]. He had an order given that from that point forward all those who had become novices were always to protect the study of the Buddha's words, shunning things that shouldn't be done such as astrology and medicine. The king, wanting to develop the *sāsana* that had diminished, took care of the *sāsana* in a number of ways. (MV 100: 50–3).

Note that the *Mahāvaṃsa* places the distinction between proper and improper monastic learning within the sphere of royal authority, portraying the king an arbiter of monastic learned culture in relation to the needs of the larger Buddhist community and the well-being of the *sāsana*.

Other sections of the work present the royal patron as the *sāsana*'s benefactor by describing him as so attentive to the benefits of Buddhist learning that he assures occasions for the transmission of religious teachings from the newly learned monks of the Siyam Nikāya to the lay community: "[Kīrti Śrī Rājasiṃha] hearing about the fruit of providing the teachings, the result of listening to the excellent teachings, and the merit in writing the excellent teachings and paying honor to the teachings thought, 'it should be done according to the excellent teachings.' He had teaching pavilions made in various places . . . having lit lamps and had seats arranged, he had exponents of the excellent teaching brought with great honor. With respect he had [them] invited and seated in the well-arranged seats. He had the excellent teachings taught by these very teachers" (MV 99: 10–20). These lines portray Kīrti Śrī as an exemplary Buddhist ruler who, in addition to learning about religious teachings himself, supports the *sāsana* by making provisions for others to benefit from monastic learning through large-scale monastic preaching events. Connections between the king's patronage, monastic attainments, and the well-being of the *sāsana* are made time and time again, as when *Mahāvaṃsa* moves smoothly between the Kīrti Śrī's command over monastic education and the way in which the monks of the early Siyam Nikāya acted to safeguard the *sāsana* from premature decline: "Thus the king, lord of Lanka, commanding the monks of Lanka in study and meditation, protected the Buddha's *sāsana*. The monks of Lanka, diligent, discerning, part of the noble lineage of virtue, diligence, and contentment [were] energetic, never lazy, acting for the Conqueror's *sāsana*. Zealous day and night they were scholars and contemplatives" (MV 100: 175–178).

The unprecedented degree of preoccupation with monastic learning becomes clearer when we compare descriptions of royal benefactors found in the sections of *Mahāvaṃsa* written during the middle years of the eighteenth century with those found in sections composed in the twelfth and fourteenth centuries. Although the earlier accounts are replete with descriptions of royal support for the construction of religious buildings, such as monastic complexes and devotional centers, the descriptions composed in the eighteenth century by Saraṇaṃkara's student Buddharakkhita insistently focus on the king's patronage of monastic education, the preservation and use of Buddhist texts, and elaborate occasions for monastic preaching to the lay community.[29] Religious instruction rather than religious construction is the emphatic theme of the later *Mahāvaṃsa* accounts, as it is of all the eighteenth-century works I have discussed. This is striking, especially since it is clear from other evidence that a substantial amount of construction and reconstruction

[29] For instance, compare *Mahāvaṃsa* chapters 73, 78, and 79 with chapters 99–100.

of religious buildings took place in the period under consideration with the support of Kīrti Śrī.[30] Although the major renovation of temples and images is mentioned in eighteenth-century accounts, it receives far less attention than the protection of educational institutions and the patronage of monastic preaching.

Further evidence that the discourse on monasticism shaped (and was shaped by) royal responses to the Siyam Nikāya is found in the royal inscriptions and land grants written at the king's command. For instance, in a *sannasa* for Bambawa Vihāraya dating to 1759, the king is described as dedicated to his own education and to the education of monks who will assure the spread of Buddhist teachings.

> [He] was like unto the morning sun on the summit of the orient hill, and dispersed his beam-like fame to all the ten points of the compass by unceasingly devoting all his time to the hearing of bana [Buddhist teachings appropriate for preaching]. . . . At this time in this Lanka—which is like unto a depository of the three gems of Buddha—there was not a single ordained priest, and Buddhism was consequently losing ground. Therefore His Majesty sent an Embassy with a great many presents to Siam, and after many endeavors brought over ten priests, headed by Upalisthavira, and under them the king had thousands of high caste youths robed. Having thus revived Buddhism (the king) repaired all the dagobas [reliquary monuments] and vihara [temples with monastic residences], which had been in ruins in all the three divisions of Lanka. [These viharas included Bamba Vihāraya which the king had restored, commanding] the produce of the land within [nearby] boundaries to be utilized for the maintenance of the priests. For the purpose of improving Buddhism with Buddha's property and priests' property, Urulewatte Piyadassi Dhammasiddhi Sami, full of virtues and piety, was interested [sic] with the same, with strict injunctions that in future he shall appoint priests of his pupillary line, who will strictly adhere to the precepts [and] interest themselves in the propagation of Buddhism . . . (Lawrie 1896, 92)

In another *sannasa* for Narēndrārāma Vihāraya, Kīrti Śrī is portrayed as a patron of learning. He is, the *sannasa* announces, "the king of the universe, whose lotus feet are resorted to by learned men like bees, whose fame resembles that of the full blown lotus at the time of the full moon, extensive and spotless" (Lawrie 1898, 801). It is implied that Kīrti Śrī sustains the men of learning who, in turn, scatter throughout the land making the honey of the Buddha's teaching available to others.

That the king's self-representation as a patron of monastic learning continued in the early years of Kīrti Śrī Rājasiṃha's successor's reign

[30] See chapter 3, as well as Duncan (1990) and Holt (1996).

indicates the degree to which the novel and pro-Siyam Nikāya discourse on monasticism had become a natural and favorable point of reference for court and monastic elites alike. The *sannasa* written for the Degaldoruvē Vihāraya in 1786, for instance, describes the new king Rājādhi Rājasiṃha as a patron identified by his own reputation as a scholar and by his respect for learned monasticism: "His Majesty having received much instruction and exhortation in the Buddhist faith and full explanation of the books Diganikaya, Upasaka-Jana-Alankaraya, Milindaprasnaya and Mahawansa from the High Priest Moratota Dhammakanda, who had a thorough knowledge of Buddhism, granted to him, his pupils, sub-pupils, in succession, to be held by them for ever, the following property . . ." (Lawrie 1896, 138). And, in a history written for the Urulevatte Vihāraya (also in 1786) as a demonstration of the temple's prestigious history, the relationship between royal patronage, monastic learning, and the life of the *sāsana* is set out in no uncertain terms.

> When His Majesty King Kīrti Śrī Rāja Sinha, the descendent of King Manu of the illustrious royal family of Mahā Sammata, was reigning in Kandy the prosperous city, he inquired as to the state of religion [*sāsana*] in Lanka, and he was told that there were no ordained Buddhist priests but only novices: on this His Majesty said, "While I am reigning it is a pity to see the religion going down;" accordingly he took to his mind to patronize the faith, assisted by the sub-king Rājādhi Rāja Sinha; he sent an embassy to Siam with presents worth one lakh of coins, and invited priests from Siam, such as Upatissa and others, who came, bringing with them bana books [books on Buddhist teachings]. Then thousands of respectable men were robed, taught [the] piṭakas; hundreds of them were daily fed; and hundreds of offerings of necessaries were made. (Lawrie 1898, 888)

Thus although the eighteenth-century discourse on monasticism consistently articulated the importance to the monastic life of learning (linked to discipline and meditation) and depicted learned monks as key participants in the revival of the Buddhist *sāsana*, it did not treat learned monks as solitary figures. Instead, monks were closely linked to the figure of the king. Royal support of learned monks and the institutions in which they lived and studied was presented as a necessary part of efforts made to arrest the deterioration of Buddhist practice and Buddhist institutions. These ideas about the king's role as a supporter of the Buddhist *sāsana*, which came to permeate the court and monastic circles of the Kandyan kingdom in the mid-eighteenth century, created favorable conditions for the king's support of the emerging Siyam Nikāya's educational institutions. They provided a persuasive devotional logic for such material support. To put it another way, the broader conversation on monasticism drew the king into the community that interpreted the Siyam Nikāya in general, and its educational institutions in particular, as natural focal points for participation and patronage. This occurred not only because of the power of eighteenth-century accounts that treated kings and monks as active participants in attempts to arrest the decline of the Buddhist *sāsana*; it was also due to the fact that these accounts resonated with long-standing images of desirable kingship within the Sri Lankan Theravāda.

IMAGES OF PROPER KINGSHIP

As scholars of the Theravāda have shown with relentless regularity, one of the most important models for kingship in Buddhist communities throughout Sri Lanka and Southeast Asia was that provided by the traditions that grew up around the Indian emperor Asoka (Dhammasoka) who reigned in the third century B.C.E.[31] Two recent studies of the Kandyan Kingdom have shown the importance of the Asokan model to Kīrti Śrī Rājasiṃha and other members of his court. Building on James Duncan's study (1990) of architectural and landscape motifs from this period, John Holt argues that the inscriptions, paintings, and court histories created during the reign of Kīrti Śrī draw on several different Buddhist understandings of kingship set forth in the literary traditions of the Theravāda. One of the most important is what Duncan and Holt both call the "Aśokan discourse." By this they mean a set of verbal and symbolic strategies through which Kīrti Śrī Rājasiṃha identified himself and his actions with the figure of Asoka. Accounts of Kīrti Śrī Rājasiṃha's actions set forth in royal inscriptions and literary works composed at the king's invitation describe Kīrti Śrī in terms vividly reminiscent of Asoka: both rulers, for instance, donate significant portions of their wealth to the monastic community, conduct festivals to honor Buddhist monks and teachings, go on pilgrimage to important Buddhist sites, request learned monks to settle doctrinal disputes and attempt to create a unified and well-disciplined monastic community (Holt 1996, 19). Both rulers also enable the transmission of Buddhist teachings by supporting the recitative compilation (Asoka) or the redaction (Kīrti Śrī) of Buddhist texts as well as monastic preaching. The eighteenth-century visions of monasticism merged smoothly with the Asokan model of kingship. Royal actions made natural and desirable by the discourse on monasticism were all the more so because they sustained and were sus-

[31] Most of these discussions have been inspired by the important work of Reynolds (1972) and Tambiah (1976).

tained by the image of Asoka who, like Kīrti Śrī Rājasiṃha, attended to the lifeblood of the *sāsana* by supporting monks committed to the threefold *sāsana* in their discipline, meditation, and learning.

This interpretation puts me at odds with standard views on Kīrti Śrī Rājasiṃha's actions as a patron of Buddhism (for example, Dewaraja 1988, and Dharmadasa 1976).[32] According to these accounts, Kīrti Śrī Rājasiṃha and the other Nāyakkar kings heavily patronized Buddhist institutions because, as members of a family with recent origins in southern India rather than in Lanka, and originally devotees of a Hindu god (Śiva) rather than the Buddha, they needed to "legitimize" their rule in the face of a suspicious local population. Subjected to substantial criticism on the grounds that it misreads the level of acculturation experienced by the ruling family (Seneviratne 1976) as well as understandings of ethnicity characteristic of the time (by importing twentieth-century communalist perceptions into historical analysis) (Gunawardana 1990), this understanding of Nāyakkar patronage has recently been resurrected in Holt's innovative study of Kandyan Buddhist painting, where it accompanies an analysis of the threat to royal power posed by Dutch presence on the island. As Holt puts it, "During his long reign, what Kīrti Śrī sought to do, then, more than anything else, was to articulate a royal discourse that appealed to Buddhist religious sentiments, sentiments that could affirm his public identity as a pious Buddhist king intent on supporting the religious culture and society that, for virtually all of the known history of civilization in Sri Lanka, had been the province and guardian of Theravāda Buddhist tradition" (1996, 13). And:

> There are essentially two ways of understanding the religious works of Kīrti Śrī. The first is to understand them as spontaneous acts of religious piety generated by a genuinely righteous Buddhist king who was guided by his deep spiritual knowledge of the Buddha's *dhamma* and his great veneration of the *sangha*. No doubt, this is precisely how Kīrti Śrī wanted to be viewed by his subjects. Without capitulating to an unwarranted cynicism, the second way is to understand Kīrti Śrī's religious endeavors as politically expedient acts, as discourses in response to the various powerful constituencies that brought pressure to bear on his ability and right to rule. Though the various discourses of Buddhist kingship to which Kīrti Śrī appealed provided for a legitimizing religious foundation for royal rule, it should never be forgotten that kingship is primarily an exercise in political power and that all royal actions have, or can be construed as having, placating or

[32] See also chapter 2. For criticisms of this view see Gunawardana (1990) and Seneviratne (1976; 1978).

inciting effects on various constituencies. Indeed, kingship is always reactionary or responsive in character; religion in royal hands is always marked by expediency. (1996, 22)

In other words, Holt argues that, faced with substantial political constraints, Kīrti Śrī Rājasiṃha was deeply motivated to create self-consciously a public vision of himself as a dedicated Buddhist king.

Holt is right to draw attention to the ways in which Kīrti Śrī Rājasiṃha (like many Buddhist kings before him) appears to have been involved in a process of self-representation modeled on representations of Asoka within the Theravāda and to query the relationship between royal patronage, representations of royal patronage, and the power relations in play within the Kandyan Kingdom. I would argue, however, against the views put forth by Holt and others that assume a stark dichotomy in the attempt to interpret Kīrti Śrī Rājasiṃha's actions. By building on the idea that the discourse on monasticism intersected with a traditional model of ideal Buddhist kingship and thus drew the king into an interpretive community predisposed to find certain actions natural and desirable, it is possible to argue for the intelligibility of Kīrti Śrī Rājasiṃha's actions to his subjects, and the positive impressions they are likely to have evoked, without overemphasizing a view of consistently intentional royal strategy.

The discourse on monasticism popular during Kīrti Śrī Rājasiṃha's reign set forth ways to interpret monasticism, kingship, the relationship between them, and the consequent dictates for royal action in a manner closely compatible with the Asokan ideal for kingship. What I have called the discourse on monasticism and what others call the Asokan discourse combined to shape an understanding of kingship in relation to monasticism in which there could be no "purely spontaneous acts of religious piety." Royal actions in eighteenth-century Sri Lanka were necessarily informed by expectations that made certain sorts of action meaningful and desirable. This does not necessarily mean, however, that the king's actions were always "politically expedient acts." Although the actions of Kīrti Śrī (and other kings in Buddhist and non-Buddhist communities) were undoubtedly informed at times by a self-conscious attempt to gain and to sustain power, we should be wary of an oversimplified view of royal agency that assumes constant, consistent and uniform intentions. Some royal acts were powerful because they made sense to communities disposed by prevailing ideas to interpret monasticism and kingship in certain ways. They possessed this powerfully authoritative character, however, whether or not the king and his subjects stopped to reflect about the power of discourse and representation.

CONCLUSION

Buddhist histories written in the latter two-thirds of the eighteenth century were important to the emergence of the Siyam Nikāya as an authoritative monastic order. The impact of these works on the institutional context of the time can be shown in many ways. I have emphasized the power of identifications made between the new order and the revival of the *sāsana*. In addition, I have shown that the new discourse on monasticism sustained the Siyam Nikāya by linking the order to privileged Pāli learning and providing a charter for monastic education. Moreover, the importance accorded to royal patrons within this discourse affected royal responses to the Siyam Nikāya. In other words, textual representations eased the formation of the Siyam Nikāya because they shaped the views on natural and desirable Buddhist practice shared by lay people and monastics in eighteenth-century Sri Lanka. A new textual community was created in eighteenth-century Lanka as a result of the Siyam Nikāya's rise and the educational developments that occurred during stages two and three of the order's formation. Without a sizable group of lay and monastic Buddhists disposed to interpret the Siyam Nikāya in a favorable light, the later stages of the Siyam Nikāya's formation would have been impossible. Thus, the innovative discourse on monasticism articulated by eighteenth century Buddhist histories played an important role in the reformulation of Lankan Buddhism. It helped to sustain the attitudes toward Siyam Nikāya monasticism needed to assure lay patronage of, and monastic participation in, the new monastic order. In time, as I show in subsequent chapters, this patronage and participation altered the way that Lankan Buddhists learned about Buddhist teachings, as well as their attitudes to textual authority.

These conclusions are quite different from the usual analyses of this period in which the framework of decline and revival is transferred from eighteenth century texts (sometimes with additional evidence on ordination or textual transmission) in order to describe conditions prior to and after the advent of Saraṇaṃkara and the Siyam Nikāya.[33] My argument here is not intended to suggest that historians are wrong to note the lack of monastic higher ordination and the diminished levels of monastic bureaucracy that characterized Lankan Buddhism immediately

[33] In English, see for instance, Dewaraja (1988), Gombrich (1988), and Malalgoda (1976). In Sinhala the most influential examples are Sannasgala (1964) and Vācissara (1964).

before the Siyam Nikāya's rise. It is, however, meant as a demonstration that the basic terms in which analyses of the period have proceeded—incorporating the accounts of decline-and-revival into contemporary historiography without attention to their highly rhetorical character—are indebted more to the powerful histories composed in the eighteenth century than we have realized. That every historian of this period until now has described Saraṇaṃkara and his students as revivalists and reformers rather than as innovators attests to the success of the eighteenth-century narratives in their construction of an authoritative lineage.

CHAPTER FIVE

"He Benefited the World and the *Sāsana*"

THE SIMULTANEOUS and interdependent rise of the Siyam Nikāya and its new monastic educational system altered the character of Lankan Buddhism.[1] This is a bold claim: that changes in the social organization and intellectual practices of monasticism had a profound and lasting impact on the entire Lankan Buddhist community. Such a claim cannot be sustained without close attention to the ways that monks engaged texts, and to the ways that this engagement affected lay and monastic Buddhists. By examining the Lankan context with the idea of textual communities in mind, we are able to attend closely to the nature and implications of eighteenth-century monastic education. Doing so, we discover that the central texts and interpretive perspectives of Siyam Nikāya monasticism changed the way that lay and monastic Buddhists encountered Buddhist teachings, as well as Buddhist understandings of textual authority.

I contend that one form, or genre, of Buddhist text played a particularly important role in the emergence of a new Buddhist textual community in eighteenth-century Lanka. This genre—the *sūtra sannaya* commentary—became important to the Siyam Nikāya in several ways. *Sūtra sannaya*s served as symbolic capital in a prestige economy. They also functioned as guides to monastic discipline. Most importantly, these commentaries played a central role in preacher training. In this chapter and the two that follow, I examine the life of the *sūtra sannaya*s in relation to the life of the Siyam Nikāya. I show the importance of these commentaries to stages two and three of the order's development, and explore the lasting impact of the *sūtra sannaya*s on Lankan Buddhism. By developing a detailed case study of one influential genre used within the Siyam Nikāya's educational system, I am able to make my claims for the reformulation of Lankan Buddhism more convincing. At the same time, the detail with which I look at the role of the *sūtra sannaya*s in socially located acts of composition, transmission, and reception suggests something about the processes through which desirable knowledge was defined and privileged in pre- and early-colonial South and Southeast Asia. These chapters are written in sympathy with Sheldon Pollock's claim that "literature is an intentional phenomenon, pro-

[1] The quotation in the title is from SV v. 101.

duced by human agents in changing but determinate conditions, with changing but determinate models of the literary, technologies, languages, and textual communities related to its production" (1995, 113).[2] At the same time as I write the Lankan *sūtra sannaya*s into a "history of literary cultures" (Pollock 1995, 113), I provide the first lengthy study of bilingual Buddhist commentary in the Lankan Theravāda, and the second for the Theravāda generally (see Pruitt 1994). For this reason, my analysis attends simultaneously to the impact of these commentaries on Lankan Buddhists and to the language and structure of the texts themselves.

Against this backdrop, the chapter develops the following three claims about the place of the *sūtra sannaya*s in stage two of the Siyam Nikāya's formation. First, in the middle of the eighteenth century, for the first time in at least three hundred years, *sūtra sannaya* commentaries became a popular genre among Lankan Buddhist monks.[3] The popularity of the genre was due in large part to the fact that the Siyam Nikāya's founder, Väliviṭa Saraṇaṃkara, composed a model *sūtra sannaya* for his monastic students in response to royal invitation. Second, Saraṇaṃkara's model *sūtra sannaya*—entitled *Sārārthadīpanī* (Illuminator of Excellent Meaning)—identified its author as a monk with a strong and bold scholarly voice, able to command the patronage of the most powerful layman on the island. Third, *Sārārthadīpanī*'s commentarial form allowed Saraṇaṃkara to articulate a distinctive vision of monasticism appropriate to his followers. *Sārārthadīpanī* offered a subtle yet powerful criticism of the Silvat Samāgama's monastic competitors and a point of orientation for what soon became the Siyam Nikāya.

SĀRĀRTHADĪPANĪ

Sārārthadīpanī was composed midway in Saraṇaṃkara's rise to leadership of the new monastic order. Although we do not know the exact

[2] Any notion of "the literary" is arguably arbitrary or historically restrictive. Pollock states that "Not everything textualized is 'literary,' though everything that is literary . . . is necessarily textualized. . . . What constitutes the literary, and if there is a literary, must always in the first instance be a local decision—or decisions, for change in, and indeed contention over, the literary occurs locally" (1995, 122–123). In thinking about the production of religious texts in eighteenth-century Lanka, I understand "literary" works as culturally valued instances of textual production that show at least partial adherence to established understandings of desirable language and style.

[3] The composition of *sūtra sannaya* texts began in the twelfth century and ceased in the fifteenth for reasons that remain unclear. It is likely that the early *sūtra sannaya*s drew on fifth- to seventh-century translations of Pāli *sutta*s into Sinhala. This cannot be confirmed, however (Godakumbura 1955, 23; Śrī Dharmakīrti 1961, 136).

date, it is evident that *Sārārthadīpanī* was written sometime between 1739 and 1747, during the reign of Śrī Vijayarājasiṃha, when Saraṇaṃkara was between the ages of forty-one and forty-nine (Sannasgala 1964, 406). In *Mahāvaṃsa*, the king's invitation to compose *Sārārthadīpanī* is described as central to King Śrī Vijayarājasiṃha's efforts to sustain the Buddhist *sāsana.*

> That king, having had dwelling places made and settled novices in various places [was] faithful and with great affection for them, showing [them] much favor with requisites such as robes, and hearing the excellent Buddhist teachings. He paid honor to that novice named Saraṇaṃkara who was faithful, a mine of [gemlike] qualities, who lived among the novices in the Uposathārama. Offering an invitation to that very one and having a commentary on the four recitation sections [*Sārārthadīpanī*] done in the language of Lanka, he protected religious learning. (MV 98: 21–24)

This account makes clear the importance of *Sārārthadīpanī*'s composition as a matter of public display to those within the highest levels of the court and the monastic community. The king's invitation to Saraṇaṃkara to compose the text was part of the formal activities through which Śrī Vijayarājasiṃha demonstrated his support for Saraṇaṃkara's monks as well as his propriety as the leader of Lanka's Buddhist community.

It is not surprising that Saraṇaṃkara received such patronage at the hands of King Śrī Vijayarājasiṃha, since he had risen to a position of eminence under the previous king, Narēndrasiṃha, and had served as Śrī Vijayarājasiṃha's tutor. Despite such signs of the king's support, the period in which *Sārārthadīpanī* was composed remained a challenging period for Saraṇaṃkara and his followers. The attempt to develop a more fully institutionalized monastic order through the educational activities at Niyamakanda, and the simultaneous attempt to reintroduce higher ordination from Southeast Asia,[4] made Saraṇaṃkara and his followers more visible and more vulnerable to attack by their *gaṇinnānse* detractors. Such opponents had reason to fear that the growing power of the Silvat Samāgama would lead to a reorganization of the monastic community and the formalization of Saraṇaṃkara's leadership at their expense. Under these circumstances, the invitation to compose *Sārārthadīpanī* provided Saraṇaṃkara with an important opportunity to demonstrate his fitness as an educated monk, alive to the authoritative traditions of the Lankan Theravāda and committed to the ideals of monastic discipline. At the same time, as the number of monks associated

[4] The first embassy was sent to Pegu in 1741 and the second to Ayutthaya in 1747 (Vijayavardhana and Mīgaskumbura 1993, xvi).

with Saraṇaṃkara grew, it was appropriate for Saraṇaṃkara to underscore his position as a teacher, and to set out a vision of educated and disciplined monasticism for his students at Niyamakanda.

CONTENTS AND STRUCTURE OF SĀRĀRTHADĪPANĪ

An analysis of *Sārārthadīpanī* cannot be understood properly without an introduction to this bilingual commentary, so I provide here a brief sketch of the content and structure of this work. The focus of *Sārārthadīpanī*'s commentary is a set of canonical Pāli texts considered to be the Buddha's own words (Pāli *buddhavacana*). At least as early as the fifth century, certain texts included within this set had been identified as special texts whose recitation would help to assure the protection of human communities from natural and supernatural harm. The collective term given to these protective texts was *paritta* (Pāli) or *pirit* (Sinhala). Both terms were based on a verbal root meaning "to protect." By the ninth century, the set of canonical texts included in *Sārārthadīpanī* had been identified as a set collection of *paritta*, and also became known as the *catubhāṇavārapāḷi* or the *catubhāṇavāra*: the "four recitation sections" taken from the Pāli *tipiṭaka*.[5] Their contents are as follows.

Saraṇagamana	*Going for Refuge*
Dasasikkhāpada	*The Ten Training Precepts*
Sāmaṇerapañha	*Questions for a Novice*
Dvattiṃsākāra	*The Thirty-two Characteristics*
Paccavekkhaṇā	*The Reflections*
Dasadhammasutta	*The Discourse on the Ten Elements*
(Mahā)maṅgalasutta	*The (Great) Discourse on What is Auspicious*
Ratanasutta	*The Jewel Discourse*
Karaṇīyamettā sutta	*The Discourse on Appropriate Acts of Loving Kindness*
Khandaparitta	*The Protective Account of the Aggregates*

[5] For a more detailed account of the history of *paritta* and forms of contemporary protective recitation, see de Silva (1983).

Mettānisaṃsasutta (or *Mettā sutta*)	*The Discourse on the Benefits of Loving Kindness*
Mittānisaṃsasutta	*The Discourse on the Benefits of Friendship*
Moraparitta	*The Protective Account of the Peacock*
Chandaparitta	*The Protective Account of the Moon*
Sūriyaparitta	*The Protective Account of the Sun*
Dhajaggasutta/Dhajaggaparitta	*The Discourse on the Standard's Tip*
Mahākassapa(tthera)-bojjhaṅga	*The Factors of Enlightenment—With Reference to the Great Monastic Elder Kassapa*
Mahāmoggallāna(tthera)-bojjhaṅga	*The Factors of Enlightenment—With Reference to the Great Monastic Elder Moggallāna*
Mahācunda(tthera)-bojjhaṅga	*The Factors of Enlightenment—With Reference to the Great Monastic Elder Cunda*
Girimānandasutta	*The Girimānanda Discourse*
Isigilisutta	*The Isigili Discourse*
Aṭaṇātiyasutta	*The Aṭaṇātiya Discourse*

Buddhist commentators writing in Lanka in the fifth century composed commentaries in Pāli for the texts contained in the four recitation sections but did not group them together or provide fully systematic commentary to the texts. In the thirteenth century, however, commentarial treatment of these texts changed radically. The first commentary on the four recitation sections as a textual collection was composed at this time, in Pāli, and given the name *Sāratthasamuccaya*. It brought the fifth-century commentaries on the *paritta* texts together in a single unit and added bridge sections between the texts. These bridge sections placed the individual *paritta* texts in a developmental sequence and suggested an interpretive framework for them. However, *Sāratthasamuccaya* retained the unsystematic character of the fifth-century commentaries with respect to the individual texts, making no attempt to provide synonyms or explanations for every textual unit.[6]

In *Sārārthadīpanī*, Saraṇaṃkara sought to create a fully comprehensive and systematic commentary on the four recitation sections in Sinhala. His composition retained all of the Pāli texts taken from the four recitation sections, as well as a substantial portion of the previous Pāli commentaries on these texts, making detailed attention to the four recitation sections his highest priority. In reproducing the Pāli texts of the four recitation sections, Saraṇaṃkara provided a brief Sinhala-language gloss for each word or phrase. He added a more detailed commentary to nearly every word or phrase of each text. This commentary included fuller explanations, examples, and references to other texts. In some cases, Saraṇaṃkara's commentarial detail was set within the glossing section. More often, the elaboration was written in a variable combination of Pāli and Sinhala following the initial brief gloss for the section under comment. The detailed commentary composed by Saraṇaṃkara was most often first introduced in Sinhala. In some cases, this Sinhala commentary clearly drew on the earlier Pāli commentaries, often presenting a slightly enlarged or more elaborate version of them.[7] From there, Saraṇaṃkara sometimes introduced portions of the Pāli commentary directly into *Sārārthadīpanī* as an accompaniment to his Sinhala commentary. Students who read or listened to *Sārārthadīpanī* encountered its contents as an integrated three-part work containing the four recitation sections taken from the Pāli *tipiṭaka*, a Sinhala commentary based partly on early Pāli commentaries, and parts of the Pāli commentaries themselves. The dominant voice in *Sārārthadīpanī* is clearly Saraṇaṃkara's Sinhala-language commentarial voice, since this orchestrates the audience's encounter with the texts of the four recitation sections through a careful attention to their contents. A schematic account of *Sārārthadīpanī*'s structure may make it easier to follow the intertextual and bilingual relationships discussed in the remainder of this chapter. It is presented in the following list.

1. A passage from the four recitation sections (usually not an entire Pāli text but only a passage from it) is reproduced in Pāli.
2. A Pāli word or phrase from this passage is provided with a

[6] On *Sāratthasamuccaya*, see de Silva (1983) and Blackburn (1996; 1999b).

[7] Close similarities between *Sāratthasamuccaya* and *Sārārthadīpanī* in the contents of the bridge sections connecting one canonical Pāli text to another, as well as Saraṇaṃkara's introductory reference to *Sāratthasamuccaya*, indicate that Saraṇaṃkara drew heavily on this work. It is thus likely that he approached Pāli commentaries composed in the fifth century through *Sāratthasamuccaya* rather than by examining the fifth-century commentaries directly.

Sinhala word gloss, perhaps with some brief additional details on the word or phrase.

3. A more detailed commentary on the Pāli passage is written in Sinhala, often with a substantial debt to fifth- to thirteenth-century Pāli commentary.

4. A section from the fifth- to thirteenth-century Pāli commentary is usually but not always included. It may treat the same matter as that in step 3 or introduce a slightly different topic.

5. The next passage from the same Pāli text is reproduced in Pāli (if the entire text was not reproduced in step 1).

6. Steps 2–5 are repeated until the entire Pāli text from the four recitation sections has been commented upon.

7. A bridge section, usually based on *Sāratthasamuccaya*'s bridge sections, is often but not always included between this text from the four recitation sections and the next.

8. Steps 1–7 begin again.[8]

BILINGUAL COMMENTARY, THE COMMAND OF LANGUAGE, AND THE LANGUAGE OF COMMAND

Pollock's work on the rise of local/vernacular languages offers a useful place to begin my reading of *Sārārthadīpanī*.[9] He draws attention to the fact that patrons and authors choose the languages in which works of literature are composed and argues that this choice should be a matter of historical inquiry. In other words, the language in which a text is composed is understood as a social fact to be analyzed for its meaning to particular communities. In Pollock's words, "One of the great challenges of a history of literary cultures in South Asia, as elsewhere, is to exhume the conditions that make possible and desirable the creation of new literatures *and to understand more subtly what other choices, social, political, religious, are being made when a given language is chosen for literature*; . . . what there is that needs to be said, now, in Kannada rather than Sanskrit, in English rather than Kannada, in Latin rather than Greek, in Italian rather than Latin" (Pollock 1995, 129, emphasis

[8] In the first lengthy example from *Sārārthadīpanī* discussed below, I have indicated stages 1–4.

[9] The subhead plays on the title of Cohn's influential essay (1996) on the relationship between learning and authority in the British Raj. Pollock uses both terms—local and vernacular—and contrasts them to "translocal" languages. He prefers "local language" to "vernacular," however, since the first term draws attention to the possibility of regionally based relations of power, and since it is less easily assumed to refer to a rustic or unsophisticated form of language.

added). Pollock's work is concerned primarily with the rise of local-language literary traditions in tension with well-established translocal literary cultures. In drawing on his ideas to frame this inquiry, it is important to note the differences between the context of *Sārārthadīpanī*'s composition and the situations that are the focus of Pollock's work. Saraṇaṃkara did not write *Sārārthadīpanī* at a time when a local-language literature was just beginning to emerge in tension with Pāli and Sanskrit. By the eighteenth century, Pāli, Sanskrit, and Sinhala were all well-established languages in Lankan literary circles, and compositions were also made in Tamil and Telegu, with greater use of the former than the latter.[10] Moreover, the composition of *Sārārthadīpanī* did not involve a choice between the local language of Sinhala and the translocal language of Pāli but, instead, a choice to bring these two languages together in a particular way. Despite these points of difference, Pollock's comments on authorial intention and the values attached to linguistic choice provide the basis from which to ask the following questions about *Sārārthadīpanī*'s composition: What claims to authority was Saraṇaṃkara able to make by virtue of his bilingual commentarial composition? How did the text's bilingual structure allow him to speak simultaneously to an audience of court and monastic elites who became acquainted with *Sārārthadīpanī* by repute, and to the group of students whom he intended to work through the commentary in a careful fashion?

Linguistic and Commentarial Pedigrees

As I argued in chapter 4, Pāli occupied a special place within the textual cultures of Lanka because it was considered to be the language of the Buddha, the "root language" appropriate to the communication of ultimate truth, and the language that linked together the Theravādin Buddhist world of Sri Lanka and Southeast Asia. The fact that the Theravādin *tipiṭaka* was redacted in Pāli, and that the most authoritative (fifth-century) commentaries on it were composed in Pāli, helped strengthen the assumption that a person knowledgeable about Pāli was a person with access to the intellectual and devotional foundations of the Theravāda. Values attached to Sinhala, or at least to particular forms of Sinhala used in literary works, were different but also quite

[10] Although works concerned with Buddhist ideas and practices were often written in Pāli and Sinhala, sophisticated participation in the literate culture of the time required knowledge of Sanskrit, since Sanskrit grammar and aesthetics were foundational for many compositions in the other languages.

important.[11] From the eleventh century onward, because of the composition of Buddhist devotional treatises and narratives in Sinhala that became central to Buddhist understandings of religious practice, Sinhala was associated with literary sophistication and devotional intensity.[12] The cluster of influential Buddhist commentaries composed in Sinhala within the prestigious monastic communities of the Dam̆badeṇi period, and the poetic works composed between the fourteenth and sixteenth centuries, further added to the positive associations attached to literary Sinhala. Thus, by the time of *Sārārthadīpanī*'s composition, Pāli and Sinhala were both well established as languages suitable for Buddhist literary compositions and both possessed powerful associations with particular authoritative scholastic, monastic, and devotional traditions. In this context, bilingual composition, especially in the form of detailed and systematic commentary in one language on the contents of another, was a sign of complete mastery over and fluidity of movement within and between Pāli and Sinhala literary traditions. The power of such bilingual composition is strikingly indicated in a letter composed by Saraṇaṃkara and presented to King Narĕndrasiṃha in 1727 on the occasion of Saraṇaṃkara's receipt of a relic and casket for installation at the Niyamakanda Vihāraya. In this letter, Saraṇaṃkara composed an *aṣṭaka*—the form of verse most highly valued as a demonstration of poetic skill—in Pāli and accompanied it with a Sinhala gloss (Paranavitana 1981, vii; 7–8).

With these ideas about the social meanings of language use in mind, it is easier to understand that *Sārārthadīpanī* appropriated earlier Pāli literary traditions in a way that reflected positively upon its author. Whether or not Saraṇaṃkara self-consciously composed the commentary as he did to display his status as a Buddhist scholar (and there is some indication that he did, as we shall see), *Sārārthadīpanī*'s bilingual commentarial structure helped to shape an image of Saraṇaṃkara as a scholar with a commanding grasp of earlier literary traditions. For instance, his decision to reproduce the Pāli texts from the four recitation sections in their entirety along with large passages taken from Pāli commentarial sources demonstrated his knowledgeable respect for the interpretive lineage of the Theravādin tradition and his determination to make these sources available to the students of his day. By making these texts the object of systematic translation and explanation in his work, Saraṇaṃkara showed himself to be a dutiful and skilled participant in processes of textual transmission, someone who dared to compose a

[11] There is a sharp difference in vocabulary and grammatical structure between colloquial Sinhala and the several forms of literary Sinhala.

[12] See Hallisey (1988).

complete translation of the four recitation sections even as he embraced Pāli texts as an authoritative focus of interpretation.

The significance of this mastery had as much to do with specific Lankan monastic identities as it did with the positive values generally attributed to Pāli and literary Sinhala. In the composition of *Sārārthadīpanī*, Saraṇaṃkara drew on Pāli commentaries attributed to the famous fifth-century commentator Buddhaghosa and to the prestigious thirteenth-century forest-dwelling lineage of Medhaṃkara. He also attempted to adopt the style of literary Sinhala used in the prose works composed by the esteemed monks of the thirteenth-century Daṁbadeṇi period.[13] In doing so, Saraṇaṃkara unmistakably identified the strands of Lankan monasticism with which he sought association. Significantly, his choices passed over the literate traditions of the more recent past that were more closely associated with his monastic contemporaries and competitors. Instead, Saraṇaṃkara forged a symbolic connection to earlier moments of celebrated monasticism that most closely matched the identity he sought to constitute for the emerging Siyam Nikāya. In a literate world of considerable sophistication, it was no minor matter for Saraṇaṃkara to show his conversance with the works of Buddhaghosa, the most celebrated scholar-monk of the Theravāda, whose commentaries and compendia were foundational works for the entire Theravādin tradition. Nor was it unimportant to link his work to the forest-dwelling monks of the Daṁbadeṇi period, whose reputation as scholar-ascetics provided a useful juxtaposition when charges of ignorance and monastic impropriety were made against Saraṇaṃkara's *gaṇinnānse* predecessors and contemporaries.[14]

Mediating and Rewriting Pāli Traditions

In the composition of *Sārārthadīpanī*, Saraṇaṃkara did more than locate himself within a series of desirable pedigrees and show his mastery of existing textual traditions. A close look at the work shows that Saraṇaṃkara chose not to rest with a recapitulation of earlier works but to mediate them and rewrite them through his Sinhala commentary. The product was a work bearing Saraṇaṃkara's stamp.

When thinking about Saraṇaṃkara's relationship to the earlier Pāli texts on which he commented, I have found it helpful to draw on Rita Copeland's account of the rhetorical and appropriative nature of local-

[13] This observation was made to me separately by Charles Hallisey and P. B. Mīgaskumbura.

[14] On Saraṇaṃkara's favorable views of Daṁbadeṇi period monks, see also Blackburn (1999b).

language translations of works in the classical Latin tradition. Copeland places her discussion of translation in the broader context of medieval ideas about commentary and rhetoric, showing that according to the rules followed for the exegesis of nonscriptural texts, a commentary "rewrites and supplants them" (1991, 3). "Even though medieval commentary works around the text, alongside the text, as addenda to the text, it can take on a primary productive character: it continually refashions the text for changing conditions of understanding" (64). Commentarial practice is rhetorical since the exegesis rewrites the text according to the exegete's views on the text's significance (76). According to Copeland, local-language (or to use her term, "vernacular") translation of the classical authorities occurred in two forms, both of which were determined by the expectation that commentary be rhetorical and transformative of the text on which it comments. These two forms, which Copeland identifies as "primary" and "secondary" translations, differ in the degree to which translation follows a commentarial model. Primary translations "exhibit a close alliance with the aims and methods of exegetical practice, and like exegesis define their purpose in terms of service to a source text" (7). In other words, although they do in fact appropriate the texts they translate, primary translations appear to remain subordinate to these texts. Secondary translations, on the other hand, "stand in a 'secondary' relationship to the exegetical tradition. . . . [T]hey do not define themselves through exegetical models of service and supplementation, but rather through rhetorical models of invention" (7). In such translations the rhetorical transformation is so successful that they are more often identified as independent vernacular texts than as vernacular texts in service to a Latin authority.[15]

Sārārthadīpanī is, in these terms, a primary translation. It creates a new, local-language version of the Pāli texts from the four recitation sections through its systematic provision of synonyms for the text while remaining closely tied to the structure of the Pāli original. By choosing to comment on the four recitation sections in particular ways through the medium of literary Sinhala, however, Saraṇaṃkara engaged in the rhetorical work of exegesis, orchestrating his readers' encounter with the texts in ways that privileged his understanding of their significance. Another way of thinking about this process is to draw on Martin Irvine's observations about the "ongoing negotiations between the authority of the text and the newer authority of the gloss" that occurred when texts were received and transmitted within a formal scholarly

[15] Copeland uses the discussion of the relationships between commentary, rhetoric, and translation to develop her argument about the subtle transformation in Latinate literary traditions that led to a "confrontation between Latinity and vernacularity" (1991, 223) and challenges to the "official [Latin] culture of academic discourse" (106).

tradition based on the discipline of *grammatica* (1994, 390). Commentarial compositions helped to assure the importance of particular texts throughout the centuries. At the same time, as the phrase "ongoing negotiations" suggests, commentarial practice played a role in changing textual norms and the social relations influenced by the composition, transmission, and reception of texts. Shifting exegetical emphases recreated authoritative texts for particular literate communities, while commentarial practice helped to mark out certain texts and the people associated with them (authors, readers, patrons), as important. As Irvine notes, "Only certain kinds of texts received the institutional validation necessary for becoming serious objects of interpretation" (391). Their interpreters were similarly privileged as people able to speak for, and about, "tradition."

With such ideas in mind about the subtle takeovers made possible by bilingual commentary and the ways in which acts of interpretation reflected a certain authority back on the interpreters (when they functioned within broadly acceptable parameters, of course), I return to Saraṇaṃkara's commentary on the four recitation sections. In the opening to *Sārārthadīpanī*, the author emphasized his indebtedness to earlier commentators while establishing his work as an act of devotion to the Triple Gem. The opening lines also indicate the work's character as a translation, since even the opening lines of homage are presented in both Pāli (below in bold) and in a Sinhala translation (below in roman type).

Homage to the blessed one, worthy one, fully enlightened.

I honor the Buddha, hero, honored by the world, conqueror, unequaled, possessing knowledge of the ocean of all that is to be known, an ocean of virtues.

I honor the *dhamma*, taught by the Conqueror, spotless, subtle, excellent, deep, difficult to perceive, dispelling evil.

And I honor that monastic community, [composed of those] whose faculties are tamed, whose conduct is pure, whose wealth is the heat of asceticism, who have acted correctly, who are offspring of the Sage.

Thus, having destroyed all misfortunes with whatever merit is accumulated by my act of proper homage to the Triple Gem, and having considered the commentary *Sāratthasamuccaya* and the condensed explanation, previously composed, which are excellent and pure,[16]

[16] "The condensed explanation" (*saṃkhepa vivaraṇa*) probably refers to a Sinhala gloss, no longer extant, made for portions of the four recitation sections. According to Somadasa's analysis, the work may have been composed in the fifteenth century (1987, Vol. 1, 104–105).

I will write another elucidation of meaning for the four recitation sections, from one perspective, desiring its long duration.

The Lord Buddha, an ocean of virtues, with knowledge for crossing the ocean of all that is to be known, unequaled, conqueror, hero, honored by all the world [including creatures] such as *brahmās*, *suras*, *asuras*, snakes, *kinnaras*, and men;[17]

and the excellent *dharma* taught by the conqueror, dispeller of evil, excellent, difficult to perceive, deep, subtle, spotless;

and the monastic community, sons of the Omniscient One, who have acted correctly, whose wealth is the heat of asceticism, possessing pure conduct and tamed faculties:

I honor [these three] properly with the three doors: body, speech and mind.

Thus, having destroyed completely all misfortunes existing within [me] and outside [me] through the power of the merit accumulated by properly honoring the Triple Gem,

looking at the commentary to the four recitation sections called *Sāratthasamuccaya*, which was composed by a former teacher, and also at the condensed explanation, and following those [texts],

I make another elucidation of meaning for the four recitation sections in one way. (SD, 1–2)

Saraṇaṃkara's debt to the author of *Sāratthasamuccaya* is presented quite emphatically in the introductory passage that follows these lines of homage to the Triple Gem, when *Sārārthadīpanī* quotes introductory comments from *Sāratthasamuccaya*. These comments define the four recitation sections, explain that its texts were compiled from the *nikāyas* (groups of *sutta* texts) of the *tipiṭaka*, define the *nikāyas* and give the *nikāya* locations for all of the texts contained in the four recitation sections (SD, 2–3; SS, 1–2).

Sārārthadīpanī's respectful representation of the Pāli four recitation sections and its indebtedness to the earlier Pāli commentaries is evident throughout the work. The example below shows Saraṇaṃkara's commentarial style. After reproducing *The Discourse on the Ten Elements* (a Pāli text from the four recitation sections) in a single passage because the text is a short one, Saraṇaṃkara provided a gloss in Sinhala for each word or phrase in the Pāli text. I have reproduced a section of this below with the words from the Pāli text printed in bold. The Sinhala gloss appears in roman type. I have also indicated the first four steps in Saraṇaṃkara's glossing procedure described above.

[17] The first three of these creatures reside in Buddhist heavens. A *kinnara* is a bird with a man's head.

> **evaṃ me sutaṃ me** mā visin **evaṃ sutaṃ** meseyin asanaladī **ekaṃ samayaṃ** ek samayekhi **bhagavā** bhāgyavatvū budurajatema **sāvatthiyaṃ** sävätnuvara samīpayehivū **jetavane** jetanam rājakumārayāgē uyanhi karaṇaladabävin jetavananamvū **anāthapiṇḍikassa ārāme** anēpiḍu mahasiṭāṇangē aramhī **viharati** vädhaväsa vadāraṇa sēka tatra kho ehilā hevat eklabhi vanāhi **bhagavā** budurajatema **bhikkhavo iti** mahaṇeniyi kiyā **bhikkhu āmantesi** bhikṣūnṭa amantraṇayakara vadāḷasēka **te bhikkhū** e bhikṣuhu **bhadante iti** svāmīnvahansäyi kiyā **bhagavato** bhagyavathaṭa **paccasosuṃ** prativacana dunnāhuya **bhagavā** budurajatema **etad avoca** me matukiyanulabana tepula vadāḷasēka **bhikkhave** mahaṇeni **ime dasa dhammā** mē daśadharmayō **pabbajitena** gihigeyahära pävidivūvahu visin **abhiṇhaṃ paccavekkhitabbā** ekvan sälakiyayut tāhuya **katame dasa** ē daśadharmayō kavurudayat (1.) **vevaṇṇiyaṃ (2.)** vivaṇṇibavaṭa **ajjhupagato amhī ti** pämiṇiyemiyi **pabbajitena** pävidivūvahu visin **abhiṇhaṃ paccavekkhitabbaṃ** nirantarayen sälakiyayutu. (SD, 23–24).[18]

After providing these brief Sinhala glosses to words from the Pāli text (in the section reproduced just above), Saraṇaṃkara moved on to a more elaborate commentarial response. Commenting more closely in Sinhala on the Pāli word *vevaṇṇiyaṃ*, which means "appearance," Saraṇaṃkara then quoted the section of *Sāratthasamuccaya* on which he drew in the Sinhala comment. The quotation from the Pāli commentary *Sāratthasamuccaya* is printed here in italics, and Saraṇaṃkara's Sinhala commentary remains in roman type.

> (3.) In this regard there are two explanations, saying "of distinct appearance physically" and "of distinct appearance with respect to [monastic] requisites [such as the robes and bowl used by a monk]." What does this mean? Having experienced in lay life things listed here such as [the use of] fine spoons in various colors, fine food mixed as desired, goods made of

[18] **Thus has it been heard by me by me** by me **thus has it been heard** it has been heard in this manner **at one time** at one time **the blessed one** the lord Buddha who became the fortunate one **in Sāvatthi** that was near the city of Sāvatthi **in Jeta's Grove** that had received the name Jeta's Grove because the park had been created by a royal prince named Jeta **in Anāthapiṇḍika's monastic meeting place** in the monastic meeting place of the great disciple Anāthapiṇḍika **resided** taught [honorific verbal form] while in residence **then** once or at one time **the blessed one** the lord Buddha **"monks!"** having said "monks!" **addressed the monks** made an address [honorific verbal form] to the monks **those monks** those monks **"venerable sir"** having said "lord" **to the blessed one** to the blessed one **replied** made a reply **the fortunate one** lord Buddha **said this** made [honorific verbal form] this following statement **"monks"** "monks" **these ten elements** these ten elements **by someone who has renounced** by someone who has renounced, giving up a layman's home **should be reflected upon repeatedly** should always be reflected upon **which ten?** which are these ten elements? **on a different appearance** on the existence of a different appearance **"I have reached"** "I have arrived at" **by one who has renounced** by one who has renounced **should be reflected upon repeatedly** should be reflected upon without interruption.

gold and silver, sleeping on high beds in bedrooms, and using medicines like ghee and butter, after the novitiate ordination [I have] cut robes into pieces, shaved hair and beard, donned clothes that appear different, eaten mixed food received from various homes in iron or clay dishes, set out branches on a bed of cloth and grass, and taken medicine like cow's urine. Because of this I have arrived at a different appearance with respect to the requisites. Having cut [my] facial hair, having become bald, I have [also] developed a different physical appearance. For someone reflecting thus again and again, no depression or anger or pride arises for any reason. In order to show how to abandon all these [states of mind] the [Pāli] commentary [*Sāratthasamuccaya*] says:

(4.) *that state of the alteration of appearance, that state of unattractiveness, is a twofold alteration of appearance: alteration of the appearance of the body and alteration of the appearance of the requisites. Here, by shaving the hair and beard, alteration of the body should be understood. Having dressed in various pleasant and pure clothes, having lain on beds in fine bedrooms, having used ghee, butter, and so on as medicine, after the time of the novitiate clothes cut from old robes should be worn, mixed foods given by others should be eaten in iron and clay bowls, one should lie down on grass mats with seats and beds such as the base of a tree, one should lie down on mats of skin, [and] medicine like cow's urine should be taken. Thus it is in this way that an alteration in the appearance of the requisites should be understood. Thus anger and pride are abandoned for someone who reflects in this way.* (SD, 24)

Despite the apparent respect for earlier commentarial perspectives, the reader's initial impression of *Sārārthadīpanī*'s conservatism gives way to an experience in which the intensity of Saraṇaṃkara's attention to Pāli texts eventually shifts the audience's attention from these Pāli texts to Saraṇaṃkara's own commentary. As Copeland remarks on the power of paraphrastic translation, "This linguistic application to the text, a form of attention to the quomodo of the text, works as a radical displacement of the text: the paraphrase itself takes on the originary authority of 'proper' speech" (1990, 85–86). The following example, taken from *Sārārthadīpanī*'s commentary on part of the Pāli *Discourse on What Is Auspicious* illustrates the way that this text from the four recitation sections (printed here in bold type, first in a complete English translation and then in Pāli within the exegetical passage) is deconstructed and overtaken by the detailed Sinhala commentarial response (printed in roman type).

Living in a proper place, the state of merit done before, and proper self-resolve; that is an excellent auspicious thing [maṅgala]. Patirūpadesavāso ca, living in a proper place (where the ten meritorious acts such as gener-

> osity and virtue exist, where all four divisions of the Buddhist assembly [monks, nuns, lay men and lay women] are present, where the Triple Gem shines, in some village, town or royal capital); **pubbe ca katapuññatā**, the existence of merit done in a previous life (to buddhas, pratyekabuddhas or noble disciples); **attasammāpaṇidhi ca**, the proper establishment (in the personal attainment of virtue, faith and renunciation which is distant from poor virtue and lack of faith); **etaṃ**, that; **uttamaṃ maṅgalaṃ**, excellent auspicious thing. (SD, 31)

The ongoing pattern of separation and paraphrase that characterizes Saraṇaṃkara's approach to the Pāli texts from the four recitation sections eventually makes the Sinhala paraphrase more accessible than the original Pāli text itself. Something similar occurs in Saraṇaṃkara's treatment of the Pāli commentaries on which he drew. While composing *Sārārthadīpanī*, Saraṇaṃkara often appropriated the content of earlier Pāli commentarial material and incorporated it into his own Sinhala commentary without indicating this incorporation. At other times, he quoted earlier Pāli commentaries to strengthen the position taken in the Sinhala commentary. In doing so, he inverted the relationship of subservience to the Pāli commentaries with which he opened *Sārārthadīpanī* by using them to serve the rhetorical aims of his own Sinhala composition.

In another section of *Sārārthadīpanī* that comments on *The Discourse on What Is Auspicious*, for instance, Saraṇaṃkara's composition of a Sinhala gloss plus minor explanatory additions draws on phrases from the earlier Pāli commentaries.[19] In the example that follows, Saraṇaṃkara's Sinhala commentary is once more printed in roman type. The passage taken from the Pāli discourse is printed in bold type, as in the previous example

> **A mind that doesn't shake when touched by the elements of the world, lack of grief, faultlessness, peace; that is an excellent auspicious thing. Phuṭṭhassa lokadhammehi**, being crushed or destroyed by the elements of the world (eight, such as *lobha, alobha*); **yassa**, to someone (elder, new or middling [in seniority]; **cittaṃ**, mind; **na kampati**, doesn't shake (the mind of such a person has the defilements destroyed); **asokaṃ**, without the affliction of grief (because the wind of grief is spirited away by the knowledge of the *arhat* path). (SD, 33)

Saraṇaṃkara's debt to the Pāli commentaries is clear from a comparison to *Sāratthasamuccaya*'s commentary on the same passage:

[19] Once again, it is likely that he drew on fifth-century commentaries as mediated through the thirteenth-century *Sāratthasamuccaya*.

> **Phuṭṭhassa lokadhammehi cittaṃ yassa na kampati,** the mind of someone touched or overcome by the eight elements of the world such as *lobha* and *alobha,* doesn't shake, doesn't tremble, doesn't quiver. The mind of that person is to be understood as an auspicious thing by anyone, because it brings a supreme state not to be disturbed. Why doesn't the mind of someone [so] touched by these things shake? [Because] it belongs to an *arahat*, someone whose defilements are destroyed, not to anyone else. (SS, 95)

Something similar occurs in *Sārārthadīpanī*'s treatment of *The Jewel Discourse*, another text from the four recitation sections.

> **Therefore, creatures, may you all listen. Do acts of loving kindness [mettā] for human beings. They bring offerings day and night; therefore protect them zealously. . . . ye,** those humans; **divā ca,** day; **ratto ca,** and night; **baliṃ haranti,** just as much as they show devotion [pūjā] with flowers, etc. at temples and other places where they have made images of deities, and make offerings—showing devotion during the day by giving an offering of rice, or at night by having the *dharma* preached, [with] lamps and flowers, and offering merit; **tasmā,** for that reason. . . . (SD, 41)

Once again the comparison with *Sāratthasamuccaya* is instructive.

> **Divā ca ratto ca haranti ye baliṃ tasmā hi ne rakkhattha appamattā.** The meaning of this: those people, having created the deities in mind or form, go to a *stūpa*, tree, etc. and make offerings for the deities in the day, and they make an offerings of a lamp *pūjā* on full-moon nights, etc. (SS, 104)

For those among *Sārārthadīpanī*'s audience who came to recognize his debt to the Pāli commentaries, this structure would have indicated the degree to which Saraṇaṃkara had assimilated his Pāli sources and thus would have served as another favorable indication of skilled authorship, given the long history of composition through compilation in the Lankan Theravāda. For those who did not recognize the borrowing, Saraṇaṃkara's work would have simply appeared creative and comprehensive.

When Saraṇaṃkara quoted earlier Pāli commentaries in the service of *Sārārthadīpanī*, these quotations were framed by his own commentarial perspective. For instance, he clearly established when and where his audience should refer to the Pāli commentary, and made the Pāli quotations relevant to his own aims. The section from *Sārārthadīpanī*'s commentary on *The Discourse on the Ten Elements,* quoted earlier, offers one example of this. The Sinhala commentary on the first part of the text adopts the ideas of the Pāli commentary, and then includes the relevant section of the Pāli commentary. Although Saraṇaṃkara's Sinhala commentary draws heavily on earlier Pāli commentaries, *Sārārthadīpanī* does not emphasize its debt to the earlier Pāli commentarial material. Instead, it uses this material as an extension of the Sinhala commentarial trajectory. One of *Sārārthadīpanī*'s sections on *The Discourse on Appropriate Acts of Loving Kindness* also reverses the expected hierarchy of Sinhala commentarial deference to Pāli commentarial tradition, though in a slightly different way. After a long Sinhala commentary on the word *karaṇiyaṃ* found in the *sutta*, in which Saraṇaṃkara explains what it means to be good at self-cultivation, he introduces the Pāli commentary to elaborate this point. By way of introduction, he writes: "here, in order to show what's intended, that is, [that] they are clever with respect to development, with respect to increasing [their attainments] or are skilled with respect to aims." Saraṇaṃkara then immediately quotes a passage of Pāli commentary that echoes the Sinhala passage with which Saraṇaṃkara began his commentary (SD, 58–59). Similarly, later in its treatment of another verse from the same discourse (quoted in bold type below), Saraṇaṃkara composes a Sinhala comment (in roman type) on what is meant by competence and the absence of physical and mental crookedness (in a gloss on the Pāli terms *sakko,* meaning "able" and *uju,* meaning "upright"), before bringing in a section of Pāli commentary (in italics) as a proof text for the Sinhala interpretation.

> **He should be able, upright, very firm, gentle, of sweet speech, and without pride. Sakko assa** he should be clever [Sinhala *dakṣa*]. What does this mean? A forest monk lives [this way] after arriving at the tranquil foundation [of action] by being endowed with the second aspect of exertion [characterized by good health] which destroys the unskillful states that have arisen and with the fourth aspect of exertion [characterized by wisdom] which increases and spreads the protection of the skillful states that have arisen. Whatever, great or little, which should be done by an ascetic with respect to his robe and bowl requisites, with respect to fulfilling duties, with respect to everything [is done] without dwelling on body and life. He should be clever in this respect, without negligence. **Uju assa** although clever in this way he should be without deceit, he should be upright **su uju assa** he should be properly upright, should be properly upright because he is without delusion, should be properly upright because of the absence of crookedness in both speech and body, should be properly upright because of the absence of mental crookedness, or should be upright by developing the [positive] qualities that are missing in himself, thus should be properly upright by not accepting gains that come from [falsely assumed and] absent qualities.
>
> This is well said,
>
> *Wanting to live having reached the tranquil foundation, or, having reached that through mundane wisdom [and] continuing after that attainment, a*

> *forest-dwelling monk, being without affection for life and body by completely reaching the second and fourth exertion, is able to conduct himself through insight into the truth. Thus, whatever, great or small, ascetic practices are [incumbent upon] him—preparing for meditation, undertaking duties, looking after the robe and bowl—he should be capable of these. Intelligence, diligence and calm are possible for one living [in this way]. Furthermore, by having completely reached the third exertion [characterized by honesty], he should be upright. And for someone who is upright, without becoming self-satisfied with the existence of his own upright nature, he should be upright by acting well [and] by acting without laxity over and over again as long as he lives. Or, he [should be] upright by not deceiving, upright through honesty, or upright by destroying crookedness of body and speech, upright by destroying mental crookedness. Or, upright by not manifesting qualities that are [actually] absent, upright by not accepting gain which accrues from [manifesting] absent qualities.* (SD, 60–61)

Saraṇaṃkara's interpretive voice is confident, drawing the "well said" words of earlier teachers into his own local-language exegesis. Although his Sinhala commentary was crucially indebted to the earlier Pāli commentaries, here Saraṇaṃkara reframed indebtedness as fortunate agreement.

Scholarly Self-consciousness

The composition of a bilingual commentary that, as a primary translation, was intended to attend closely to the letter of the Pāli texts from the four recitation sectons on which it commented provided opportunities for Saraṇaṃkara to engage in a critical reading of the texts with which he worked. It is this aspect of *Sārārthadīpanī*'s commentarial style that provides the clearest indication of Saraṇaṃkara's authorial intentions. The nature of Saraṇaṃkara's commentary strongly suggests his awareness that commentarial composition offered an opportunity to display himself to students, rivals, and courtiers as a well-educated scholar monk. Within *Sārārthadīpanī*, Saraṇaṃkara's critical reading of the Pāli texts takes three forms: the detailed discussion of difficult textual passages, the inclusion of references to other textual authorities, and the inclusion of references to Saraṇaṃkara's own works. Once again, several examples bring this point into sharper relief.

In his commentary on *The Protective Account of the Moon* Saraṇaṃkara commented on the following Pāli passage: "**Bringer of light to those who are blind; shining with its orb whose brilliance has arisen; Rahu don't swallow my son who wanders about the sky; Rahu free my Chandima.**" His Sinhala commentary proceeds as follows:

> This verse doesn't belong to *The Protective Account of the Moon*. Why is this? This verse doesn't appear for *The Protective Account of the Moon* in this spot in the gloss commentary made for this text by earlier teachers. Asking the reason for that, I looked at the commentary on the four recitation sections called *Sāratthasamuccaya* which earlier commentary teachers made for this book of protection. This verse isn't in *The Protective Account of the Moon* there, either. Asking why this is the case, I compared both *The Protective Account of the Moon* and *The Protective Account of the Sun*. Having seen that [the word] *vairocano* is particularly put down for the sun in the Pāli word-list called *Abhidhānapradīpikā*,[20] that the third plural [for "verses"] is used in *The Protective Account of the Sun*, which says "**then the Buddha spoke to Rahu, lord of the *asuras*, about Chandima the deity with the verses**" and that the third singular [for "verse"] was used in *The Protective Account of the Moon*, [where it] says, "**then the Buddha spoke to Rahu, lord of the *asuras*, with a verse**," I thought that perhaps this verse was mistakenly included in *The Protective Account of the Moon* and so I haven't provided a commentary for it. Therefore look at it as clarified below [in *Sārārthadīpanī*'s commentary on *The Protective Account of the Sun*]. (SD, 103)

The detail in which Saraṇaṃkara described his exegetical choices in this passage, and the emphatic first person voice he used to do so, helps to create an identity for Saraṇaṃkara, in the eyes of *Sārārthadīpanī*'s audience, an identity as a careful and able scholar intent on the reconstruction of learned traditions. This impression is enhanced by the passages in which Saraṇaṃkara referred his audience to other authoritative sources. We see this in the preceding example, where Saraṇaṃkara made careful reference to *Sāratthasamuccaya* and *Abhidānapradīpikā*, and in many other passages that direct *Sārārthadīpanī*'s audience to a range of stories that can be used to augment Saraṇaṃkara's own gloss and commentary. In commentary on the Pāli *Discourse on the Benefits of Friendship*, for instance, Saraṇaṃkara wrote: "*na pasahanti* means 'are not able to overcome.' This should be clarified by the *Story of the Novice Saṃkicca*. *Na atimaññeti khattiyo* should be clarified by *The Story of Jotipala*" (SD, 96). Directions like these heighten the audience's impression that the author of *Sārārthadīpanī* has a breadth of command over Pāli and Sinhala textual sources. Where Saraṇaṃkara did not consider a matter sufficiently important to be brought fully into the body of his commentary, he placed the commentary in a web of intertextual relationships.

In this regard, the most striking passages in *Sārārthadīpanī* for a twentieth-century reader of Theravādin commentaries—and probably

[20] A lexicon, on which see chapter 3.

an eighteenth-century reader, as well—are those in which Saraṇaṃkara made elaborate references to his own written works rather than remaining content with references to standard authorities such as Buddhaghosa's fifth-century Pāli compendium *Visuddhimagga*. The frequency and forceful possessiveness of these references is unusual in a commentarial tradition that typically privileges authorial anonymity and the view that exegesis and translation simply provide access to earlier learned traditions. In his commentary on *The Discourse on the Benefits of Loving Kindness*, for instance, Saraṇaṃkara made a brief reference to a monk named Visakha before referring his audience to other sources on this monk: "The story of the elder Visakha has been put down in detail in the explanation of meditation on loving kindness in the *Visuddhimagga*, and has been included in the *Exposition of the Discourse on What Is Auspicious* [*Maṅgalasūtrakathā*] in my *Sārārthasaṅgrahaya* [the compendium composed by Saraṇaṃkara at the invitation of King Narēndrasiṃha]" (SD, 88). There is a similar remark at the end of *Sārārthadīpanī*'s commentary on *The Discourse on What Is Auspicious*: "The origin of *The Discourse on What Is Auspicious* should be understood as it appears in my *Sārārthasaṅgrahaya*. Here, with respect to [the discourse] only the word meaning has been presented" (SD, 34). *Sārārthadīpanī*'s introduction to *The Discourse on the Benefits of Loving Kindness* made a similar move: "And the *Aggikkhandopamasutta* [mentioned in this introduction] should be understood by looking at the way it appears in *The Exposition of the Discourse on What Is Auspicious* at the end of my *Sārārthasaṅgrahaya*" (SD, 82).

What is most noteworthy about these passages and others like them is not Saraṇaṃkara's references to his own work, *Sārārthasaṅgrahaya*, but the insistence with which he informed his audience that *Sārārthasaṅgrahaya* is *his* work. Saraṇaṃkara's unusual commentarial stance is thrown into sharp relief when contrasted with that of Buddhaghosa,[21] arguably the model commentator for Theravādin writers. Looking at his commentary on the *Saṃyutta Nikāya* of the *tipiṭaka* (selected at random from the Buddhaghosa corpus), we see a decided authorial reticence. Like Saraṇaṃkara, Buddhaghosa had composed a compendium (*Visuddhimagga*) prior to beginning his celebrated commentaries on sections from the Pāli canon. Unlike Saraṇaṃkara, however, Buddhaghosa usually mentioned only briefly his authorship of *Visuddhimagga* at the beginning of his commentary, after which all references to *Visuddhimagga* make no mention of Buddhaghosa's status as its author.[22]

[21] Or, as Ñāṇamoli would have it, the voice of "the committee called Buddhaghosa" (1971, 235).

[22] See, for instance, Sāratthappakāsinī II, 6, 10–11, 17, 94, 106, 164, 175, 288, 355, 368.

Access and Appropriation in Primary Translation

I hope by now to have made clear some of the ways in which Saraṇaṃkara composed *Sārārthadīpanī* with a boldness and thoroughness that made the commentary a significant one within eighteenth-century Lankan literary culture. The composition of *Sārārthadīpanī* enhanced Saraṇaṃkara's image as a scholar-monk, just as Saraṇaṃkara began to consolidate the position of his monastic community by introducing new educational institutions and seeking the reintroduction of higher ordination. As I have shown, the courtly and monastic audiences for whom *Sārārthadīpanī* was composed assumed a strong relationship between public displays of learning and the attainment of high social position. The formal literary aspects of *Sārārthadīpanī*—its bilingualism, its appropriation of earlier Pāli traditions, and its critical textual references—were social facts, meaningful in the context that characterized its composition and early reception.

In thinking about these aspects of *Sārārthadīpanī* more abstractly, I find it useful to take up another distinction made by Copeland. Copeland's discussion of European theories of translation is developed in part on the basis of a contrast between access and appropriation theories of translation. These theories are found in the European tradition itself and point to the different expectations for the translation of the classical Latin authors and for the translation of Christian scripture. Those engaged in the translation of secular works (that is, on philosophy and rhetoric) were expected to resignify the source text in the process of translation; a well-trained translator understood the skillful reconfiguration of meaning as a proper and creative task and appropriated the source text during the act of translation. This stood in contrast to a long-standing view that translations of scripture should follow a theory of access which held that translation must resist the possibility of appropriation and alteration in order to make the transcendent truth accessible to the reader. In the European context, according to Copeland, the two types of translation were theorized as completely incompatible (1990, 225–226). The opening lines of *Sārārthadīpanī* initiate a primary translation of the Pāli four recitation sections in terms entirely consistent with an access theory of translation. There, as I have already shown, Saraṇaṃkara signaled his intention to make the Pāli texts available to readers through a Sinhala commentary rooted in an inherited commentarial tradition. In practice, however, as we have seen, Saraṇaṃkara's translation of the four recitation sections also bears the marks of appropriation through translation. By drawing the source text into his own composition, by providing it with a new Sinhala voice, and by framing his readers' understanding of previous commentarial traditions with his own concerns, Saraṇaṃkara engaged the earlier Pāli traditions rhetorically, reconfiguring them while providing access to the Pāli texts contained in the four recitation sections.

LOCALIZING COMMENTARY

The fact that *Sārārthadīpanī* was composed at the king's invitation and therefore had to satisfy certain performative expectations did not prevent Saraṇaṃkara from using the composition as an opportunity to set forth his own ideas about monasticism. A close reading shows that Saraṇaṃkara consistently emphasized topics having to do with monastic discipline and asceticism. Since such topics were important in the competitive monastic environment that characterized the early development of the Siyam Nikāya, it is likely that Saraṇaṃkara intended his monastic students to reflect on their teacher's views at the same time as they studied the texts of the four recitation sections that were part of the basic education for novice monks.[23] *Sārārthadīpanī* was intended to speak to two audiences: the circle of elite monks and nobles who encountered the work as a literate performance made at the king's behest, and the group of monastic students who studied at Niyamakanda during stage two of the Siyam Nikāya's rise.

Dialogical Interplay in Bilingual Commentary

Saraṇaṃkara's ability to speak to two audiences through the composition of *Sārārthadīpanī* had much to do with the bilingual nature of the commentary. The combined use of Pāli and Sinhala in *Sārārthadīpanī* not only displayed linguistic command to advantage but also allowed subtle but unmistakable patterns of authorial emphasis within the text. With respect to its bilingual commentarial form, *Sārārthadīpanī* bears a strong resemblance to many of the texts composed in England during the ninth and tenth centuries, during which time a new textual culture emerged that was characterized by a bilingual intertextual system. Irvine notes that, during this period, "[t]he vernacular, English culture appropriated the textual values and some of the genres of Latin gram-

[23] This is evident in the developmental structure of *Sārārthadīpanī*, which clearly presupposes a monastic readership (Blackburn 1999b; Piyadassi 1981). According to Śrī Narēndrasiṃhārāma Rajamahāvihārayē Adhipati Paññāsāra Thero, the texts contained in the four recitation sections were foundational to monastic education. Personal communication, 30 June 1997.

matical culture, which it paralleled and often interpreted in an English form" (1994, 405). Latin culture remained the primary model for textuality, but there was a "dialogical interplay" between textual traditions in Latin and English to the extent that "English textual culture provides examples of writing in utraque lingua, two literary languages . . . that formed, and were formed by, a bilingual, intertextual system" (405). Most Old English texts were "textual hybrids" created by the "interweaving" of Old English and Latin (420–421).

These comments on textual hybridity and the dialogical interplay of local and translocal languages provide a helpful framework within which to think about the way that *Sārārthadīpanī* communicated Saraṇaṃkara's views on appropriate monasticism. Although the eighteenth-century Lankan case is quite different from that discussed by Irvine in many ways (not least of which is the long tradition of local language use in Sri Lanka by that time), Irvine's description of textual hybridity fits Saraṇaṃkara's commentary remarkably well.[24] I take up the idea of a dialogical interplay between translocal and local languages because it draws attention to the possibility that the ideas set forth in one language emerge in conversation with those set forth in the other, and that the interweaving of languages may serve a commentator's rhetorical aims. Although Irvine does not use the term to argue that the commingling of languages provided a way for an author to introduce or to privilege particular ideas, I have taken up the notion of "dialogical interplay" to make this point. In Saraṇaṃkara's bilingual commentary, the movement back and forth between Pāli and Sinhala underscores certain topics specifically relevant to the context in which *Sārārthadīpanī* was composed.

Crossing the Lay-Monastic Threshold

Saraṇaṃkara worked with the dialogical interplay between Pāli and Sinhala to compose a commentary that taught monks the contents and meaning of the *paritta* texts contained in the four recitation sections at the same time as he elaborated his views on what constituted proper monastic conduct. In doing so, he made *Sārārthadīpanī* a work that offered constructive guidelines for the monks affiliated with him and criticism of the monks who stood apart. Although, as so often, it is

[24] Indeed, it is not unreasonable to state that the composition of *Sārārthadīpanī* helped to inaugurate a new interest in hybrid literary traditions that was sustained by the educational practices described in Chapter 3. The eighteenth century was a period in which both Pāli and Sinhala texts could be written by the same writers, copied by the same scribes, and included in the same libraries.

impossible to speak with complete certainty about authorial intentions and the degree to which the text contains textual strategies, the patterns of Saraṇaṃkara's exegetical reworking of *Sārārthadīpanī* are consistent enough to suggest that they are the result of a self-conscious composition. This suggestion fits well with the unusually clear first-person intervention in the text and with Saraṇaṃkara's strong interest in monastic pedagogy. Two commentarial strategies are particularly important to Saraṇaṃkara's elaboration of monastic guidelines and criticism within *Sārārthadīpanī*, and both are made possible by the work's bilingualism. The first is the addition of commentarial content in Sinhala that is not derived from earlier Pāli commentarial works, and the second is the orchestration of doubled exegesis created through the repetition of closely similar statements in Pāli and Sinhala.

In *Sārārthadīpanī*, Saraṇaṃkara frequently added small details in Sinhala that do not originate in the earlier Pāli commentaries and, as I have shown, he integrated parts of these earlier commentaries within *Sārārthadīpanī* in a way that altered their impact. It was rare for Saraṇaṃkara to interpolate passages longer than a few lines into his commentary, however. Relevant narratives were typically indicated only by a brief textual reference, such as those discussed above. It is striking that the only supporting story narrated in full concerns the hazards of unbridled monastic sensuality. This appears early in *Sārārthadīpanī*, where Saraṇaṃkara developed his commentary on *The Reflections*, a list of statements prescribed by the Buddha for regular monastic reflection. Included in the list is the statement that a monk should collect alms only to assure the basic level of physical well-being necessary to continue his work on the path to liberation. There Saraṇaṃkara first took a passage from the earlier Pāli commentaries that underscores the distinction between collecting food for basic sustenance and collecting food in order to enhance beauty through one's diet or to attract others who might be encountered while walking about on the alms round. He translated this Pāli commentarial passage into Sinhala as part of his Sinhala commentary on *The Reflections*. Thereafter he made an emphatic addition not found in his primary source text, *Sāratthasamuccaya* (SS, 58–59):

> Here the story should be told of a monk who fell into the hands of a woman who wanted him to disrobe and marry her daughter. She ignored many monks who were dedicated to asceticism and had calm senses, but saw a stupid monk with unbridled senses going past [on his alms round] looking all around him. He was conspicuously dressed, had makeup on his eyes and was chewing betel. [Thinking,] "that fool will do for us," she invited him into her own house as if she were just going to offer him a meal. (SS, 18–9)

The vignette is a humorous one, but its message to Saraṇaṃkara's monastic students was more pointed than we would assume without knowledge of eighteenth-century monastic struggles in the Kandyan Kingdom. In this context, in which those affiliated with Saraṇaṃkara asserted that their rivals lacked authority because they were too closely involved with the lives of the laity and thus contributed to the decline of the Buddhist *sāsana*, the story was a bold reminder of Saraṇaṃkara's position.

Turning to *Sārārthadīpanī* with an eye to the points at which Saraṇaṃkara provided a double commentary in Pāli and Sinhala, we find that this bilingual repetition is consistently used to isolate and emphasize discussions of proper monastic conduct, including the importance of meditation. In his commentary on *The Reflections*, Saraṇaṃkara emphasized the second reflection (SD, 18–20), focusing attention on the juxtaposition between lay and monastic life made by the reflection, which says:

> **Carefully I follow the alms round: not for play, not for decoration, not for ornamentation, not out of pride. Only as far as [needed for] the maintenance of this body, to follow ascetic conduct. Thus I destroy old sensation. I don't cause new ones. For me there will be blameless living and a pleasant lifestyle.** (SD, 18).

With his commentary Saraṇaṃkara chose to emphasize the monastic alms round as a symbol for the distinction between lay and monastic life and the path that should be taken by monks who correctly follow the ascetic monastic ideals. This was in keeping with the emphasis he is said to have placed on the alms round in the lives of the Silvat Samāgama, about which a dramatic story is told in *Saṃgharājasādhucariyāva*. There Saraṇaṃkara is described as determined to proceed on the alms round, but he was confronted with lay Buddhists so used to less disciplined monasticism that they failed to prepare food for wandering monks. Eventually Saraṇaṃkara instructed a pious lay woman in the practice (SSC, 17). This and other related images are so vivid that it is not surprising that, even in the late twentieth century, Saraṇaṃkara's most common epithet was "alms-going Saraṇaṃkara." Taking up a similar theme in his commentary on the first element identified by *The Discourse on the Ten Elements* as suitable for monastic reflection, Saraṇaṃkara doubled his commentarial attention to the canonical Pāli statement, "**'My appearance is now different' should always be reflected upon by someone who has gone forth'**" (SD, 23). Including a closely similar Pāli commentary and Sinhala commentary, Saraṇaṃkara used *Sārārthadīpanī's* framework to set forth a strong view of the contrast between lay life and monasticism that focuses on the activities basic to human existence such as eating and sleeping (SD, 24).

From these and other double commentarial passages (some of which are discussed at length in chapter 6), it is clear that Saraṇaṃkara was preoccupied with distinctions between lay life and monasticism, and that he missed few opportunities to drive home the point that the passage from the lay world to the monastic community should be seen as a dramatic change and as the acceptance of a demanding asceticism. His interest in the transformation of social roles and behaviors extended to the practice of meditation, a practice possible for all Buddhists but particularly enjoined upon monastics. Thus *Sārārthadīpanī*'s commentary on *The Discourse on the Benefits of Loving Kindness* describes the results of a mind freed by meditation on loving kindness with a double commentary to show that such meditation brings good dreams, peaceful sleep, and plentiful friendships. This bilingual commentarial repetition makes a forceful claim on *Sārārthadīpanī*'s audience by using the weight of a long commentarial tradition to advocate the practice of meditation. I reproduce part of this section below. Once again, the passage from the Pāli four recitation sections is in bold, the Sinhala commentary in roman type, and the Pāli commentary in italics.

> **Monks, there are eleven benefits of loving kindness—which is mental liberation—welcomed when it [loving kindness] is followed, developed, made much of, practiced, made a foundation; when it is familiar and well undertaken. Which eleven? Sleeping happily, waking happily, not having bad dreams, being dear to humans, being dear to nonhumans [gods, demons, etc.], being protected by the gods, being unaffected by fire, poison, and swords, being able to concentrate the mind quickly, having a shining facial complexion, experiencing death without confusion, and birth into the *brahma* world[25] immediately if one does not reach the ultimate [*nibbāna*]. Monks, these are the eleven welcomed benefits of loving kindness—mental liberation—which is followed, developed, made much of, practiced, made a foundation, when it is looked after and well undertaken.**
>
> **bhikkhave**, monks **āsevitāya** which has been engaged in with respect **bhāvitāya** which has similarly been increased through development **bahulīkatāya** which has been developed by increasing [it] again and again **yānīkatāya** which has been used in the way a plow is set down as it is used **vatthukatāya** which has been accomplished, as a thing is, in the sense of being established **anuṭṭhitāya** which exists following [practice] or which is looked after **paricitāya** which has been made completely familiar **sus-**

[25] A supramundane rebirth state. See Collins (1998).

amāraddhāya which has been well begun **cetovimuttiyā** mental liberation is the same as loving kindness or, as the commentary says: *because the mind is linked [to loving kindness] it is freed from impediments and obstructions; therefore the mind is freed from the enemy. Mental liberation is a synonym for loving kindness which has attained [a level of] meditative concentration.* For that reason, if the mind which has attained mental liberation is freed from enemies such as the impediments because of that; because of this loving kindness the mind is freed from enemies. This loving kindness is called mental liberation. Or, loving kindness which is linked to the loving kindness-meditational attainment [Sinhala *maitri dhyāna*] [and] which has found a meditative focus is called mental liberation. Belonging to that loving kindness which is mental freedom [are] **ekādāsa ānisaṃsā pāṭikaṃkhā** eleven benefits that are praised or liked **katame ekādasa** which eleven benefits? **sukhaṃ supati** pleasant sleep. Or, as it is said in the following way: *while other people sleep unhappily, tossing and turning, and prattling [in their sleep] one doesn't sleep like that. Descending into pleasant sleep one is like someone reaching a [meditative] attainment.* If other people sleep tossing about and prattling, he doesn't sleep like that [but] sleeps like someone who has reached a [meditative] attainment. Or, as it is said: *while others wake unhappily, rolling over, yawning, and moaning, one doesn't wake thus. One wakes steadily and happily like a blossoming lotus.* If other people wake up unhappily while tossing, constricting [their bodies] and feeling uneasy, the person doesn't wake this way [but rather] comfortably, without movement, like an opening lotus. (SD, 87–88)

The most striking instance of bilingual repetition through commentary is a lengthy story included as an introduction to *The Discourse on the Benefits of Loving Kindness*. Many *sutta*s from the *tipiṭaka* were provided with introductory stories called *nidāna kathā*s when Pāli commentaries to these *sutta*s were composed by the fifth-century commentators. The introductory story typically describes the occasion on which the Buddha first preached the *sutta* in question and sometimes provides hints as to how it might be interpreted by its audience. *Sāratthasamuccaya* included long introductory stories for four of the texts found in the four recitation sections, all of which Saraṇaṃkara included in Pāli when he composed *Sārārthadīpanī*.[26] However, Saraṇaṃkara translated only one of these into Sinhala in his commentary, which indicates that he considered the story to contain matters of particular interest. It is striking that this introductory story concerns the challenges of the monastic life and the importance of meditation to proper monastic practice.

[26] These are: *The Jewel Discourse, The Discourse on Appropriate Acts of Loving Kindness, The Discourse on the Benefits of Loving Kindness,* and *The Discourse on the Benefits of Friendship.*

This introductory story, written for *The Discourse on the Benefits of Loving Kindness* (SD, 81–85), recounts that the Buddha once decided to teach a particular *sutta*, *The Discourse on the Simile of the Great Mountain of Fire* (Aggikkhandopamasutta) to a group of monks. This *sutta* had powerfully positive effects on those ready for liberation but devastated some of those who were not. After hearing the Buddha's teaching, sixty monks were freed from mental defilements and became enlightened, but sixty more realized that they should give up the monastic life to become householders. Describing them, the story says, "if [they] hadn't heard this . . . *sutta*, they would certainly have committed the two types of [major and minor] monastic offenses. But having heard this *dharma* teaching, some reflected on [monastic] training and concluded that 'the Buddhist teachings and institutions developed for monasticism are very pure and it is not possible for us to fulfill that [standard of] conduct until the end of our lives. But by fulfilling the teachings for lay followers, we are liberated from suffering.' Thus they became lay people." In other words, they decided to revert to lay life in order to avoid the intense suffering in hell experienced by monks who fail to meet the requirements of monastic life, comforted by the thought that, in time (perhaps many lifetimes), they would gain enough wisdom to attain complete liberation from suffering in the cycle of rebirth. Later the Buddha returned from his travels and was surprised to see that the temple was empty, no longer shining "with yellow cloth and bustling sages." When the situation was explained to him, he preached *The Discourse on the Benefits of Loving Kindness* in order to explain that meditation on loving kindness could be used to develop a person's mind, and that this type of meditation was suitable for monastic practice. A monk who practices meditation on loving kindness, announced the Buddha, "doesn't uselessly consume the alms of the country dwellers. [Rather,] he enacts the Buddha's advice and instruction." The Buddha used *The Discourse on the Benefits of Loving Kindness* to reassure his monastic followers that even the less advanced among them could make significant progress on the Buddhist path by using the techniques of meditation on loving kindness within the positive structures of monastic practice.

This story, which Saraṇaṃkara says he has "specially presented" (SD, 86), draws together themes emphasized elsewhere in *Sārārthadīpanī*. It emphasizes the importance of correct monastic behavior by voicing the unenlightened monks' fear that they will be reborn into hell for violating rules of the monastic code and offers a vivid example in support of the idea that monks should carefully reflect on the distinctions between lay and monastic life. Monks are urged not to take up monastic practice carelessly, since such negligence has uncomfortable results. On the other hand, the narrative also provides some reassurance with regard to monastic practice because of the Buddha's statement that monks who practice meditation on loving kindness are proper monks who deserve the support of the laity. As the story concludes, even those monks not very advanced on the path to final liberation from suffering can make progress within monastic institutions. They cannot do so, however, unless they make the decision to meditate as the Buddha instructed them to do.

The pattern taken by the dialogical interplay between Sinhala and Pāli in *Sārārthadīpanī* was not inevitable. It was, rather, the product of an authorial imagination specific to Saraṇaṃkara who took up the possibilities of bilingual commentary, using them to emphasize certain aspects of monastic life while retaining the larger framework of preexisting Pāli Buddhist texts. The patterns of interpolation and repetition visible in *Sārārthadīpanī* combine to make statements about desirable monasticism that resonated with and helped to sustain themes in the discourse on monasticism characteristic of the early Siyam Nikāya. *Sārārthadīpanī*'s images of reflective, meditative monasticism aloof from the enticements and distractions of lay Buddhist life were by no means neutral in the context of the commentary's composition. Instead, they participated in a debate about monasticism that characterized the formative period of the Siyam Nikāya and that pitted Saraṇaṃkara and his followers against well-established *gaṇinnānse* monks in the Kandyan Kingdom's monastic centers.

Paritta, Protection, and Propriety

The local claims about the nature of proper monastic practice made by *Sārārthadīpanī* were not limited to the themes discussed in the previous section. When King Śrī Vijayarājasiṃha invited Saraṇaṃkara to compose a commentary on the Pāli *paritta* texts contained in the four recitation sections, he indicated that he considered the protective recitation of *paritta* a practice appropriate to Buddhist monks. Saraṇaṃkara, by making *paritta* texts the subject of systematic translation and explanation, made his own compatible but slightly different claim: that *paritta* recitation was appropriate to monastics but only to monks who approached the *paritta* texts with an eye to their meaning as well as to their potency as protection against human and supernatural harm. The importance of *Sārārthadīpanī*'s composition in this regard is not clear unless it is recognized that polemics about proper and improper monastic participation in ritual practices of protection were central to the ways in which monks of the early Siyam Nikāya dismissed their monastic predecessors and rivals. In the texts associated with the Siyam Nikāya and produced in the middle of the eighteenth century, the *gaṇinnānse* monks who held sway in the Kandyan kingdom prior to Saraṇaṃkara's rise are described in consistently unfavorable terms. These monks are characterized as greedy for material possessions and sensual experience, as well as overly attached to the family ties ideally abandoned by monastics. Most important in the present context, these monks are also portrayed as committed to the practice of astrology in order to protect humans from human and supernatural harm, and as participants in rituals to destroy the harmful control of demons, or *yakṣa*s, over their human subjects. This comes through clearly, for instance, when the first Kīrti Śrī Katikāvata describes the condition of the Buddhist monastic community from the late fifteenth century up to the rise of the Siyam Nikāya: "only a few novices remained. Of these novices, too, apart from some who avoided impropriety and were well-disciplined, many remaining [monks] studied the scorned sciences such as astrology, medicine and demon-sorcery which were prohibited by the Buddha. The customary conduct of the *sāsana* diminished and [it] was on the brink of destruction (Ratnapala 1971, 97). The consistently negative links between astrology, demon-sorcery, undisciplined monasticism, and the decline of the Buddhist *sāsana* are matched by a series of positive associations between Saraṇaṃkara's monks, the revival of the Buddhist *sāsana*, disciplined monasticism, the pursuit of religious learning, preaching, and *paritta*.[27] Although it is unlikely that the monks of the early Siyam Nikāya were strangers to astrology and demon sorcery, and it is most realistic to assume that they combined such practices with the recitation of *paritta* that already had a long history of popularity on the island, eighteenth-century texts paint a picture of radically opposed views on protective practices appropriate to monastics. Thus in *Saṃgharājavata*, Saraṇaṃkara fulminates against monastic impropriety, saying "I have no use for those who drive away demons, know medicine and astrology, and look after their relatives!" (SV: 80). In contrast, *paritta* recitations are elsewhere described in favorable terms, as in *Mahāvaṃsa*'s account of ceremonies to mark the restoration of Ridī Vihāra by Kīrti Śrī Rājasiṃha (MV 100: 274–275) and other monastic activities commanded by the king (for example, 99: 14–26). In works written during the eighteenth century by authors connected to Saraṇaṃkara's community, the contrast between *paritta* on the one hand and astrology and demon sorcery on the other condensed a broader set of

[27] This was not the first time that polemics over protective and devotional practices had entered into statements made by competing monastic communities. For information on such polemics in the Kōṭṭe period, see the scattered remarks in Sannasgala (1964, 244) and Godakumbura (1955, 189–207, 245–246).

tensions and oppositions between the monks connected to Saraṇaṃkara and those displeased at the prospect of Saraṇaṃkara's growing eminence. Under these circumstances, Saraṇaṃkara's ability to invest *paritta* with authority and social value through the composition of a commentary on the *paritta* texts at royal invitation was an important step forward in efforts to align the early Siyam Nikāya with the protective recitation of *paritta* rather than with other types of protective practice. Composing *Sārārthadīpanī* gave Saraṇaṃkara an opportunity to emphasize that the practice of *paritta* recitation was proper practice because it was sanctioned by the Buddha and used the Buddha's own words as the source of protection. It also signaled that *paritta* recitation was compatible with the vision of educated and disciplined monasticism with which Saraṇaṃkara intended to characterize the new monastic order.

CONCLUSION

Given the attitudes toward literary display characteristic of Saraṇaṃkara's time, the composition of *Sārārthadīpanī* reflected positively on its author, disposing some members of the Kandyan Kingdom's elite circles to see Saraṇaṃkara's rise as natural and desirable. Because the text identified Saraṇaṃkara as a learned monk who sought to preserve earlier teachings and to make them accessible to his own monastic students, *Sārārthadīpanī* enhanced Saraṇaṃkara's position as a monastic leader. At the same time, the work was intended as a tool for the inculcation of monastic identity in the monks already connected to Saraṇaṃkara. Its efficacy in this regard was strengthened by the possibilities of bilingualism, since Saraṇaṃkara's choice to arrange translation and repetition in particular ways appropriated the Pāli four recitation sections in the interests of specific and local concerns about monastic practice. *Sārārthadīpanī* was simultaneously a step forward in the identification of Saraṇaṃkara as a monk to be taken seriously and an expression of his determination to associate himself and his students with classic monastic ideals. Written shortly after his death, *Saṃgharājavata* reminded its audience that the composition of *Sārārthadīpanī* had made a difference: "he learned the Buddha's words by heart, translated the four recitation sections into Sinhala and pleased everyone; creating [this work] he benefited the world and the *sāsana*" (SD, 101).

CHAPTER SIX

Readers, Preachers, and Listeners

A THIRD STAGE in the development of the Siyam Nikāya and its educational institutions began, as we have seen, in 1753, when the new order was inaugurated through a higher ordination ceremony performed by monks from Ayutthaya (Siam). Thereafter, the authority and institutional reach of the Siyam Nikāya grew rapidly. The educational institutions of the Siyam Nikāya, and the textual practices (composition, transmission, and reception) that occurred within them, brought into being a group of male monastic readers who understood themselves as a community. They were bound together by certain text-focused experiences through which they were inculcated into monastic life. The most important of these experiences was reading. Because monastic readers were also preachers, however, the impact of their reading experiences deeply affected the Lankan Buddhist community. The genres and interpretive strategies that dominated monastic textual practices became part of a wider—lay and monastic—understanding of textual authority and Buddhist teachings. Thus the rise of widespread and standardized temple-based monastic education after 1753 provided the necessary conditions for the creation of a new textual community in eighteenth-century Lanka and, following from this, a reformulation of Lankan Buddhism.

Far from being stable over many centuries, pre- and early-colonial Lankan Buddhism was shifting, multiplex, and human. In the latter two-thirds of the eighteenth century, readers, preachers, and listeners, through complicated and varying interactions, altered the face of Buddhism in Lanka. And, importantly, they did so before the cultural forms of Protestant colonialism drew Lankan Buddhism into an (at times uncomfortably) tight embrace. We see this clearly when looking at the life of the *sūtra sannaya*s, which played a critical role in the constitution of a new Buddhist textual community and the subsequent reformulation of Lankan Buddhism.

This chapter develops three specific claims. First, during the third stage of the Siyam Nikāya's formation, the newly popular *sūtra sannaya* genre had a powerful impact on the collective identity of the new monastic order. Using *Sārārthadīpanī*—Saraṇaṃkara's model *sūtra sannaya*—as the object of a close and historically contextualized reading, I show how monastic experiences of reading and interpretation sustained a collective sense of what it meant to be a Siyam Nikāya monk in the latter half of the eighteenth century. Unwilling to accept too simple a view of textual practice in relation to monastic identity, however, I develop a second claim; I distinguish between more and less constrained instances of monastic reading, and argue for interpretive variation within the community of Siyam Nikāya monks. Finally, I argue that monastic uses of the *sūtra sannaya*s were crucial to the emergence of a new Buddhist textual community, since lay Buddhist understandings of Buddhist teachings and textual authority were shaped by their experiences of listening to monastic preaching. Once again, using *Sārārthadīpanī* as an example, I show how *sūtra sannaya*s entered the lives of lay men and women in Lanka.

READING OR LISTENING TO SĀRĀRTHADĪPANĪ?

We have several reasons for thinking that students in the early Siyam Nikāya's educational centers studied *Sārārthadīpanī*. First, as I showed in the previous chapter, the patterns of emphasis within the commentary suggest that Saraṇaṃkara wrote the text in part for his monastic students. The careful developmental structure of the first part of *Sārārthadīpanī*, which I discuss at greater length below, is another indication; the work unfolds in a way that presupposes a monastic audience. This, in conjunction with the degree to which Saraṇaṃkara appears to have influenced education at Niyamakanda and the centers established thereafter, makes it likely that *Sārārthadīpanī* was used by monks in the emerging order. Moreover, because *Sārārthadīpanī* was the model for all subsequent *sūtra sannaya* production at this time, monks who had reached stage four of the educational system were likely to refer to it again as a guide to their own expositions, especially in the early years of the Siyam Nikāya. Finally, manuscript collections at key Siyam Nikāya-connected temples in the Kandyan area show *Sārārthadīpanī* among the holdings. Copies of *Sārārthadīpanī* also appear in the British Library's Nevill Collection and in the manuscript collection at the Sri Lanka National Museum Library.[1]

[1] One copy of *Sārārthadīpanī* is listed on the handlist of manuscripts at Mädavela Rajamahavihāraya, another on the handlist held in the Malvatu Vihāraya's Saṃgharāja Pansala, which incorporates manuscripts from Gaḍaladeṇiyē Saddhammatilaka Rajamahavihāraya. In addition, three copies appear in the library of the Daḷada Maligāva and one in that of Hanguranketa Potgul Vihāraya, both of which contain materials drawn from several temples in the Kandyan region (Blackburn 2001). The library of the Sri Lanka National Museum retains a copy, 1465.Foll 106, as does the British Library's Nevill Collection, OR6600 (151).

Some students may have encountered *Sārārthadīpanī* in partial form, since the *sūtra sannaya*s included in it were often included in eighteenth-century monastic handbooks.[2] In whole and in part, *Sārārthadīpanī* was thus included in the eighteenth-century manuscript tradition that developed in the Siyam Nikāya's educational centers. From this pattern of manuscript circulation, however, we should not automatically assume that students encountered *Sārārthadīpanī* by reading from a manuscript, since there is ample evidence of oral-aural learning in the Theravāda. For instance, writing of the "earliest phase of Buddhist textual tradition," Collins notes that "we have no knowledge of any large-scale writing of texts before the statement in the early chronicles [fourth-fifth centuries C.E.] that both the tipiṭaka and its commentary were written down . . . in the first century" (1992, 121). The terms used to describe learning in the texts from the *tipiṭaka* and their commentaries redacted in the fifth century include "listening to in silence," "making a verbal recitation," and "teaching others," all of which suggest the importance of auditory learning and memorization. Later references in *Mahāvaṃsa* refer to the process of writing a text as one in which writing occurs after the writer has learned through listening, and in which oral recitation is used to check the text. Collins notes similar evidence from the fifteenth century for a three-part process, in which students were given an oral dictation of Pāli text plus Sinhala gloss, which they wrote down in order to use it again in recitation before

[2] The incumbent at the Śrī Narēndrārāma Rajamahavihāraya notes that all or part of the first sixteen *paritta* texts found in the four recitation sections were often included in monastic handbooks with their *sūtra sannaya* commentaries because they were popular texts for novice monks (personal communication, 30 June 1997). This is supported by the collection of Sinhala manuscripts held in the British Library's Nevill Collection (all of which date to the eighteenth century or are nineteenth-century manuscripts most often copied from eighteenth-century models) and by the manuscripts from the same period held in Copenhagen's Royal Library. Of the nine *baṇa daham pot* in the Nevill Collection, only one is without a *sūtra sannaya* (sometimes called *padārtha*, a term often used interchangeably with *sannaya*) (Godakumbura 1980, 97) for one or more of the texts from the four recitation sections; Somadasa 1987: Or. 6599(2), (34), (35), (37); 6600(59), (60), (120); 6601 (145). Of the two *baṇa daham pot* held in the Royal Library, the longest contains twelve full *sūtra sannaya*s, and the shortest contains a portion of one (Godakumbura 1980: PAS (Sinh.) 16 (Cod. Pal. XXVII); PAS (Sinh.) 17 (Cod. Pal. XXXV). All of these are *paritta* texts, and all but one appear in the Pāli four recitation sections. The most common *sūtra sannaya*s included in the *baṇa pot* held in the British Library and the Royal Library collections are those for the following *paritta* texts: *Maṅgalasutta*, *Ratanasutta*, *(Karaṇīya)mettāsutta*, *Khandaparitta*, *Moraparitta*, *Dhajaggasutta*, *Āṭanātiyasutta*, *Aṅgulimālasutta*, and the *Bojjhaṅgasutta*s. All of these except the *Angulimālasutta* are given *sannaya*s in *Sārārthadīpanī*'s treatment of the four recitation sections. And, as noted in chapter 3, the monastic handbook first used by Saraṇaṃkara also contains texts from the four recitation sections. After the composition of *Sārārthadīpanī*, it is likely that these circulated with *sūtra sannaya*s attached.

an audience (124–129). Walpola Rahula, describing conditions in Sri Lankan monastic circles through the tenth century, states that "[b]ooks [i.e., palm-leaf manuscripts] were used of course, but infrequently. It was not possible for every student to possess his text: the production of a manuscript was so laborious. Most probably manuscripts were available for reference at the principal monasteries" (1956, 290). Adikaram notes, however, that monks did possess small manuscripts into which they had copied essential teachings (1946, 127–28).

Evidence for the eighteenth century suggests the growing importance of reading from manuscripts. Although the sections of *Mahāvaṃsa* composed during this period recount an instance of monks learning texts from the *tipiṭaka* by listening to their teacher (MV 99: 174), there are numerous references to monks engaged in the production and use of manuscripts. *Saṃgharājasādhucariyāva* recounts that students within the Silvat Samāgama moved from temple to temple, taking their manuscripts (*pot pat*) and stylus with them (SSC 22). This suggests that monks read and copied manuscripts. The proliferation of manuscripts during the period and the greatly varied skill in orthography characteristic of the extant manuscripts strongly suggests that manuscript reading and redaction were not restricted to a small circle of monks. Other remarks in *Saṃgharājasādhucariyāva* offer further indications that much learning took place through manuscript reading. Certain monks are singled out for their skill in writing the small letters used to redact manuscripts appropriate for solitary, silent reading rather than for oral recitation (see, for example, SSC 51). Moreover, monastic biographies typically link the production of manuscripts (which could mean copying or composition) to a monk's work as a teacher and emphasize the distribution of the teacher's manuscripts to his students prior to the teacher's death (SSC 39–42). (See figs. 2 and 3 for pictures of palm-leaf manuscripts.)

It thus seems probable that monastic students most often studied *Sārārthadīpanī* by reading from manuscripts containing the entire text or portions of it compiled in monastic handbooks. It is unlikely that their reading occurred in complete independence from their teacher, given the long-standing expectation within the Theravāda that younger monks study closely with their teachers both prior to higher ordination and afterward, in the period of continued dependence known as *nissaya*.[3] The reading experiences I sketch below, however, would have been

[3] Ven. Ānanda Maitreya's autobiographical comments on manuscript reading and student lessons in the early twentieth century provide useful information about the way monks combined solitary study of manuscripts with conversations with their teachers. In these conversations they learned how to interpret their readings and were examined on the material. (See 1996, 26–36).

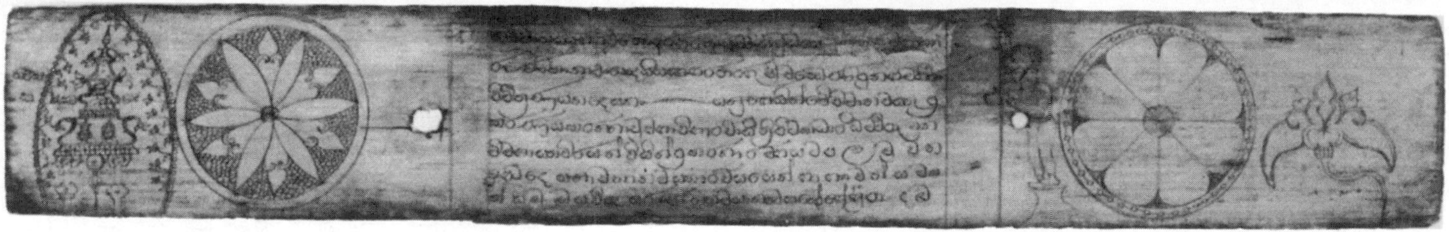

Figure 2. A manuscript leaf from *Vimānavastuprakaraṇaya*. Reproduced with permission of the Royal Library, Copenhagen.

Figure 3. A manuscript leaf from *Abhidānapradīpikā*. Reproduced with permission of the Royal Library, Copenhagen.

shared to some extent by monastic students trained to study through the linked processes of audition, memorization, and recitation. As the oral preservation of texts in the Theravāda into the early years of the common era attests, aural-oral learning is not incompatible with close attention to textual detail.[4] What I will say about the play of imagery, simile, metaphor, and intertextual association is applicable to situations in which *Sārārthadīpanī* was studied without manuscript support as well as to those in which a student read, or read and copied, from a manuscript. Therefore, in what follows, unless I make specific references to manuscripts, understand "reader/listener" and "reading/listening" when I use the terms "reader" and "reading."

CULTIVATING HABITS OF THOUGHT AND ACTION THROUGH READING

In thinking about the ways in which the students in the early Siyam Nikāya's educational institutions read *Sārārthadīpanī* it is important to pay attention to both the inside and the outside of the text. Readers' experiences were influenced by both: by aspects of the work's form and content that provoked readers to respond in particular ways, and by expectations about monastic reading that carried authority within the order and thus influenced the ways students read and internalized what they read. By looking at the first aspect—the textual characteristics that influenced reading experiences—we remain open to the possibility that students' encounter with, internalization of, and subsequent use of the text proceeded with a certain amount of individual variation. By looking at the second aspect—external expectations that affected reading experiences—we also take seriously the fact that readers' responses to texts were substantially influenced by the fact that these readers shared an institutional location, and that this location affected acts of interpretation.

Below I explore both aspects in relation to *Sārārthadīpanī*. I first look at aspects of the text and its context that would have encouraged more constrained readings of *Sārārthadīpanī* before examining characteristics of the work that are likely to have stimulated less constrained readings of the text. It is important to note at the outset that I have found no marginal comments on the manuscripts I have examined (though such comments may exist on other manuscripts). In the absence of such mar-

[4] For a discussion of the oral characteristics of *tipiṭaka* texts, see Allon (1997) on the *sutta*s of the *Dīgha Nikāya*.

ginalia from which to discuss responses by particular readers, my analysis is necessarily suggestive. It is by no means ungrounded, however, because it emerges from the sort of painstaking encounter with *Sārārthadīpanī* that would have been characteristic of monastic students in levels three and four of the curriculum. This, when combined with an understanding of Lankan monastic life and an exposure to the dominant discourses of eighteenth-century Lankan monastic circles, makes the following interpretations informed though by no means definitive. I am emboldened to continue in part thanks to LaCapra's comments on historical reading; he suggests that historians distinguish between the "documentary" and the "worklike" aspects of texts in their attempts to place texts within a larger context of social and intellectual processes.[5] LaCapra writes: "The documentary [aspect of a text] situates the text in terms of factual or literal dimensions involving references to empirical reality and conveying information about it. The 'worklike' supplements empirical reality by adding to it and subtracting from it. It thereby involves dimensions of the text not reducible to the documentary, prominently including the roles of commitment, interpretation, and imagination. . . . With deceptive simplicity, one might say that while the documentary marks a difference, the worklike makes a difference—*one that engages the reader in recreative dialogue with the text and the problems it raises*" (1983, 30, emphasis added). From this perspective, the scribe's name given in a manuscript colophon, for instance, is a documentary aspect of the text. An elaborate simile used in the colophon itself, however, is a worklike aspect because it invites a reader to exercise his or her imagination; no such imagination is needed to understand that the text was copied by the person named in the colophon. LaCapra suggests, in other words, that attention to the worklike aspects of a text that incite the historian-reader's attention and imagination has a place in a "'performative' notion of reading and interpretation in which an attempt is made to 'take on' the great texts and to attain a level of understanding and perhaps of language use that contends with them" (64). This performative approach to the historical place of texts in social processes need not devolve into a historically uninformed interpretive chaos. "Even if one accepts the metaphor that presents interpretation as the 'voice' of the historical reader in the 'dialogue' with the past, it must be actively recognized that the past has its own 'voices' that must be respected, especially when they resist or qualify the interpretations we would like to place on them. A text is a network of resistances,

[5] My appreciation for LaCapra's formulation has been greatly enhanced by Collins's use of it. See Collins (1998, esp. 41–46).

and a dialogue is a two-way affair; a good reader is also an attentive and patient listener" (64).[6]

In the attempt to think through the reading experiences of monks who encountered *Sārārthadīpanī* in the context of the Siyam Nikāya's educational institutions, I have therefore paid attention to the stylistic aspects of the text that consistently encourage my own reflective reading. I have also noted narrative moments within the work that resonate with what I know about monastic ideals and debates within the early Siyam Nikāya environment. At the same time, I have remained alert to the differences between readings of a printed text (since I consistently used a printed edition in my sustained readings of *Sārārthadīpanī*) and eighteenth-century monastic students' experiences of reading *Sārārthadīpanī* in manuscript form. If the process of reading the printed version is already slow and laborious for a novice student, think of the difference made by reading a manuscript. Copied by scribes with wildly varying levels of skill on palm leaves that quickly darken and blur, *Sārārthadīpanī*'s commentary moved regularly from Sinhala to Pāli and back again, sometimes alternating languages every word or phrase. Manuscripts of *Sārārthadīpanī* inevitably contained minimal punctuation and manifold errors of orthography. Some were copied by scribes who understood their sense; others by those with little understanding, who inevitably repeated existing small errors and added new ones.

In this context, Dagenais's remarks on the contrast between manuscript textuality and our contemporary experiences of the printed word are compelling and decidedly relevant. Commenting on the fragility and variability characteristic of manuscript transmission, Dagenais notes that "[m]anuscript culture takes up its physical residence in that same world of variation, imprecision, and error. . . . Incoherence is a powerful force in the medieval textual world, and a recognition (not suppression) of its power is fundamental to any understanding of that world" (1994, 16). Because of the incoherence characteristic of manuscript textuality (even when readers and writers are highly motivated by ideas of scriptural authority to replicate the letter of the text correctly) we should in general presume a slower reading process than that required for reading print, and a process that more often demanded the monastic student's recreation of the text before him. Such a reading experience

[6] Or, as Mark Whitaker suggests in usefully Wittgensteinian fashion, "the key, here, is whether you can discern and learn an old interpretive language game" (personal communication, 19 February 1999). Eco (1990, 45) argues that "a theory of interpretation—even when it assumes that texts are open to multiple readings—must also assume that it is possible to reach an agreement, if not about the meanings that a text encourages, at least about those that a text discourages." In this regard see also Ahearn (forthcoming).

had the positive effect, from the perspective of religious education, of making it harder for the monastic student to skim the text he used. The resulting inducement to thoughtful reading was further enhanced when reading *Sārārthadīpanī* because the breakdown and elaboration of the four recitation sections through commentary created more moments of transition and disjunction for the reader who was forced to engage in a constant process of summary and narrative recapitulation.

MORE CONSTRAINED MONASTIC READINGS OF SĀRĀRTHADĪPANĪ

As I will show in the next section, certain formal features of *Sārārthadīpanī* encouraged monastic readers to respond to the work with a high level of interpretive freedom and creativity. Monastic readings of *Sārārthadīpanī* were often, however, significantly constrained by readers' circumstances. The monks from the early Siyam Nikāya who read *Sārārthadīpanī* encountered the work as part of the monastic curriculum used at Niyamakanda and subsequent educational centers where, by virtue of their status and experiences, they formed a group predisposed to respond to the work in specific ways. As I shall show in more detail, monastic readings were most constrained when the focus of their reading was a discussion of monastic discipline. In other matters, less constrained monastic readings could prevail.

As we have seen, the patterns of bilingual commentarial repetition in Saraṇaṃkara's composition of *Sārārthadīpanī* indicate the degree to which he was preoccupied with questions about proper monastic discipline at the time he composed the work. This, combined with what we know of the eighteenth-century discourse on monasticism, strongly suggests that the monks involved with Saraṇaṃkara and his students during the early days of the Siyam Nikāya were educated in an environment characterized by insistent pressures to reflect on (if not to act on) the ideal behaviors of the monastic life, behaviors that included both outward displays of comportment and the cultivation of positive mental states. Although this alone might well have affected the way that monks read *Sārārthadīpanī*, by inclining them toward a more catechetical approach to the sections of the text that touched on aspects of monastic discipline, there were other more specific constraints on the reading experiences of monastic students: constraints created by monastic readers' personal participation in structures of monastic discipline, those created by advice on reading set out in other media, and those created for *Sārārthadīpanī*'s ideal reader by Saraṇaṃkara himself.

Disciplined Readers

By the time a monk began to read *Sārārthadīpanī*, he was already engaged in a series of physical activities and social relations that affected his interaction with the work. Although it would be misguided romanticism to overemphasize the distance from lay Buddhist life that characterized the monastic world inhabited by *Sārārthadīpanī*'s readers, it is certainly the case that these monastic students engaged themselves on a day-to-day basis in forms of comportment quite different from those of their lay peers. A monk's dress and posture, for instance, were subject to collective regulation, as were his eating habits, manner of bathing, and so on. All forms of physical comportment were open to scrutiny by other members of the community in order to assure adequate compliance with monastic rules and to evaluate the monk's progress toward desired states of equanimity and humility. His interactions with other members of the community were governed by a strict monastic hierarchy based on seniority in which monastic students occupied the lower levels. Although the monk's teacher ideally served as a guardian and nurturing figure as well as an intellectual guide, the teacher exercised a high level of control over his student, which sometimes caused the student distress. Moreover, in this rather regimented context, the reassurance provided by forthright displays of affection between mother and child that characterized lay life had no straightforward parallel.

These characteristics of monastic life inevitably affected the manner in which monastic students read and interpreted the texts before them, and especially those which touched on matters of monastic discipline. Although it is impossible to write with complete assurance on such matters, it seems reasonable to suspect that monastic students responded more sharply to images of proper and improper monasticism because they already participated in a lifestyle designed to discipline themselves. Whether the texts' insistence on the need to embody monastic ideals irked or soothed them, monastic readers would probably have been unable to ignore the didactic force of what they read. Participation in the ordered and regulated aspects of monastic life inclined many monks to accept the ideal images of monastic conduct presented by their texts, and to evaluate their own actions when they were faced with textual juxtapositions between undesirable and desirable monastic behavior. Just as reading the *Wall Street Journal* sustains and is sustained by the day-to-day activities of an entrepreneur, monastic readings of *Sārārthadīpanī* existed in a relationship of normalizing interdependence with the performance of monasticism.

Instructed Readings

In reconstructing the experience of *Sārārthadīpanī*'s monastic readers, we are fortunate to have the evidence of texts that circulated simultaneously with *Sārārthadīpanī* and that carried enough authority to influence the responses of monks within the early Siyam Nikāya community. These texts are the advisory letters composed by Saraṇaṃkara for use by students in distant temples and the first monastic regulation promulgated by King Kīrti Śrī Rājasiṃha with Saraṇaṃkara's assistance.

In *Saṃgharājānuśāsanaya* (The Instructions of the Lord of the Monastic Community; sometimes called *Saṃgharājāvavādaya*), written sometime in the late 1740s or early 1750s, Saraṇaṃkara discussed the approach his students should take to certain Pāli *sutta*s. These *sutta*s included *The Discourse on the Ten Elements* and *The Discourse on Appropriate Acts of Loving Kindness* that appear in *Sārārthadīpanī*. In his comments, these *sutta*s are identified as texts that model appropriate monastic attitudes and conduct: "You should stick to the ascetic virtues such as noncovetousness and contentment, mentioned in the *sutta*s such as *Dasadhamma Sūtra*, *Karaṇīyamettā Sūtra*, and *Dhammadāyāda Sūtra*. . . . You should be malleable in every way. . . . Thus fulfilling the virtues of asceticism praised in the various works [seek] understanding" (Dhammānanda 1969, 145). Although *Sārārthadīpanī* is not mentioned here by name, and students are not told how to approach these *sutta*s in conjunction with their Sinhala or Pāli commentaries, this passage is important. It shows the way Saraṇaṃkara sought to guide monastic students' engagement with selected texts and indicates that *Sārārthadīpanī* was seen as valuable for monastic education in part because the texts on which it comments could be used to instill positive models for monastic life.

Śāsanikasandeśaya (The Letter Relating to the Sāsana), written sometime after 1753, was intended to guide monastic teachers in their work with monastic students. It shows the same preoccupation with text-based virtues as *The Instructions of the Lord of the Monastic Community*:

> have them learn especially that the virtues of abstention from what is unskillful, contentment and noncovetousness as they are presented in the *Karaṇīyamettā Sūtra*, in the *Dasadhamma Sūtra*, in the *Dhamadāyāda Sūtra*, in the *Mahāryavaṃśa Sūtra*, and in the *Yogikathā* should be practiced, should be done repeatedly, and should be fulfilled by those with the ideas of good people, who like discipline, who are afraid of the cycle of rebirth,

who are afraid of evil, and who have been born during a period characterized by a Buddha's birth. (Dhammānanda 1969, 149)

Because these comments figured in the letters of instruction sent to temple-based educational institutions connected to the early Siyam Nikāya, it is almost certain that such guidance to student readers became a part of the dominant views on pedagogy in these institutions. It is likely that Saraṇaṃkara's insistence on reading these *sutta*s for images of disciplined monasticism affected the approach taken by teachers and students to other *sutta*s in *Sārārthadīpanī* as well.

The impact of such guidelines on monastic readers was enhanced by the references to study of the Pāli *sutta*s contained in the first *Kīrti Śrī Rājasiṃha Katikāvata*. In this monastic regulation, monks are told to include certain *sutta*s in their study at several different educational stages. "All [monks]—the elders, the newcomers [novices], and those at the middle level—should concentrate on the *Anumāna Sutta* and the *Dasadhamma Sutta* without distraction at least once a day." Novice monks were also instructed to become familiar with the four recitation sections that contained *The Discourse on the Ten Elements* and *The Discourse on Appropriate Acts of Loving Kindness* (Ratnapala 1971, 99, 101). Once again, we see that texts included in *Sārārthadīpanī* were singled out for attention as efficacious didactic texts. This had implications for monastic reading. That such instructions appeared in a regulation focused on the careful structuring of monastic life, and that this regulation was itself included in monastic educational curriculum, would have further strengthened the weight of its interpretive authority.

With this background on instructed readings in mind, it is clear that many monastic students read *Sārārthadīpanī* as a disciplinary text as well as an exegesis of the four recitation sections and a guide to Pāli language. Certain passages from *Sārārthadīpanī* lend themselves particularly well to such readings; it is no surprise that they were singled out by Saraṇaṃkara in the advisory letters. *The Discourse on the Ten Elements* contains ten statements appropriate for reflection by a monk.

> "I have a different appearance [from that of a layman]." "My life is dependent on others." "I should conduct myself differently [from the way a layman does]." "Isn't there censure in my own mind regarding my conduct?" "Do wise people who know me criticize my conduct?" "I will be separated from those dear to me." "I am my own *karma*, am an heir to *karma*, a source of *karma*, a receptacle for *karma*. The *karma* I do, good and bad: I will inherit it." "How do I spend my days and nights?" "Do I delight in an empty place?" "Do I have supramundane characteristics? Have I reached a distinction of proper knowledge and vision? In the end, questioned by ascetics, will I not be flustered?" (SD, 23)

All ten of those aspects, even in their uncommented form, lend themselves to monastic reflections on the monastic life, especially if the reader is spurred to read the text with such reflections in mind.[7] When accompanied by a *sūtra sannaya*, however, the didactic hold of the text on the monastic reader would have increased sharply, as I shall show with a few examples. Elaborating on the statement "I have a different appearance," *Sārārthadīpanī* develops the phrase into an epitome of renunciation, juxtaposing the appearance of a monk with the appearance of a layman (see pp. 120–21 above). The commentary goes on to emphasize that distinctiveness is not limited to a monk's outward appearance but should extend to his internal dispositions, as well. *Sārārthadīpanī*'s commentary continues to provide detailed and sometimes humorous images of monasticism perfectly suited to the readings advocated by Saraṇaṃkara. Elaborating on the statement "I should maintain a different deportment," the text paints another evocative picture of the physical and psychological landscape to be traversed by a monk: "A different deportment means not the postures of householders [but] the way said [to be] the proper postures for a renouncer. Therefore: not going out with restless postures and exhibiting a playful gait, with the neck drawn up high and drawing attention to [his] chest [and instead] possessing the right postures appropriate to a monk and continually reflective, he should go calmly like a cart full of water on uneven ground, looking only a short distance ahead, with tranquil posture and [sense] faculties" (SD, 25). Here *Sārārthadīpanī* sets out a guide for the most basic of daily activities—walking. Descriptions of monastic practice provided by the commentary extended to the details of collective ritual and education. Extending the reflection, "How do I occupy myself day and night?" the Pāli commentary quoted by Saraṇaṃkara in *Sārārthadīpanī* says: "[this] means for me the performance of practice and duties, or if not doing that then discussing the words of the Buddha, or if not doing that then concentrating the mind" (SD, 27). It is important to note that the commentarial additions often engaged the reader directly, with phrases like "[this] means for me," "it should be understood" or "it should be reflected," giving *Sārārthadīpanī* an interactive, interrogatory claim on the reader.

The Discourse on Appropriate Acts of Loving Kindness is a sermon said to have been preached by the Buddha to protect monks meditating

[7] Aspects of my argument in this section were worked out earlier in Blackburn (1999a). According to a monastic handbook redacted in 1795, for instance, the *sutta* could be considered an entire monastic handbook in itself. "According to the colophon this sutta is called 'Cāritra-vāritra-baṇadaham pota,' the Book of Sermons on What Should be Done and What Should be Avoided" (Godakumbura 1981, 110). Note that Godakumbura translates as "Book of Sermons" what I understand as "Monastic Handbook."

in a forest from disturbances. In the second part of the *sutta*, the Buddha explains how monks should meditate on loving kindness. In the first, however, he describes the desirable characteristics for a monk on the path to liberation.

> What should be done by one skilled in his own development, who understands the peaceful foundation [of *nibbāna*] is this:
> He should be able, upright, very resolute, flexible, of sweet speech and without pride, content and easy to support, with few cares and few needs, wise and with calmed faculties, not bold, not attached to families, and without an inferior act with regard to proper conduct because of which the wise should censure him. (SD, 57–65)[8]

Sārārthadīpanī's commentary on *The Discourse on Appropriate Acts of Loving Kindness* contains many didactic images available to a monastic reader inclined to approach the text as part of his reflection on desirable and undesirable behaviors. Consider, for instance, the extended comment on the phrase "of sweet speech," from the section quoted above. Saraṇaṃkara took up the phrase by describing a situation in which a monk is reprimanded and then fails to show that he's been chastened:

> A person who responds to the admonition "this shouldn't be done" by saying: "What have you seen? What have you heard? Who speaks of me? . . ." or who causes the [other person] discomfort by being silent, or who accepts the admonition but doesn't follow it, is a long way from special attainments. But he who, when admonished, says "It is good, sir. It is well said. My fault is really difficult for [me] to see. Seeing me in a similar state again, advise me soon out of compassion. Your admonishment has been accepted" . . . is not at all far from special attainments (SD, 61–62).

Here the contents of *Sārārthadīpanī* would have overlapped substantially with other guidelines given to the monastic reader. If obedience to authority was desirable in a monk, so too was malleability, especially during the period in which young monks were socialized to become fully competent members of the monastic order. Saraṇaṃkara's commentary on the word "flexible" that also appears in the passage from the four recitation sections quoted above transformed it into a vivid evocation of desirable attitude and deportment: "[he] should be malleable, suitable for use, like gold which has been well burned, in the fulfillment of personal asceticism and with respect to duties, without inflexibility or stubbornness . . . or should be flexible like a ford which has been made for properly crossing, not intransigent [as shown by] not speaking properly [or] looking at the ground with [one's] face wrinkled

[8] The *catubhāṇavāra* text is spread out over several pages, interspersed with Saraṇaṃkara's commentary.

up [when spoken to]" (SD, 62). Once again, *Sārārthadīpanī* touches on matters of considerable importance to monks living the structured life of the order, emphasizing flexibility in the face of collective living and the link between flexibility and obedience.

Sārārthadīpanī's reader also encountered didactic passages concerning proper lay and monastic relations. I have already shown that texts written by those connected with the Siyam Nikāya accused their predecessor *gaṇinnānse* monks of maintaining inappropriate lay contacts. That context made the following passage from *The Discourse on Appropriate Acts of Loving Kindness* particularly charged and even more likely to have claimed the reader's attention. In addition, since many younger monks studied *Sārārthadīpanī* at an age when they were still likely to have mixed feelings about their new environment, the commentary may have inspired a more personal reflection on the difficulties involved in being "unattached to families."

> Should some monk approach that family of a devout layman by himself? The condition [of being a monk] is without attachment through unsuitable ties to householders or through craving focused on that family. Here, this is what's considered unsuitable connection to lay people: [Saying], "alas, bad luck" when something sad happens to people who give requisites, gathering [the monastic community] because of this sad occurrence by informing [other monks] that this bad thing happened, saying, "A sad thing has happened to the people who give requisites." Similarly, if a good thing happens, gathering together on that account. . . . [Or,] looking after that duty, great or small, should be done [by the laity.] Thus, leaving the actions of his childhood, he goes forth for ordination as a youngster and emerges after observing the three month rains retreat without declaring that he is the own son of [his] father and mother. . . . Remembering what's superior, including the Buddha, which is praised by those parents [themselves], he should not be attached to the family of the devout layman. (SD, 65)

The passage instructs the monastic reader not to cling too tightly to lay families who provided his food and clothing, nor to indulge himself in emotional ties to a family left behind.

Structural Constraints

Saraṇaṃkara's authorial control over *Sārārthadīpanī*'s structure allowed him to draw his readers into a particular interpretive trajectory; this influenced a reader's response to single passages of the text and also inclined that reader to accept broader arguments about the nature of appropriate monasticism and the effects of meditation. In other words,

Saraṇaṃkara's ability to develop a line of interpretation across several sections of *Sārārthadīpanī* was a powerful rhetorical tool that made certain reader responses natural, and others much less so. I elaborate this claim by showing that the organization of Saraṇaṃkara's *sannaya*s for the first six *sutta*s commented on in *Sārārthadīpanī* transformed the Pāli texts from the four recitation sections into a gradually intensifying introduction to monastic discipline and meditation.[9] The connections drawn by Saraṇaṃkara's commentary were so insistent that they predisposed the reader to engage the *sutta*s in certain ways.

Saraṇaṃkara was quick to inform his reader that *Sārārthadīpanī* should be approached as an intensifying introduction to proper Buddhist practice. In his commentary on the first of the texts from the four recitation sections, *Going for Refuge*, Saraṇaṃkara explained the reason for placing this text first in the collection: The three refuges are "the path for descent into the Buddha's *sāsana* . . . gods and humans descend into the Buddha's *sāsana*, as devout lay people or novices, on the path of the three refuges" (SD, 4). The image of a path for descent signals the reader that what follows in *Sārārthadīpanī* should be approached as a teaching that is gradual, developmental, and structured. This brief explanation is followed by a long serial simile on the Buddha, *dhamma*, and *saṃgha*; the intense repetition of these similes, and their emphasis on the monastic community's role as consumer and embodiment of the teaching, creates a psychological and devotional framework within which a reader could think about his encounter with the remainder of *Sārārthadīpanī*'s contents.

After laying this groundwork, Saraṇaṃkara introduced *The Ten Training Precepts*, which are the guidelines for a novice monk or for a lay person who chooses to adopt the basic aspects of monastic practice. Here the commentary makes an explicit connection to the previous section by linking the two sections together and relating them to the theme of descent: "the training precepts are presented [showing] that which should be learned first by a devout lay person or a novice monk who has descended as far as possible into the Buddha's *sāsana* by going for refuge in the way [just] stated" (SD, 9). The ten precepts are then listed and explained. These are to abstain from "taking life, stealing, nonascetic conduct, false speech, intoxicants, eating at the wrong time, watching dancing, singing, and shows, sweet-smelling ointments, adornments and decorations, high and large beds, and accepting gold and silver" (SD, 9). There *Sārārthadīpanī* recapitulates rules that would have been recited by the novice monks who studied the text.

Then Saraṇaṃkara introduced the next section, *Questions for a Nov-*

[9] Aspects of this argument were developed in Blackburn (1999b).

ice. Once again, the commentary's introduction to the section links it to the previous ones in order to show the progress a student could make by carefully studying *Going for Refuge* and *The Ten Training Precepts*: "There was a great follower of the Buddha whose name was Sopāka. The Buddha set him questions, wondering, 'how wise is Sopāka after seven years as a monk?' In order to show the level of Sopāka's wisdom . . . the Buddha asked the [following] questions. . . . The youngster who had spent only seven years as a novice—fulfilling the ten training precepts and established in the three refuges—was able to respond to the questions with near omniscience" (SD, 12). The powerful nature of the teachings contained in *The Ten Training Precepts* and *Going for Refuge* is underscored by the abstract and technical nature of Sopāka's answers to the Buddha's questions. Both the questions and the answers are included in *Questions for a Novice* itself:

> "What is one?" "All beings subsist on food."
> "What is two?" "Name and form."
> "What is three?" "The three sensations."
> "What is four?" "The four noble truths."
> "What is five?" "The five constituents of grasping."
> "What is six?" "The six internal sense-bases."
> "What is seven?" "The seven limbs of enlightenment."
> "What is eight?" "The eightfold noble path."
> "What is nine?" "The nine abodes of beings."
> "What is ten?" "An *arahant* endowed with the ten perfections." (SD, 12)

The ten questions answered by Sopāka cover important and sophisticated aspects of Buddhist teaching. By introducing them in relation to the gradually intensifying exposure to Buddhist teachings possible for the reader of *Sārārthadīpanī*, Saraṇaṃkara made an argument for the interrelationship of regulated monasticism and liberating knowledge.

From there Saraṇaṃkara moved to the next section of the four recitation sections, *The Thirty-two Characteristics*. Once again, Saraṇaṃkara introduced the new section with a statement linking it to the preceding sections. In doing so, he instructed his monastic readers not to forget that an intellectual understanding of central Buddhist teachings must be developed in tandem with meditative practice: "When one has achieved enough wisdom to explain the questions that have just been analyzed, and has concentration as a foundation for that wisdom, the thirty-two characteristics are set down here in order to show the object of meditation on the characteristics of the body" (SD, 15). Here, Saraṇaṃkara insisted that the reader think about *Sārārthadīpanī* as an introduction to the practice of meditation. Seen from his perspective, *Going for Refuge* sets up appropriate attitudes for monastic practice, *The Ten Training*

Precepts provides the ethical foundation for mental cultivation, and *Questions for a Novice* provides a set of teachings related to the goals of meditative practice and the mental transformation required for enlightenment. Then *The Thirty-two Characteristics* provides instructions on how the practice of meditation on the impure elements of the body allows the monk to bring knowledge of meditation into the practice of meditation.

From here Saraṇaṃkara drew his readers into a consideration of *The Reflections*, a section from the four recitation sections that explains how a monk should reflect on the requisites for the monastic life (robes, alms food, and so on). Once again, Saraṇaṃkara clarified the way his readers should understand this section in relation to those prior to it. In doing so, he underscored the relationship between *The Reflections* and meditative practice, explaining that *The Reflections* provides a way to extend the mindfulness developed with respect to *The Thirty-two Characteristics* into the basic activities of monastic life. Here Saraṇaṃkara emphasized that the distinctive physical practices of the monastic life should not be seen only as a matter of external comportment. Rather, the special ways in which monks dress, feed themselves, and so on should become the focus of meditative reflection. "Thus, *The Reflections* is set down here in order to indicate the way in which one should use [the requisites] without increasing negative elements such as greed, while living mindfully with awareness of the worthlessness of individual existence, achieved through [an understanding of] the thirty-two impure characteristics [of the body]" (SD, 17).

A careful exposition of *The Reflections* followed, in which Saraṇaṃkara explained the mindful use of monastic robes, alms food, and dwellings. Following this, he again linked a new section to the previous ones, explaining that the new section on *The Discourse on the Ten Elements* is included in order to prevent the student from regressing on the path of mental cultivation. *Sārārthadīpanī* instructed the monastic student to interpret *The Discourse on the Ten Elements* as a text that offers the monk new ways to guard against unskillful mental states.

> *The Reflections* is presented because [it is said] that one should reach the city of *nirvāṇa* by fulfilling the threefold training, reflecting on the matters that have been set out for continual reflection and recollection. *The Discourse on the Ten Elements* is put down here after *The Reflections* because of the Buddha's compassionate thought, "Since the negative elements [in one's mental states, which govern progress on the Buddhist path] increase if one lives foolishly after this point [in the teaching] and the hells fill up with [unskilled beings who succumb to foolish living], it would be good to alleviate the suffering of rebirth by this means, as well as by using the requisites while reflecting on *The Reflections*." (SD, 22)

Here Saraṇaṃkara connected the two texts from the four recitation sections (*The Discourse on the Ten Elements* and *The Reflections*). He did so by accounting for the origin of the former as the Buddha's attempt to prevent dangerous regression in Buddhist practice by providing ten more statements for monastic reflection. In doing so, he reminded his reader to interpret *The Discourse on the Ten Elements* in the context of what came before and to reflect on the distinctiveness of the monastic life as a spur to religious practice. This was the last in a series of closely connected commentarial elaborations intended to frame a monastic reader's encounter with *Sārārthadīpanī*.

The first six sections of *Sārārthadīpanī* were intended to serve as a clearly articulated and gradual introduction to the relationship between monastic behavior, meditative practice, and knowledge of the Buddha's teaching. Because Saraṇaṃkara expressed his intentions so clearly in his commentary, the monk who studied this portion of *Sārārthadīpanī* was trained to approach the texts as a compendium of teachings particularly useful for members of the monastic community. He was repeatedly instructed to approach all aspects of the monastic life as opportunities through which to explore the liberating and integrated disciplines of physical comportment, learning, and meditation. The close fit between the institutional experiences of a monastic reader and Saraṇaṃkara's commentarial elaborations made it difficult for *Sārārthadīpanī*'s "empirical reader" (a certain monk in a Siyam Nikāya educational center, already disciplined by his experiences there) to distance himself from the "model reader" presumed and created by the text.[10]

LESS CONSTRAINED MONASTIC READINGS OF SĀRĀRTHADĪPANĪ

Certain worklike aspects of *Sārārthadīpanī* did, however, make it possible for readers to draw the contents of the text into their reflections on monastic discipline and Buddhist devotion in ways that left room for

[10] The terms used here are taken from Umberto Eco but used in a rather different context. Eco writes: "The model reader of a story is not the empirical reader. The empirical reader is you, me, anyone, when we read a text. Empirical readers can read in many ways, and there is no law that tells them how to read, because they often use the text as a container for their own passions, which may come from outside the text or which the text may arouse by chance. . . . [T]he model reader [is] a sort of ideal type whom the text not only foresees as a collaborator but also tries to create" (1994, 8–9). *Sārārthadīpanī* differs from the fictional narratives discussed by Eco. The empirical author, Saraṇaṃkara, was significantly invested in the responses of the empirical reader, whose reading was partially constrained by institutional experiences and authoritative instructions. Eco's terms remain useful, however, because of his notion that a text's structure assumes and shapes a particular set of responses on the part of the reader.

quite personal responses to these texts. Two such aspects were simile and metaphor, which are both examples of ruminative triggers, stylistic characteristics of the text that draw the text and the reader more closely together and thus intensify the quality of the reader's reflective experience. The presence of these ruminative triggers in *Sārārthadīpanī* made it easier for monastic readers to read selectively and to interpolate elements of their personal experience (including their relationship to other texts and to people) into the work as they read. Because of these possibilities for selective reading and interpolation, the "habits of thought" (d'Avray 1985, 191) shaped by readings of *Sārārthadīpanī* emerged through the reader's dialogue with the work itself.

Similes

Three examples of simile from *Sārārthadīpanī* provide material helpful when we consider the role of simile in a more abstract manner. The first appears as part of Saraṇaṃkara's commentary on *The Jewel Discourse* from the four recitation sections, where it is introduced as part of a discussion on improper action.

> Just as, monks, a young boy, a fool, or an infant, having stepped on a coal with his foot or hand very quickly pulls back, similarly, monks, how can an offense be committed by one who has attained [right] views through Buddhist teachings? He perceives the occurrence of such an offense and then, very quickly, he tells it to a teacher. (SD, 47)

By comparing a novice monk who has committed an offense against the monastic rule to a child burned by hot coals, the simile prompted the reader to think about propriety and impropriety and the urgency of monastic self-correction. At the same time, the simile created a conjunction between the process through which a child becomes aware of the world as it really is and the experiences that transform a novice into a monk. Although the simile could be interpreted as pressure to conform to the authority of the monastic community, and to accept the teacher as a new parental figure, one should not forget that it could also spark a series of negative associations for a young monk dissatisfied with the lack of autonomy in his monastic life or unhappy with his second childhood.

The second example is taken from the *Sārārthadīpanī*'s commentary on *The Discourse on Appropriate Acts of Loving Kindness*.

> A person who purifies [himself] having cleaned the stains of ethical conduct [Pāli *sīla*] with the water of wisdom is said to be someone who purifies ethical conduct through proper wisdom, as one purifies gold by burning in

> a flame, or purifies clothes with acidic water mixed with ash. He [is said to be someone who] protects his own ethical conduct very zealously, like an insect protecting its egg, like an animal protecting its grass, like a mother protecting her only son, like someone protecting his or her sole eye: he reflects day and night and does not reveal even a small fault. (SD, 58)

Here, activities from the lay spheres of craftsmanship, household work, and parenting are used to explore the transformative power of right action and the diligence necessary to sustain it. The similes provoked reflection on the distance between lay and monastic life and on the intensity of the new bonds that are expected to characterize the monastic world. Especially for a young novice monk, separated from his mother for the first time, the passage might have been a compelling one as he reflected on the absence of his mother and the oddity of so soon becoming his own protector.

My third example is an elaborate serial simile, or a string of related similes, that introduces the *Saraṇagamana* section of *Sārārthadīpanī*.[11] The force of the passage lies in the multiplicity of images and is therefore worth quoting in full.

> The three refuges are taught in this way: The Buddha is first [as] chief of all beings including men and *māra*s, and the *dhamma* following that because it appears as a teaching from that Buddha, and [then] the *saṃgha*, which is a receptacle for bearing that *dhamma*, like a golden bowl for lion's oil. Further, in this regard, the Buddha is like a full moon, the *dhamma* taught by the Buddha is like the moon's rays and the *saṃgha* is like people made happy by the fact that heat is calmed by the rays of the moon. Further, the Buddha is like the arc of daybreak on top of a high mountain, the *dhamma* is like the sun's rays which destroy darkness, and the *saṃgha* is like a population for whom darkness is destroyed [having] destroyed the darkness of the defilements by looking at the good teaching. The Buddha is like a person who burns the forest, because [he] burns the forest which is the defilements. The *dhamma* taught by the Buddha is like the fire. The Buddha's listeners [in this case, monks] are like an area of land that has become a pure field after burning the forest of the defilements. The Buddha, intent on delivering the rain which is the good teaching is like a great cloud. The *dhamma* that was taught is like rainwater fallen onto land. The *saṃgha*, which has destroyed the dust of the defilements, is like a stretch of land in which dust has been calmed [by the rains]. The Buddha is like a tamer of quick horses, the *dhamma* is like a way to train high-bred horses and the *saṃgha* is like a group of such horses properly trained in this way. The Buddha, because he aims to remove all visible thorns, is like a surgeon.

[11] On serial similes, see Hallisey (1993).

The *dhamma* is like a surgical method and the *saṃgha*, because of the uprooting of the thorns that are wrong views, is like a group of people healed by this surgical method. The Buddha is like an arrow because he pierces the veil which is delusion. The *dhamma* is a means of removing the veil and the *saṃgha*, with the veil of delusion removed and a clear eye of wisdom, is like a clear-eyed population because of the removal of this veil. Or the Buddha, because [he] aims to carry off the illness of the defilements, is like a clever doctor. The *dhamma* is like the medicine properly used and the *saṃgha*, with the defilements calmed by the medicine of the good teaching, is like a group of patients whose illness has been quieted by using medicine. Or, they say the Buddha is like someone who comes from a good region, the *dhamma* is like a place without fear and the proper path [to it]. The *saṃgha* is like a group of people who have arrived at that supreme location—where peace is the destination—by that path. They say that the Buddha, because [he] makes it possible to cross the ocean of rebirth, is like someone who own the right boat. The *dhamma* is the boat into which beings embark and the *saṃgha* like a group of passengers who cross by that boat. Further, they say that the Buddha is like a snowy mountain, the *dhamma* is like a medicine suddenly appearing there and the *saṃgha* like a group of people whose illness has disappeared after using that medicine. They say that the Buddha, by giving the wealth of the good teaching, is like a man who gives wealth. The *dhamma* is that wealth and the *saṃgha*, which has received that noble wealth, is like a group of people who have received it by means of [their] intention. They say that the Buddha, because he saw the treasure of the good teaching, is like a man who has seen treasure. The excellent *dhamma* is that treasure and the *saṃgha*, which has received that treasure of noble gems, is like a group of people who have attained treasure. They say that the Buddha, by offering fearlessness [to counteract] the fear of rebirth, is like a person who gives courage, the *dhamma* is that courage and the *saṃgha* is like a group of people who have properly arrived at a state without fear. They say that the Buddha is like one who comforts because of the comfort for those in distress, which is as if [he] said, "while I live, for what do you fear?" The *dhamma* is comfort and the *saṃgha* is like a group of people who have received that ease. They say that the Buddha is like a happy person because [he] causes those frightened by the suffering of rebirth to reach happiness. The *dhamma* is like the advice for that and the *saṃgha* like a group of successful people who attained [it] by mental effort. The Lord Buddha is like a gem mine, the *dhamma* is said to be like an ocean of gems appearing there, and the *saṃgha* is said to be like a group of people who have received those gems. They say that the Buddha, because of [his] purification after removal of the defilements, is like a man who has been consecrated as a royal prince. The *dhamma* is like a bathing room with proper water [used in the consecration

> ceremony] and the *saṃgha*, properly purified by the water of the good teaching, is like a group of royal princes who have bathed properly and received [it]. They say the Buddha, by decorating himself with the ornaments of virtue, is like a well-adorned prince. The *dhamma* is the ornament and the *saṃgha*, adorned with ornament of the good teaching, is like [a group of] princes who have received [such] decoration. They say that the Buddha is like a sandalwood tree, the *dhamma* is like the sandalwood produced there, and the *saṃgha*, which has received endless calm from enjoying the sandalwood that is the good teaching, is like a group of people made tranquil by the enjoyment of sandalwood. They say that the Buddha, because of his intention to give the good teaching as inheritance, is like a father. The *dhamma* is like the gift and the Buddha's listeners [monks], who have received the inheritance of the good teaching, is like a group of sons who have gained [their] father's inheritance. They say that the Buddha is like a fully opened lotus, the *dhamma* is like the honey produced within that lotus, and the *saṃgha* is like a cluster of bees who have enjoyed that honey. (SD, 4–7)

A monk reading *Sārārthadīpanī* was already an integral part of the Buddhist world evoked by the simile because he was a member of the monastic community, and he was therefore likely to find the similes significant. Because of certain relational patterns emphasized by the serial simile itself, a monk's reflection would tend to focus on the monastic community's role as recipient of the Buddha's teaching and on the idealized depiction of the monastic community as proof of the *dhamma*'s efficacy. Although the ingestion of medicine (which appears twice in the series) is perhaps the most striking of these, images of the monastic community—as the golden bowl for the lion's oil of the teaching, as parched and dusty earth that absorbs the rainwater of good teaching, as princes physically touched by the consecrating water of the *dhamma* or soothed by it as by sandalwood, as bees feeding on the honey of the *dhamma*—vividly convey the point that a very close association with the teaching is necessary for desirable mental transformations to occur. A monastic reader was given the opportunity to reflect on the satisfactions and dissatisfactions experienced during his encounters with Buddhist teaching, on the degree to which he embodied the virtues of the monastic community elaborated through the similes, and on the emotional tenor of his life as a student. Students who saw themselves as scholars may have been especially drawn to the simile of lion's oil, given an evocative exegesis by K. R. Norman:

> [The simile] is used in a simile for doing something attentively or carefully (because the oil is valuable and must not be spilled). . . . It is also used as an illustration of something remaining unchanged and not disappearing.

> The two words *kañcana-pātī* and *kañcana-nāḷī* which frequently occur with *sīhavasā* both refer to containers ("bowl" and "tube") in which the valuable oil is kept, so that it is not lost (because it is in a golden container, and not an earthenware one, through the walls of which seepage might take place). . . . The compound is very appropriate to the work of authors and scribes, who hope that their work will not disappear. (1993, 61–62)

Thinking more abstractly about the impact of similes on the experiences of monastic readers, it is useful to observe that the very act of stating "is like," "like," and "just as" highlights the tension between difference and similarity that exists in simile and, in so doing, enhances the level of the reader's attention to the relationship expressed by the simile itself. These overt markers of a simile simultaneously indicate likeness and difference, emphasizing that the image presented is a verbal creation that gestures toward experience rather than directly describing it. This in turn provides what might be called an interpretive opening, or a point of entry for the reader to reflect upon the types of experience that the text describes. The reader is inspired to think about what he or she has read precisely because the simile's avowed failure to elaborate identity puts the attentive reader to work. Responding in this way, an eighteenth-century monastic reader might have asked himself whether his own experience of the *dhamma* was one of increased calm and pleasure, and whether he was as single-minded about his monastic discipline as the simile suggested he should be. Such self-questioning was possible even for a student whose command of abstract teachings was minimal. As Hallisey notes, "analogies, similes, and metaphors are a common feature of Theravādin homiletics. Indeed, analogy and simile were apparently considered very effective teaching tools, appropriate for even the dullest student" (1990, 163).[12]

Metaphor

Turning to metaphor, examples from *Sārārthadīpanī* once again provide the basis for exploring the importance of metaphor to monastic reading more generally. The metaphor of the three sense doors first appears at the devotional beginning of Saraṇaṃkara's composition and of his readers' encounter with the work.

> The Lord Buddha, an ocean of virtues, with knowledge to cross the ocean of all that is to be known, unequaled, conqueror, hero, honored by all the world . . .

[12] That analogy was a powerful tool for the good students as well is suggested by Collins's analysis of analogy in his discussion of Pāli textual descriptions of Buddhist kingship (1998, 475).

And the good teaching, taught by the Conqueror, dispeller of harm, excellent, difficult to perceive, deep, subtle, spotless, excellent,
And the monastic community, sons of the Omniscient One, who have acted correctly, whose wealth is asceticism, whose actions are pure, whose sense faculties are tamed.
I honor [them] properly with the three doors: body, speech, and mind. (SD, 1)

Here, the reader is alerted both to the fact that each of these thresholds onto the external world should be traversed with discipline and to the ideal unity of the three. As *Sārārthadīpanī* unfolds, the hold of the metaphor on the reader's imagination is likely to intensify. References to the three doors—body, speech, and mind—interact with each other across the many sections of the work as a series of verbal echoes, or as a refrain to that reader's encounter with *Sārārthadīpanī.* Thus, in the commentary to *The Discourse on the Ten Elements*, an elaborate comment upon the self-regulation of morality concludes by linking the comment back to the opening lines of *Sārārthadīpanī*: "because of protecting the mind like someone who lives conducting himself according to the reproach of [his] own mind, such stray thoughts [of avoiding responsibility] do not arise. Shame regarding wrongdoing arises in the mind. Because of this shame there is covering of both doors, body and speech. Thus there is restraint of the three doors. Or, the three doors themselves are without impropriety" (SD, 25). Remarks on the need to control what passes through the three doors brings the comment to a close, linking restrained action to shame in the face of those more virtuous: "He becomes fearful with respect to the others described [as virtuous]. Because of that fear the three doors are restrained" (SD, 26). Repetition of the metaphor within *Sārārthadīpanī* would have brought the image of well-developed and integrated action firmly into the consciousness of many monastic readers. At the same time, however, the ways in which the refrain of the three doors metaphor would have triggered associations in the reader's mind necessarily varied from person to person.

In my second example, in *Sārārthadīpanī*'s commentary on part of *The Discourse on What Is Auspicious*, a monk is said to know well how to cut and sew the monastic robes that are the most visible badge of his monastic identity. At the same time, however, the metaphor of delicate clothwork is used to evoke images of proper monastic behavior. *Sārārthadīpanī* tells the reader that the four pure *sīla* (aspects of ethical conduct) that should characterize a monk's behavior are to be "properly and seamlessly learned without holes, in an unbroken fashion" (SD, 31). Here the metaphor of clothwork creates an important juxtaposition between the most obvious but superficial sign of monastic life (the orange robes) and the less obvious but most important sign—unfailing attention to all aspects of monastic discipline. The monastic reader was given the opportunity to think about the care required to stitch together monastic conduct that fits him without imperfections, and about the frustrations inevitably present for a monk still learning how to make, and fit, his costume. Metaphors like these demanded hard but creative work on the part of a monastic reader; they assume connections without elaborating them and thus require a careful reader to explore what might have been an instinctive sense that the metaphor made sense. The "locked image" of the metaphor incited the reader to explore certain causal connections for himself.[13] "In what sense are body, speech, and mind doors?—Doors that open out onto beautiful rooms? Doors that let in unwelcome strangers? Doors difficult to close?" "What exactly is seamless action?—Action that never stops? Action that is elegant? Action that is very discrete?"

The impact of simile and metaphor on the monastic reader's experience would in all likelihood have been enhanced by the reader's growing knowledge of multiple texts at least loosely united by their subject matter: monastic discipline and Buddhist devotion. Many similes and metaphors are used with considerable consistency and frequency throughout the texts used by eighteenth-century monks. Such texts included favorite Pāli *sutta*s such as those included in the four recitation sections, a variety of Sinhala and Pāli commentaries (including the *sūtra sannaya*s), and a range of whole or partial texts related to monastic discipline and included in the monastic handbooks. In this context of wider reading, it would have been natural for a monastic student reading *Sārārthadīpanī* to make associations between them, and to read one text with the echoes of another in his ears. This can be considered a form of intertextuality, created not by one text's overt reference to another but by one reader's experience of multiple texts in ways that create connections between them in the reader's mind. The metaphors and similes used in the *sūtra sannaya*s entered into a process of expanding literary associations that affected a monastic reader's propensity to think about the monastic life in certain terms. Through multiple encounters with these ruminative triggers, the memory of monastic readers became saturated with images, and also with an awareness of the moods and moments in which previous responses to these images had occurred. Michel de Certeau's comments on reading as an "everyday practice" are welcome at this juncture, since they conjure up the complex and unpredictable processes through which readers place themselves in the texts they read and draw these into their own mental and emotional worlds. The reader "insinuates into another person's text

[13] This pleasing phrase was suggested to me by Mark Whitaker.

the ruses of pleasure and appropriation. . . . Words become the outlet or product of silent histories. The readable transforms itself into the memorable" (1984, 11).[14]

A COMMUNITY OF READERS

The effects of *Sārārthadīpanī* on the monastic readers of the Siyam Nikāya extended well beyond the individual experiences of readers on which I have focused until now. Saraṇaṃkara's composition of *Sārārthadīpanī* inaugurated a period in which the *sūtra sannaya*s became immensely popular forms of composition and central to the education of Siyam Nikāya monks. The result of this was the emergence of a community of readers bound together not only by their experiences of reading *Sārārthadīpanī* but also by their collective encounter with a group of other *sūtra sannaya*s modeled after Saraṇaṃkara's composition.

As I have noted, *sūtra sannaya*s often circulated as part of monastic handbooks. In addition, these works, composed following the *Sārārthadīpanī* model, circulated in large numbers as single manuscripts or as part of a double manuscript set containing a *sūtra sannaya* and a companion text, the *sūtra pada änuma*.[15] The British Library's Nevill Collection of Sinhalese Manuscripts makes clear the popularity of the *sūtra sannaya*s. The first two volumes of the catalogue for that collection contain separate *sūtra sannaya* manuscripts, many of which are paired with *pada änuma*s. My own study of manuscript collections at temple sites connected to the early Siyam Nikāya confirms the centrality of *sūtra sannaya*s to eighteenth- and nineteenth-century manuscript production. The *Dhammacakkappavattana Sūtra Sannaya*, *(Mahā)Satipaṭṭhāna Sūtra Sannaya*, and the *Brahmajāla Sūtra Sannaya* were by far the most popular (Blackburn 2001). Other favorite *sūtra sannaya*s were those written for *Kālakārāma Sutta*, *Hatthipadopama Sutta*, *Vyagghapajja Sutta*, *Bālapaṇḍitopama Sutta*, *Dakkhiṇāvibhaṅga Sutta*, *Velāma Sutta*, *Kālāma Sutta*, *Ālāvaka Sutta*, *Aṅgulimāla Sutta*, *Āsīvisopama Sutta*, *Cakkavattisīhanāda Sutta*, *Vasala Sutta*, and *Parābhava Sutta* (Adikāri 1991, 246).[16]

[14] Others of de Certeau's views on reading work much less well for the Buddhist case, and for the context of manuscript reading, such as when he emphasizes the transience of the reader's "habitation" of the text. This contrasts with my view that monastic readers retained inhabited texts within their memories, where they influenced the possibilities for action and interpretation.

[15] The *pada änuma* contains the Sinhala syntax created by the *sūtra sannaya* but without the *sannaya*'s Sinhala-language explanations. See Bechert (1969).

[16] See also Bechert (1997).

In other words, these *sūtra sannaya*s became a central part of the "practical canon" (Blackburn 1999a) characteristic of Siyam Nikāya educational institutions. As such, they helped to determine which sections of the Pāli *tipiṭaka* were actually read by monks connected to the new monastic order, and shaped the interpretive approach taken by these monks to the Pāli *sutta*s. The importance of the *sūtra sannaya*s in this regard comes through most clearly when the presence of *sūtra sannaya* manuscripts and *sutta piṭaka* manuscripts are compared in a single temple collection. At Pādeniya Rajamahavihāraya, where the library was constructed during the reign of King Kīrti Śrī Rājasiṃha (Chutiwongs et al. 1990, 36), the handlist of manuscripts held by the incumbent provides rich clues with respect to the relative importance of *sūtra sannaya* and *sutta* manuscripts. One hundred and two manuscripts contained single *sutta*s or collections of two or three *sutta*s bound together. Ten are clearly identified as *sūtra sannaya*s, and another nine are identified as *sutta*s with Sinhala commentary, using terms like *padārtha* or *arthavyākhyāna* usually considered synonymous with the term *sannaya* (Godakumbura 1980). An additional fifty-two are likely to contain *sūtra sannaya*s because the *sutta* is labeled on the handlist as *sūtra* rather than *sutta*.[17] In contrast, the list indicated only two copies of the *Saṃyutta Nikāya*, two copies of the *Aṅguttara Nikāya* (one partial), one copy of the *Khuddaka Nikāya*, and one of the *Dīgha Nikāya*. This evidence, borne out by the data from other temple collections (Blackburn 2001), strongly suggests that most monastic students knew only a handful of Pāli *sutta*s well, and that they studied them by reading *sūtra sannaya*s. The *sūtra sannaya*s did more than determine which portions of the Pāli *tipiṭaka* figured verbatim in the practical canon of the early Siyam Nikāya educational community. They also provided a standardized set of interpretations for these Pāli *sutta*s, since the authors of *sūtra sannaya* compositions were often respected scholars whose work was redacted with considerable conservatism. The result of this was a community of students linked not only by their monastic status but also by their (at least partly) constrained experiences of reading selected Pāli *sutta*s within the *sūtra sannaya* framework.

[17] In the manuscripts I examined during 1997, many manuscripts labeled *sutta* and *sūtra* included *sūtra sannaya*s, with a higher proportion of *sūtra sannaya*s present in those labeled *sūtra*. With the exception of the *Dhammacakkappavattana-* and *(Mahā)Satipaṭṭhāna-sutta*s, which appear to have been extremely popular as donative texts and may appear as *sutta* fragments only in Pāli, the majority of separately circulating *sutta* manuscripts contained some form of commentarial apparatus, which was occasionally a *pada änuma* but most often a *sūtra sannaya*.

RESISTANT READINGS

We have been examining the combination of text-internal and contextual factors that are likely to have constrained (though not determined) monastic readings of *Sārārthadīpanī*, and thus helped to strengthen a collective identity shared by monks of the Siyam Nikāya. It is important not to overstate the case for constrained reading, however. We must also remain open to the possibility that some monastic readers resisted these pressures to interpret sections of *Sārārthadīpanī* in accord with monastic ideals and Saraṇaṃkara's expectations. As many readers know from personal experience, certain circumstances dispose them to read against the grain of external expectations that frame their reading, and against the persuasive flow of the text before them. Among these circumstances, temporary emotional preoccupations and pervasive feelings of disenchantment with authority are perhaps the most conducive to readings against the grain, or what one might call resistant readings. Since it is difficult enough to write convincingly of resistant readings in a time and place close and familiar, it is tempting to avoid the matter altogether, and remain content with a tidier vision of didactic readings undertaken by monks in eighteenth-century Lanka. However, the failure to attend to the possibility of resistant readings hides the fact that the Lankan monks of the early Siyam Nikāya were often creative, independent, and alive to the ironies of their time. Therefore I now suggest two resistant readings of *Sārārthadīpanī* that make sense in the context of eighteenth-century Lankan monasticism. As with the analyses presented earlier in the chapter, these are suggestive readings. We cannot know how and when monks resisted conservative, didactic readings of *Sārārthadīpanī*. My attempt to describe some possibilities should be seen in part as a reminder of the perils of totalizing analyses and of the limits of our knowledge.

I find it helpful to think about resistant readings in terms of ethical responses to the exemplary images and narratives set out in *Sārārthadīpanī*. By "ethical responses" I mean moments in which the monastic readers responded to the work by assessing its depictions as positive or negative models for their own lives, and by reflecting on the degree to which their lives overlapped with these models. In the eighteenth-century Lankan Buddhist context, as in the "medieval" Christian ones analyzed by John Dagenais (1994) and Mary Carruthers (1990), a person's storehouse of memory contained narrative snapshots that could be used in analogical reflection on his or her actions and decisions. It also contained a series of exemplary characters linked to particular virtues.

In other words, one of the ways that Lankan Buddhists developed an ethical repertoire from which to understand themselves and those with whom they associated was through the cultivation of narrative memory. This is made clear by the rich collection of narrative preaching texts composed in Sinhala and by the consistent presence of stories in Buddhist compendia composed to describe specific virtues and the path to liberation.[18]

Carruthers wrote of the place of narrative in Christian memory: "One sometimes gets the impression that a medieval person . . . could do nothing (especially in duress) without rehearsing a whole series of exemplary stories, the material of their experience built up board by board in memory . . . so that even in moments of stress the counsel of experience will constrain a turbulent and willful mind" (1990, 180). Carruthers' words overstate the case slightly in the Buddhist context, since the discipline of meditation was identified as a crucial part of Buddhist ethical cultivation. Nonetheless, they provide a helpful model for thinking about the importance of reading and reflection on reading in the constitution of personhood and of ethical understanding. As Gananath Obeyesekere puts it, "The abstract ethics and abstruse concepts of the doctrinal tradition were given an immediacy, a concreteness and an ethical salience in peasant society through storytelling" (in R. Obeyesekere 1991, x). The process Obeyesekere describes is true of reading and listening. That this continues in our own day (although perhaps in a somewhat diminished form) is clear from the ways Sri Lankan Buddhists debate the ethical implications of the *Mahāvaṃsa*'s Dutthagämunu narrative,[19] and from the experiences of Cambodian refugees discussed by Charles Hallisey and Anne Hansen (1996).

I have chosen two passages from *Sārārthadīpanī* for which to suggest resistant readings. The first is taken from Saraṇaṃkara's commentary on *The Discourse on Appropriate Acts of Loving Kindness*, where he responds to a Pāli verse praising the virtue of humility.

> [You] should be humble, not criticizing others because of their status, family, and so on, and without pride in learning, education, family, and birthright status. [Be] like the Sakyan [a reference to the Buddha's birthright community] sons Aniruddha and Ānanda, who were both praised by the Buddha for bringing things to him and requesting him to ordain them only after someone of lower rank. They said, "In order to destroy pride in birth by creating opportunities fɔr humble acts [that would arise] because of the

[18] See Godakumbura (1955), Hallisey (1988), Mahinda (1995), and R. Obeyesekere (1991). It is instructive to note the presence of narratives in Buddhaghosa's *Visuddhimagga*, on which see Norman (1983).

[19] See, for example, G. Obeyesekere (1991), Spencer (1990) and Seneviratne (1999).

customs of seniority . . . it would be good if you were to ordain us first after ordaining the barber [a low-status occupation in the South Asian context] Upāli." (SD, 62)

Here *Sārārthadīpanī* introduces a brief story about two monks, Aniruddha and Ānanda, who exemplify the absence of pride and caste-based prejudice ideally characteristic of a Buddhist monk. These monks are said to have requested ordination after the low-caste barber, Upāli, in order that they would benefit from the opportunity of serving him. Because monastic seniority is calculated from the time of ordination, Aniruddha and Ānanda would have been obliged to show humility before Upāli, despite the fact that they were superior to him according to the logic of caste status.

As we have seen, the newly formed Siyam Nikāya relatively quickly became a caste-exclusive order in which only monks of the highest status, called the *goyigama* or *govikula*, were eligible for higher ordination.[20] According to southern monastic traditions discussed by Hēvāvasam, one of Saraṇaṃkara's earliest students, Siṭināmaluvē, received higher ordination under the Siamese monk Upāli but later returned to novice status, perhaps in the aftermath of the caste-exclusive decree set out by Kīrti Śrī Rājasiṃha (Hēvāvasam 1966, 35). The Siyam Nikāya's exclusivity caused disenchantment, especially in the southern maritimes where men of more varied status sought to participate in the institutions of the new order. Although non-*goyigama* men were able to become novices and to study in the Siyam Nikāya's educational centers, they were unable to become full members of the community through higher ordination. The frustrations this created are exemplified by a petition sent by the erudite novice monk Mihiripänna Dhammaratana to King Śrī Vikrama Rājasiṃha (r. 1798–1815), in which he requested that the caste-exclusive pattern of higher ordination be reversed. When this was unsuccessful, he remained active as a teacher to lay and monastic students and as a writer known best for his poetry (80). That a considerable number of monks shared Mihiripänna's disenchantment with the Siyam Nikāya is also clear from evidence of independent higher ordinations performed as early as the late 1770s. These eventually gave way to the formation of a new monastic order, the Amarapura Nikāya, in 1800 (Malalgoda 1976, 97–98).

The presence of sharp caste-based tensions in the early Siyam Nikāya strongly suggests that some monastic readers would have responded with anger or irony to the story about Aniruddha, Ānanda, and Upāli recounted in *Sārārthadīpanī*. For a novice monk unable to receive

[20] Prior to the decree, several non-*goyigama* men received *upsampadā* (Malalagoda 1976, 91).

higher ordination in the Siyam Nikāya and its consequent benefits (both material and symbolic), it is unlikely that the story was digested as a straightforward reminder about the merits of monastic humility. Rather, for such a monk and perhaps for others, it was more likely to have contributed to ethical reflection on the distance between model and action in the life of the order.

My second example is also taken from the commentary in *Sārārthadīpanī* on *The Discourse on Appropriate Acts of Loving Kindness*, in a section focused on the *sutta*'s description of a monk as ideally "content and easy to support."

> [This] means [one] is easily supported, it is said that [such a] one is easily cared for. A monk who fills his bowl with rice, meat, etc. while acting depressed and wearing a sad face because of what's been given, and who blames the donors: "Why has this been given as alms? Give it to the novices and the laity!"—that's someone who's a real burden! Seeing that, people far and wide shun [him], saying, "A burdensome monk can't be supported." That monk who happily receives alms whether great or small, with a pleased face—that is someone who's a slight burden. Seeing that, people are exceedingly faithful, agreeing, "Our Sir is a slight burden; he is pleased with just a trifle. We will care for him indeed." And they do so. (SD, 62)

A monastic reader inclined toward a catechetical reading of *Sārārthadīpanī* might have been inclined to read the story without much care, accepting it as a simple gloss on the merits of monastic contentment. The exemplary vignette, however, contained the basis for a critical reading of monastic organization in eighteenth-century Lanka that some readers were sure to notice. What we know of donative patterns during the period indicates that certain temples, such as the key Kandyan educational centers, received lavish contributions from lay patrons and came to command large areas of productive land plus the services of male and female laborers. In such contexts, although monastic residents may have occupied themselves diligently with other activities expected of a monk, the material interdependence of monks and laity worked in ways quite different from those described by *Sārārthadīpanī*'s didactic image. Lay men and women in these situations had little freedom to turn away from a greedy monk, since their obligations to the monastery were commanded by the king and monitored (to some extent at least) by members of the monastery and of the royal administration. Other temples remained less well endowed; we know less about them because they received less munificent grants.

Because monks seeking higher ordination were required to travel to Kandy in order to receive it, those from poorer temples scattered throughout the Siyam Nikāya's periphery had occasion to observe the lives of wealthier monks in the central temples of the Kandyan region. Some of these monks were, in the words of *Sārārthadīpanī*, "heavily laden," and offered a significant contrast to the idealized image of a monk "who goes happily about . . . like a bird flying, without impediments" (SD, 63). It is unlikely that this experience failed to impress upon some monks the disjunction in living standards that characterized the order. This, in turn, may have spurred some readers to reflect on the relationship between *Sārārthadīpanī*'s exemplary models and the conditions in which they found themselves, leading to an ironic and critical perspective on the actual organization of monastic life.

PREACHING ON THE BASIS OF *SŪTRA SANNAYAS*

Whether monastic readers read with or against the grain of disciplinary expectations and collective pedagogy, they were united by their exposure to the *sūtra sannaya*s, which helped to weave the monastic community together, "providing it with shared experience and a certain kind of language" (Carruthers 1990, 12). In addition to such monastic readings, a related process of textual reception contributed to the creation of a new Buddhist textual community in eighteenth century Lanka. This occurred when Siyam Nikāya monks preached sermons on the basis of the *sūtra sannaya*s to audiences of lay men and women. Because of monastic preaching and lay Buddhist responses to this preaching, the development of new forms of organized Buddhist learning for Siyam Nikāya monastics had a profound effect on the entire Lankan Buddhist community and not just the circle of monks connected with the Siyam Nikāya. Once again using *Sārārthadīpanī* as a point of orientation, let us examine how the *sūtra sannaya*s entered the lives of lay men and women, drawing them—along with their monastic preachers—into the new textual community that developed within the institutional context of the new Siyam Nikāya. Looking at the impact of the *sūtra sannaya*s in this way provides a new perspective on the relationship between literacy and religious learning in an era before widespread, print-medium education.

Eighteenth-century acounts of the Lankan monastic community stressed the fact that Siyam Nikāya monks were effective and dramatic preachers. Saraṇaṃkara's expository skills were heralded, for instance, and Moratoṭa Dhammakkhanda was described as someone who "delighted the faithful people by preaching the *dharma* declared with various distinguished and elaborate meanings in the middle of an assembly of monastic leaders, kings, and royal ministers using Pāli texts . . . and their commentaries" (SSC, 49). Monastic biographies contained in *Saṃ-*

gharājasādhucariyāva repeatedly mention other monks' dedication to preaching, as in the description of Däramiṭipala Dhammarakkhita as someone who "preached to many people" (SSC, 46–47) and of Maḍabāviṭa Unnānsē, who passed his time "preaching to many faithful people" (SSC, 40) while serving as a scholar-teacher. Such examples indicate that preaching was considered an important part of monastic labor and that it was performed by monks who studied in the Siyam Nikāya's educational institutions. Moreover, they show that monks were prized for their ability to preach to people at all levels of society: to the higher circles of court and monastic leaders as well to the ordinary laity described as "the people" or "the faithful people." Preaching events were sometimes elaborate performances; they could also be shorter, simpler affairs done in the course of ordinary monastic duties for the benefit of lay and monastic audiences.

The frequency with which preaching is identified with well-known monks and monastic education in eighteenth-century sources indicates that monastic preaching was considered important enough for monks to receive formal training as preachers. The emphasis on educated preaching characteristic of the early Siyam Nikāya was another way in which the monks of the new order distanced and distinguished themselves from their monastic predecessors and contemporaries. Prior to the rise of the Siyam Nikāya, *gaṇinnānse*s preached, but from a different repertoire that most often emphasized the recitation of popular *jātaka* stories composed in verse and other poetic devotional texts (Sannasgala 1964, 391; Vācissara 1964, 71). By preaching from a larger selection of texts (often in prose) on the basis of Pāli and Sinhala commentaries, monks of the early Siyam Nikāya once again identified themselves as learned in a very public way. In addition, however, this interest in trained preaching should be seen as an outgrowth of broader devotional expectations within the Lankan Buddhist community. The composition and transmission of unprecedented numbers of *dharmānisaṃsa* texts—texts that extol the benefits of writing, preaching, and listening to the Buddha's *dhamma*—signaled a new formalization of attention to the benefits of preaching and preaching-related activities.[21]

[21] This does not mean, of course, that Lankan Buddhists were previously uninterested in preaching. See Godakumbura (1955), Hallisey (1988), Mahinda (1995) and Sannasgala (1964) on pre-eighteenth-century preaching texts. However, Mīgaskumbura (personal communication) and Mirando (1985, 113–114) draw attention to rising interest in *dharmānisaṃsa* texts in the seventeenth and eighteenth centuries. Their view is supported by Sinhala manuscripts held in the British Library's Nevill Collection and by Buddhist compendia composed by Saraṇaṃkara's student Tibboṭuvāvē Buddharakkhita. See Amaramoli (1956) and Sannasgala (1964, 420–421). Note also that the chapters of *Mahāvaṃsa* composed by Tibboṭuvāvē Buddharakkhita (97–101) emphasize preaching and recitation of

It is difficult to reconstruct fully the styles of preaching in use during the eighteenth century. However, the evidence available indicates that preaching was done by single monks and by groups of two, and that some preaching performances were quite elaborate. The references in *Saṃgharājasādhucariyāva* to Moratoṭa, Däramiṭipala, and Maḍabāvita seem to assume one-man preaching events. Such an event is described in an account by a Sri Lankan monk who studied in the early part of the twentieth century; it can only be used to suggest the form and mood of an ornate one-man preaching event.

> First of all awnings are tied in the entire hall and the preaching pavilion is decorated in great beauty by hanging lotus flowers and coconut fronds. In the middle of the pavilion a traditional preacher's seat is made by placing cushions so that the orator of the dhamma can comfortably sit in the lotus posture with curtains drawn in a circle around it. About twenty to thirty coconut oil fueled brass lamps are lit and hung all over the preaching hall. . . . No later than 9:00 in the night the venerable orator of the dhamma is placed on a chair and carried up to the preacher's seat with great honor and love by two strong and pure men, amidst exclamations of "Sadhu." The venerable dhamma orator (preacher) . . . stands near the preacher's seat, and leaning against it and holding with both hands the great fan, chants the grant of merit for the preacher's seat. He is helped to the preacher's seat only after this grant of merit. . . . Now preparations are made to perform the invitation to preach by offering and placing popped rice, the fivefold flowers, incense and sandalwood water in the area surrounding the preacher's seat everywhere on the pavilion, and by playing the drums of the first watch [of the night]. One or two beautifully dressed handsome boys kneel down in worshipping posture and facing the direction of the preacher's seat chant verses . . . inviting the preacher to deliver his sermon. This may also be done by grown ups. . . . Now the preacher administers the five precepts and chants the invitation to the gods. . . . Next the preacher chants in a beautiful metre three or four verses of worship and in a lullabic voice chants a [verse] that extols the good effects of worshipping the Triple Gem. . . . Next, the preacher chants the benefits of (hearing) the dharma, preaches a considerable portion of the text (*sutra*) that is the subject of the sermon, and explains it drawing out the explanations in the commentary. The dawn portion of the sermon is concluded with the chantings of the Extolling of Maitreya [the next Buddha] and the Donation of Merit. (in Seneviratne 1999, 43–45)

As Mahinda has shown, however, a style of preaching in which two monks participated became popular in the eighteenth century. Called

---

the *dhamma* far more than any other section of that work.

two-seated preaching (Sinhala *āsana deke bāṇa*), this type of preaching was used largely for more elaborate preaching performances and became characteristic of the Siyam Nikāya (Mahinda 1995, 143–149). His reconstruction of such an event draws on his study of eighteen-century manuscripts and his education as a Sri Lankan monk.

> A two-pulpit preaching manuscript adds a poetic dimension. . . . "White canopies are tied like the full-moon which shines in the middle of the sky. Oil lamps which are lighted to remove darkness are like the shining stars in the background. [Pots] are set at the doorways which are decorated with garlands of flowers. . . ." All these passages describe the way that the preaching hall and its surroundings were decorated as an offering to the Buddha. In the middle of the preaching hall, two pulpits . . . are set up for the two preachers. According to the traditional custom, one pulpit faces east while the second pulpit is positioned to the right of the first seat but facing north. . . . The way the two pulpits are ritually positioned . . . has been influenced by the traditional account of the First Council [organized to recite the Buddha's teachings after his death]. . . . In addition to the arrangement of the pulpits, the preaching hall is divided into two sections to accommodate the audience: on one side men, on the other side women; both groups sit on the floor on mats. . . . At the scheduled time, the two preachers are conducted to the preaching hall with traditional demonstrations of honor. . . . Once the two arrive at the preaching hall, they stand in front of the main seat . . . holding their hand-fans before their faces and facing the audience. The devotees make obeisance to them and cry "sādhu! sādhu! sādhu!" which means "excellent or well done." Then the preachers bless the audience. . . . After the two preachers have given blessings, they are lifted to their seats where they sit cross-legged until morning. After they have taken their seats, as a custom, the two seats are covered with a piece of white cloth . . . so that only their faces appear above the curtain. [After aesthetically pleasing recitation of verses extolling the Three Refuges and chanting the Five Precepts (five foundational aspects of moral conduct)] . . . [t]he lay devotees invite the preachers to commence the preaching by singing eight Sinhala poems [or by chanting an alliterative prose invitation]. . . . [Then the preaching proper begins, with one monk reading out of a Pāli manuscript in alternation with the other, who] provides detailed explanations with innovative interpretations of his own as a Sinhala commentary on the sermon. . . . The Laudatory Account of the Buddha Maitreya marks the climatic [sic] conclusion of two-pulpit preaching. (Mahinda 1995, 155–198)[22]

[22] I have rearranged sections from Mahinda's description in addition to making substantial elisions.

Mahinda stresses that what he calls "late medieval" Buddhist preaching was intended to maintain a balance between form (Pāli *vyañjana*) and content (*attha*), "by emphasizing primarily the form in the early parts of the ritual, while focusing on the presentation of the content in the later parts" (165–166). Thus the verses in honor of the Triple Gem, the Five Precepts, the invitation to the gods to join in the benefits of the occasion, and the invitation to preach were often performed in a musical style that maximized the play of alliteration and intonation. The preaching and explication of the Pāli text (the *sūtra* in the first example) was driven principally by the goal of "persuading average people about the teachings of the Buddha" (121). One should not assume, however, that the explication of a Pāli text in Sinhala was always fully understood by the listeners. Comprehension depended heavily on the listeners' education and the preacher's skill. Benefits were ascribed to the experience of listening to aesthetically pleasing passages even when they were not understood. As P. B. Mīgaskumbura writes, the objective of preaching was often described as the development of both confidence (Pāli *saddhā*) and wisdom (Pāli *buddhi*). Thc type of vocabulary used in the Sinhala exposition and a listener's level of education determined when a member of the audience developed confidence and when he or she developed wisdom. In other words, "some of the expressions and descriptions [used in exposition] were mainly for the ear and not for the mind."[23]

SŪTRA SANNAYAS AS PREACHING GUIDES

The Siyam Nikāya's interest in trained preaching influenced monastic interest in the *sūtra sannaya* genre, since these works modeled on Saraṇaṃkara's *Sārārthadīpanī* were seen as particularly useful for training monks as preachers. Writing about the *sūtra sannaya*s, Sannasgala notes that "[t]he group of students in [Saraṇaṃkara's] lineage made a great effort to put down the form of exposition characteristic of Pāli *dharma* and used in Pāli compilations in Sinhala language. . . . It is evident that the composition of these *sannaya*s was due above all to their usefulness in preaching in Sinhala" (1964, 491–492). In other words, the Sinhala commentaries composed for Pāli *sutta*s in the *sūtra sannaya* style were used as the basis for monastic preaching. It is unlikely that the monks of the early Siyam Nikāya read from the *sūtra sannaya* manuscripts themselves during preaching performances, because the script used in these

[23] Personal correspondence, 10 April 1995.

manuscripts is small and difficult to read. Manuscripts prepared in the eighteenth and nineteenth centuries were copied in a larger hand if they were intended to be used in a public reading.[24] At times monks may have chosen to recite an entire *sūtra sannaya* from memory. However, the fact that the *sūtra sannaya*s continually moved back and forth between Pāli and Sinhala, introducing short passages in Sinhala for the most part, strongly suggests that monastic students most often memorized the contents of the *sūtra sannaya*s during their education and then drew on their memory to introduce portions of them at fitting moments during their preaching.[25] G. H. Vijayavardhana notes that "what I am inclined to think is that these sanna [= *sannaya*] books were intended more for the preacher and not so much for the listening audience. They would have helped the preacher to understand the Pāli text, and he in turn would have based his exposition on the sannaya. More correctly, he would have used the material from the sannayas to make his exposition clear to the audience. . . . Particularly in the eighteenth century it is rather hard to believe that the general audience was

[24] See, for instance, the manuscripts containing *catubhāṇavāra* texts without commentary copied in a large and regular hand for easy consultation: Somadasa 1987, 63 and OR 6599(36), Malvatu Vihārayē Saṃgharāja Pansala No. 36 (Blackburn 2001) and Ridī Vihāraya no. 52–52 (Blackburn 2001).

[25] The creation of printed versions of the *sūtra sannaya*s in the nineteenth century is likely to have altered their role in monastic preaching. Because printed texts were more legible than manuscript copies, it was possible for preachers to read from the actual text of a *sūtra sannaya* if they wished. Such use is suggested by Copleston's report in 1892 that "the monks who are the guests at a [preaching event] take it by turns to read the Pali Suttas, with their Sinhalese comment or explanation. . . . In the Kandian country, about which I have learned the most, the suttas most read are the Dhammacakkappavattana and the Satipaṭṭhāna Suttas; after these, Kālakārāma Sutta, Subha Sutta, and Sigālovāda Sutta. And for the rest, those to which there are explanations (sannas) [= *sannaya*s] . . . are most in use. Few leaf-books are now written, for printing has almost superseded them" (1984, 258, 266). Moreover, some printed versions of the *sūtra sannaya*s introduced a new form of commentary called the *bhava sannaya*, not found in any of the manuscript versions I have examined. The *bhava sannaya* drew together the sections of Sinhala commentary found in the *sūtra sannaya*, presenting them in a single coherent piece at the end of the commentarial work. The publication of *sūtra sannaya*s with a *bhava sannaya* added made it easier for monks to memorize the *sūtra sannaya*s in a form suitable for recitation during a preaching event. This view is supported by Somadasa's comments on the use of the *bhava sannaya* for *asana dekē baṇa* (personal communication, 21 October 1994). See, for instance, the print edition of *Sārārthadīpanī* (1891) in comparison to the manuscript held in the British Library (OR.6600 [151]) and the Sri Lankan National Museum (1465 Foll. 106). Some printed *sūtra sannaya*s even included all of the introductory and concluding recitations to be used in an elaborate preaching performance. One copy of the *Mallikovāda Sūtra Sannaya* held in the British Library, for instance, contains all of the elements to be said by a monk at a major preaching event, including the invitation to preach (HN14098.d.85).

literate enough (literate at all, in fact) to read and understand the vistara [detail] sannaya."[26]

His views are consistent with statements made by the incumbents at two Buddhist temples in contemporary Sri Lanka. In a series of discussions about contemporary monastic educational practices and those used in the eighteenth century, these monks stated that it was natural for monks to preach based on the *sūtra sannaya*s, since preaching is always based on the ideas a monk has studied himself and the forms in which he has encountered these ideas.[27] Because the *sūtra sannaya*s contained Pāli text plus Sinhala commentary, they were ideal for training monks to undertake two-seated preaching.[28] The commentary provided by the *sūtra sannaya*s, however, also provided a framework for exposition appropriate for a preaching event performed by a single monk. In this regard, the comments of Hendiyagala Silaratana are informative, despite the fact that they describe an early-twentieth-century monastic education: "I memorized new sutras, about one a month, and crafted *baṇa* [exposition] for preaching. I trained to preach from the *Mahamangala*, *Vasala* and *Parabhava sutras* as well. Now I know from memory everything I need to perform (all) night sermons. Even if I had to preach several consecutive days at the same place, I could do so without repetition, by alternating among five or six *sutras*" (in Seneviratne 1999, 44–45). Here, where the monk writes of "crafting" his exposition, it is almost certain that he used *sūtra sannaya*s as guides, since all of the *sutta*s mentioned were the subject of *sūtra sannaya*s. Silaratana also notes his reliance on the preamble to another *sutta*, which would have been included in its *sūtra sannaya*.

Sārārthadīpanī and the *sūtra sannaya*s written after it became central to the processes by which monks were trained as preachers in the educational institutions of the early Siyam Nikāya. Using such texts, monastic students memorized popular *sutta*s from the Pāli *tipiṭaka* and also learned to interpret these texts according to the commentary set down in Sinhala (sometimes with Pāli commentary also, as in *Sārārthadīpanī*) by respected monastic scholars. Trained in this way, Siyam Nikāya monks were prepared to make certain sections of the authorita-

[26] Personal correspondence, 25 April 1995.

[27] The incumbent of the Śrī Narēndrārāma Rajamahavihāraya, 30 June 1997, and the incumbent of the Mulkirigala Rajamahāviharaya, 6 July 1997. Their comments suggest that *sūtra sannaya*s became part of a repertoire on which monks were able to draw as they attempted to make certain points to an audience.

[28] K. D. Somadasa notes that "[t]he Pali text with the Sinhalese paraphrase lent itself to a style of delivery by two monks seated on two pulpits (āsana dekē baṇa). They recited alternately: one would recite a portion of the Pali sūtra, the second its Sinhala paraphrase" (1987, Vol. 1, ix).

tive Pāli tradition available to a larger eighteenth-century Buddhist audience, and to do so according to eighteenth-century local interpretations (which were sometimes heavily influenced by the fifth-century Pāli commentaries). Drawn upon in this way, the *sūtra sannaya*s epitomized several points of orientation characteristic of the early Siyam Nikāya: elaborate, public attempts to preserve and transmit authoritative Pāli texts; the acceptance of systematic monastic education as an ideal; an appreciation for the interdependence of learning, performance, and prestige; and an interest in localizing Buddhist textual transmissions through commentary and translation.[29]

Drawing on *Sārārthadīpanī*, which comprised *sūtra sannaya*s composed for each text of the Pāli four recitation sections, it is possible to identify six aspects of these commentaries that increased their usefulness as guides for Buddhist preaching. These are the impetus to mental association created through repetition, the possibilities for elaboration provided by simile, the conceptual and aesthetic appeal of etymological interpretation, the identification of appropriate introductory stories, the elaboration of confidence-inducing descriptions, and explicit expository guidance.

Repetition-association

We have seen that the *sūtra sannaya*s in *Sārārthadīpanī* reproduce the *sutta*s from the Pāli *tipiṭaka* as part of the commentary and, in doing so, create a new layered and multilingual work. The presence of the *tipiṭaka* passages within the commentary creates an intense repetitiveness within *Sārārthadīpanī*, since words and phrases drawn from the Pāli passage under comment are repeated in the Sinhala commentarial sections that follow each section of the Pāli texts from the four recitation sections. By repeating words and phrases taken from the Pāli *tipiṭaka* text in two languages—Pāli and Sinhala—and by then providing detailed guidelines for the reader's interpretation of these words and phrases, the *sūtra sannaya* helps to develop expository patterns in the reader's mind that subsequently allow individual words and phrases to trigger specific narrative associations.[30] By this I mean that the commentary first sets words and phrases very firmly in the reader's memory, and then links them to other ideas, establishing a natural connection be-

[29] On the latter point see also Blackburn (n.d.a).

[30] On this point I am indebted to Ebersole's discussion of oral performance and the way that formulaic phrases may trigger a series of associations in a performer's or listener's memory (1989, 211) as well as to discussions with Shantanu Phukan about narrative associations possible for educated readers of Hindi and Persian. See also Phukan (1999).

tween certain Pāli words and the ideas elaborated by the commentary. If the reader of the *sūtra sannaya* later began an oral exposition, he was thus disposed to use the commentarial elaboration when talking about words or phrases treated by the commentary. An example makes this clearer. Verse 3 of *The Discourse on What Is Auspicious* includes the Pāli phrase "**and living in a proper place.**" In *Sārārthadīpanī*'s *sannaya* for this discourse, the Sinhala comment for this phrase proceeds as follows: "living in a proper place where the ten meritorious acts—such as generosity and moral conduct—exist, and the four groups of people [monks, nuns, laymen, and lay women] move about, and the Triple Gem shines; in some village, town, or royal capital" (SD, 28). The monastic reader of the *sūtra sannaya* here learned that, if he was preaching on the basis of *The Discourse on What Is Auspicious* and chose to elaborate verse 3, it was advisable to link the propriety of place to the meritorious behaviors of its inhabitants and to the presence of a devoted Buddhist community. He was also reminded to insist that a place even as small as a village can be "proper" in this sense. In addition, however, since this part of the *sūtra sannaya* helps to sustain a train of thought on what constitutes a good or proper dwelling place—that is, certain relationships between place, social organization, and religious devotion—it would have been accessible to a preacher for use in a number of expository situations requiring an excursus on good living. For instance, a monk working from another text might have enhanced his sermon by drawing on the *sūtra sannaya*'s treatment of "living in a proper place" to describe the relationship between social ethics and the prospects for enlightenment.

Elaboration through Simile

The similes in the *sūtra sannaya*s added much to the power of these commentaries as preaching guides because their aesthetically pleasing vividness engaged the imagination of a reader alert to didactic possibilities. An example is the way in which simile brings to life a standard Buddhist view that moral conduct, concentration, and wisdom arise together and reinforce each other as progress is made along the path to liberation. A gloss to the word "faithful," found in *Sārārthadīpanī*'s *sūtra sannaya* on *The Jewel Discourse*, explains that certain people are faithful because they possess "the virtues of moral conduct, concentration, and so on, which arise simultaneously because of movement along the path, as the color and scent of flowers like the *vampaka* and the *vakula* arise together" (SD, 43). This simile would have been retained by a talented preacher as an image that could be used to make an abstract point more straightforwardly accessible and more aesthetically appealing. It not only underscores the ideal of the absolute inseparability of morality, concentration, and wisdom for proper Buddhist practice; it also carries within itself the seeds of other didactic similes and metaphors. It would not have been difficult for a trained preacher to move from this section of the commentary on *The Jewel Discourse* to a discussion of the auspicious complexion that accompanies a tranquil mind or to an evocation of the fully balanced beauty of *nirvāṇa*.

Another fine example of the expository possibilities provided by the similes in *sūtra sannaya*s can be found in *Sārārthadīpanī*'s commentary on *The Discourse on Appropriate Acts of Loving Kindness*. Describing the final verse of the *sutta* said to be the words of the Buddha that describe the attainment of liberation, the *sūtra sannaya* elaborates the Buddha's finale with the words: "He thus put the finishing touches on the teaching through arhatship or he adorned the palace which is the teaching with the pinnacle which is the declaration of arhatship" (SD, 68). Here the commentary's assertion that liberation, or arhatship, is the highest embellishment on an already impressive structure provided the reader with a powerful image to be used in preaching. The obvious positive associations between the palace, spiritual power, and the wealth that results from proper Buddhist practice provide several rich starting points for exposition. Moreover, the commentary's comparison between the Buddha's teaching and a royal palace invited a preacher's elaboration on the capaciousness of Buddhist teaching, the way that it is possible to move from one room-aspect of the teaching to another, and the many adornments of the Buddha's words.

Etymological Interpretation

For readers of the *sūtra sannaya*s preparing to use the texts' contents in preaching, etymological interpretation was another aspect of the commentaries particularly well suited to incorporation in oral exposition. The use of etymological interpretation, called *nirukti* in Sanskrit and *nirutti* in Pāli, has a long history in Buddhist and other South Asian literatures.[31] The popularity of this form clearly owes much to the flexible and sophisticated manner in which it creates connections between ideas through word play. Through the verbal work of a *nirutti*, word play becomes an important focusing device. Although the conceptual contents of a particular *nirutti* might have been accessible only to a rather sophisticated listener (among the preacher's fellow monks or the

[31] See, for instance, Bond (1982, 151–152).

best-educated laymen in the audience), nearly every listener was able to recognize the existence of the word play and to appreciate its sonorous aesthetic.

One example, is a *nirutti* for the word *nirvāṇa* from *Sārārthadīpanī*. *Nirvāṇa* [Pāli *nibbāna*] as the ultimate goal of Buddhist practice, has naturally been a favorite focus for etymological interpretation. The commentary in *Sārārthadīpanī* on *The Discourse on What Is Auspicious* contains a passage that exemplifies the potential for a *nirutti* to communicate ideas vividly and in an aesthetically pleasing manner. Building on the Pāli verse that runs

> **Ascetic exertion, sexual restraint, seeing the Noble Truths and an act of truth in relation to *nibbāna*; that is an excellent auspicious thing**

the Sinhala gloss to "an act of truth in relation to *nibbāna*" plays on a favorite etymological interpretation for the word *nirvāṇa*.

> For instance, investigation of and entry into the city of *nirvāṇa*, which is said to be *nirvāṇa* because of the absence of craving which is understood as an obstacle [*nīvaraṇa*] to the five places of rebirth." (SD, 32–33)

The force of the *nirutti* hinges on the tension between *nirvāṇa* and *nīvaraṇa* created at once by the similarity of sound and the causal relations sketched between the words by the Sinhala commentary. Such an etymological interpretation provided a preacher with the opportunity to ring the changes on the meaning of the term *nirvāṇa* by stressing that *nirvāṇa* is characterized by an absence of craving; that craving is an obstacle to release from the cycle of rebirth. A preacher inclined to develop the metaphor of the "city of *nirvāṇa*" under the influence of this creative etymology could, for instance, elaborate on the way the Buddhist path opens doors into the city of *nirvāṇa* while closing off/creating obstructions to the undesirable experiences of rebirth.[32]

Identifying Appropriate Introductory Stories

A *sūtra sannaya* very often includes a *nidāna kathā*, or introductory story, which gives the circumstances in which the *sutta* was first preached by the Buddha. This story often provides a detailed description of the *sutta*'s original context and thus provides a ready-made narrative frame upon which a preacher might draw in his exposition of the *sutta*. By drawing on the story set out in the *sūtra sannaya*, a preacher was able to emphasize the powerful and authoritative quality of the *sutta*'s message, reminding his listeners that the *sutta* was the Buddha's

[32] On the city of *nirvāṇa*, see Hallisey (1993).

own teaching and that its history as liberating discourse was a long one. Because the introductory story often suggested that the *sutta* was particularly effective as a teaching for certain personalities and/or for people in particular circumstances, it also helped the preacher to choose occasions on which to preach from the contents of the *sutta* and its *sūtra sannaya*. Although it was certainly possible for the preacher to memorize the entire introductory story and recite it in full as a preamble to his discussion of the Pāli *sutta*, there was also a great deal of room for the preacher to draw indirectly on the story's narrative frame in his exposition. As Somadasa notes, "The sermon proper begins with the origins of the sutta: when, where and why it was preached" (1987, Vol. 1, ix). For instance, the introductory story included in *Sārārthadīpanī*'s *sūtra sannaya* on *The Jewel Discourse* included the story of the Buddha's first recitation of *The Jewel Discourse* to destroy the threats to the city of Vesāli (SD, 37–40); this could be used to emphasize the power of the Buddha's words and the importance of listening to them, or the fact that the Buddha's power was greater than that of any human ruler. The introductory story included in Sāraṇaṃkara's *sūtra sannaya* for *The Discourse on the Benefits of Loving Kindness* (SD, 79–86)—concerning the sixty monks who reverted to lay life in order to avoid suffering in hell, and who were assured of the benefits experienced by diligent monks who meditated on loving kindness—could be used, for example, to frame a sermon on the importance of certain types of meditation, on the propriety of lay donations to meditating monks, or on the fact that life as a lay Buddhist is appropriate for people at certain stages along the path to liberation. The idea that the material crafted for a sermon often drew on a *sūtra sannaya*'s introductory story is supported by the comments of Hendiyagala Silaratana: "Because the Ālavaka sutra is prefaced by a long *nidāna kathā* (preamble) I can manage to preach [an exposition] for a couple of hours from that" (in Seneviratne 1999, 45).

Confidence-inducing Descriptions

The *sūtra sannaya*s frequently include long and dramatic passages that describe the Buddha's superhuman characteristics, the transformative power of Buddhist preaching, and the array of supernatural beings who played a role in Buddhist cosmology. Some of these passages were composed in a highly Sanskritized form of Sinhala comprehensible to the educated monks and laity in a preacher's audience but not to the majority of the listeners. We would be mistaken, however, to assume that such portions of the *sūtra sannaya*s were unimportant to the preparation of monks as preachers. Since Buddhist preaching was intended to develop both wisdom and confidence, certain forms of expression were valued for their transformative, confidence-inducing, quality rather than for their power to develop a listener's wisdom through conceptual understanding. Such passages, according to Mīgaskumbura, "had some air of grandiloquence which heightened the spirit and the *saddhā* (confidence) of the audience. The alliteration and other sound effects, and severe mutilation of words to bring about sonority may have contributed to such an effect."[33] *Sūtra sannaya*s were used in preacher training in part as source texts from which the students were to memorize aesthetically pleasing passages appropriate to spur the audience's confidence in Buddhist teachings. By reading the *sūtra sannaya*s with an attention to such portions of the commentary, monastic students added dramatic images and musical descriptions to their storehouse of memory. Thus, in the *sūtra sannaya* composed for *The Aṭanāṭiya Discourse* by Saraṇaṃkara, a description of the land of Uttarakuru inhabited by the king of the demons, Vessavaṇa/Kuvēra, includes a description of a jeweled assembly hall where the demons gather. In *Sārārthadīpanī* it is presented first in Pāli and then glossed in Sinhala. The Pāli passage would have been the most useful to a preacher concerned with the power of form rather than the accessibility of content.

> **there the demons pay honor. There [there are] ever-flowering trees and various groups of birds pleasantly resounding: peacocks, herons, geese, and so on. Then, [there is] the sound of the *jivaṃjīvakās*, [also birds called] *otthavacittakā* and *kukutthakā*, crabs, and those [creatures] belonging to lakes and forest. [There is] the sound of birds called *sātakās*, parrots and *sālikas*, and the *daṇḍamāṇavakānis*. That *kuvera* pond shines splendidly always, in every season.** (SD, 163)

Because the qualities of the passage have much to do with repeated sounds that are clearer in the Pāli passage, I reproduce that also.

> yatha yakkhā payirupāsanti tatha nicca phalā rukkhā nānā dija gaṇa yutā mayura [read māyura] koñca abhirudā kokilā abhi hi vaggubhi jivaṃjīvakasadd' ettha atho otthavacittakā kukuthakā kulīrakā vane pokkhara sātakā suka-sālikasadd' ettha daṇḍamāṇavakāni ca sobhati sabbakalāṃ sā kuvera nilinī sadā.

Expository Guidance

Another aspect of the *sūtra sannaya*s that allowed them to serve as guidelines for preaching is explicit expository guidance included in the

[33] Personal correspondence, 10 April 1995.

commentaries. This takes two primary forms. In one, the reader is provided with references to other texts that could be used to provide additional detail in the course of exposition. In Saraṇaṃkara's commentary on *The Ten Training Precepts*, for example, the reader is told to turn to the *Brahmajāla Sutta* (a Pāli *sutta*) and *Dasasīlagathā* (verses in Pāli on the ten moral precepts to be followed by a novice monk or devout lay person) for additional details on these injunctions (SD, 10). Similarly, the *sūtra sannaya* written for *The Discourse on What Is Auspicious* instructs the reader to turn to Saraṇaṃkara's compendium, *Sārārthasaṅgrahaya*, if he wishes to know the origin story for this discourse: "The origin of *The Discourse on What Is Auspicious* should be understood as it is set out in my *Sārārthasaṅgrahaya*. Here, with respect to the discourse, only the meaning of the words has been presented" (SD, 34). If a monk wished to make this origin story the centerpiece of his sermon, he knew where to turn for the details needed to preach a full and convincing narrative. Something like this also occurs in the commentary on *The Discourse on the Benefits of Loving Kindness*, where the *sūtra sannaya*'s origin story refers to *The Discourse on the Simile of the Mountain of Fire*. A monk who wanted to elaborate on why *The Discourse on the Simile of the Mountain of Fire* frightened so many monks into becoming householders knew where to find a fuller account. "And *The Discourse on the Simile of the Mountain of Fire* should be understood after looking at it the way it appears in the *Exposition of the Discourse on What Is Auspicious* in the *Sārārthasaṅgrahaya* of which I am the author" (SD, 82). Such expository guidance was sometimes quite clearly defined. Thus, for instance, the commentary on *The Discourse on the Benefits of Friendship* elaborates on the phrase "he is dear to people" as follows: "he is dear to nonhumans, like the elder [monk] Visakha. The story of the elder Visakha was set out in detail in *Visuddhimagga* and has been included in the *Exposition of the Discourse on What Is Auspicious* in my *Sārārthasaṅgrahaya*. This should be understood, looking at it as written [there]" (SD, 88).[34]

The second form of expository guidance frequently took the form of

[34] Visakha Thera was known as "[a] rich householder of Pataliputta [on the Indian subcontinent] who, hearing that there were many [Buddhist] shrines in Ceylon, made over his property to his family and left home with one single coin wrapped in the hem of his garment." He was ordained and set out traveling after five years. With the help of a minor deity, he found his way to a certain temple where he stayed for four months. As he was about to leave, the deity that inhabited the tree standing at the head of his meditation walkway appeared before him, weeping. The tree-deity explained that while the monk was there, nonhumans lived in peace, but that when he had gone they would start quarreling and talking loudly. Several times he tried to leave but was thus prevented until he eventually was liberated from the cycle of rebirth and died (Malalasekere 1938, 898–899).

instructing the reader/preacher to develop certain lines of argument for maximum rhetorical effect. Thus, in *The Reflections* section of *Sārārthadīpanī*, the commentary explains the disadvantages of feeding oneself in order to become more attractive, before adding in no uncertain terms: "Here the story should be told of a monk who fell into the hands of a woman who wanted him to disrobe and marry her daughter" (SD, 18). The *sūtra sannaya* then presents the recommended story (quoted in chapter 5 above). Similarly, *Sārārthadīpanī*'s *sūtra sannaya* composed for *The Discourse on the Benefits of Friendship* elaborates this phrase from the Pāli four recitation sections: "**He eats well when away from his own home; many support him, one who doesn't cause harm to friends—**" with the words, "This is to be explained by the Story of Sīvalī" (SD, 94).[35] The same *sūtra sannaya* provides instructions for elaborating on other portions of the Pāli four recitation sections stating that freedom from thievery "should be clarified by the Story of the Novice Saṃkicca," and the ability to overcome all enemies "should be clarified by the Story of Jotipāla " (SD, 95), and provides similar references for yet further portions of the *sutta*.[36] The numerous guides to exposition found in this *sūtra sannaya* offer important evidence of the way that such commentaries informed monastic preaching. It is no accident that this proliferation of references comes in *The Discourse on the Benefits of Friendship*, since the discussion of the benefits of friendship contained many themes relevant to lay audiences. By providing points of access for a preacher who sought to explicate a particular Pāli *sutta* and by providing the details necessary for an effective exposition, the *sūtra sannayas* helped monastic students to develop their preaching repertoire while they became familiar with the contents and meaning of popular texts from the Pāli *tipiṭaka*. The impact of what may first appear to be abstruse forms of exegesis was not limited to a narrow circle of scholastic elites.[37]

[35] "Sivali was declared by the Buddha preeminent among recipients of gifts. It is said that when the Buddha visited Khadiravaniya and Revata, he took Sivali with him because the road was difficult and provisions scarce. [Later] Sivali went to the Himalaya with five hundred others to test his good luck. The gods provided them with everything" (ibid., 1,163–1,164).

[36] Saṃkicca was a novice monk who intervened with thieves to save the life of one of their victims. He was taken instead, and was on the point of death by sword when he entered a meditative state. As a result the sword bent and split upon contact with Saṃkicca's body. The thieves honored Saṃkicca, listened to his preaching and asked to be ordained as Buddhist monks (ibid., 975–976). Jotipāla was a monastic elder who was assaulted after defeating his rivals in debate. An ulcer appeared on his assailant's hand (ibid., 972).

[37] Several discussions of the interrelated use of exegetical texts, model sermon collections, *floreligia*, and university sermons in England and the continent between the twelfth

LISTENING TO *SŪTRA SANNAYA*-BASED SERMONS

My consideration of the ways an audience of lay men and women might have responded to a preaching performance inspired by a *sūtra sannaya* is necessarily tentative, as we have no evidence from which to reconstruct specific audience responses during this period. It is more important for my purposes, however to indicate ways in which monastic preaching drew the *sūtra sannaya*s into the life of a larger Buddhist community than it is to defend the detailed reconstruction of any one such listening experience. The commentaries on which I focus are *Sārārthadīpanī*'s *sūtra sannaya*s for *The Discourse on the Benefits of Loving Kindness* and *The Discourse on the Standard's Tip*. Manuscript evidence shows that these *sūtra sannaya*s were of sufficient interest to readers for them to circulate independently of *Sārārthadīpanī*.[38]

Preaching from the Sannaya *on* The Discourse on the Benefits of Loving Kindness

This *sutta* would have been an appropriate focus for preaching on occasions like *poya* (Pāli *uposatha*) day festivals held to honor the Triple Gem and to commemorate the Buddha's enlightenment experience. Such festivals were times for lay Buddhists to gather at their local temple, perhaps to meditate, to listen to sermons preached by the temple monks and to make offerings to the various shrines on the temple property.[39] If *The Discourse on the Benefits of Loving Kindness* was the focus for a sermon, for instance, the audience might first have been introduced to the *sutta* with comments drawn from the origin story of the *sūtra sannaya*. Thus they might have been told that the *sutta* was first preached by the Buddha to show that a monk who cultivates *mettā*, or loving kindness, as a meditative technique deserves the support of the laity. This would have alerted the audience to the idea that meditation on loving kindness was a desirable form of meditation and not some-

---

and fourteenth centuries shed new light on the possible uses of several genres of commentary and compilation in the Theravāda. See, for instance, Carruthers (1990, esp. 189–220), d'Avray (1985, esp. 64–203), and Rouse and Rouse (1979). In this section, despite significant difference between the *sūtra sannaya*s and scholastic commentaries, I have found D'Avray's work helpful in thinking about the ways in which preachers familiarize themselves with themes and rhetorical constructions.

[38] See Godakumbura 1980, 109; Liyanaratne 1983, 39; Somadasa 1987, OR6600(21), 6600(78).

[39] For a twentieth-century description, see Gombrich (1971, 273–274).

thing to be dismissed as a practice less serious than the meditations, such as those focused on the fragility and loathsomeness of the body, that might be performed by more advanced practitioners. The audience might then have had the pleasure of a chuckle at the expense of monastics, since the origin story goes on to explain that the Buddha taught the *sutta* in order to arrest an exodus of monks from the order caused by one of his previous sermons, *The Discourse on the Simile of the Mountain of Fire*. The *sutta* describes the effects of this discourse in dramatic terms: "The Buddha sat down on [a folded robe] and addressed the monks. He told *The Discourse on the Simile of the Mountain of Fire* which begins, "monks, did you see that great mountain of fire?" When this *Discourse on the Simile of the Mountain of Fire* teaching was done, hot blood poured forth from the mouths of sixty monks. Sixty monks, reflecting on the training, left for the inferior status of a householder" (SD, 82). The audience might well have welcomed an account of this *sutta* developed by the preacher on the basis of the reference to *Sārārthasaṅgrahaya* given in the *sūtra sannaya* on *The Discourse on the Benefits of Loving Kindness*. After enjoying the tension of the origin story's account of a monastic community depleted and restored by the Buddha's instructions on meditation, the audience was perhaps disposed to appreciate the conclusion to the origin story that refers to the benefits of meditation on loving kindness: "That is the origin. The Omniscient One spoke this *Discourse on the Benefits of Loving Kindness* showing that there were thus great benefits by cultivating [loving kindness]. . . . For one who becomes accustomed to and develops a mind [characterized by] loving kindness . . . having thus entered into a state of mental focus, there is a full [attainment of an advanced meditative state] and fruitful consumption of the country's alms" (SD, 83).

The preacher was then likely to begin a recitation of the *sutta* itself, in Pāli, and to comment on aspects of it himself or to listen while his fellow preacher did so. Thus the audience would have heard the eleven benefits of loving kindness announced by the Buddha:

> there are eleven welcomed benefits of loving kindness—mental liberation—[that are] welcomed [by the practitioner] when it is followed, developed, made much of, practiced, made a foundation, when it is familiar and well undertaken. Which eleven? Sleeping happily, waking happily, not having [lit. seeing] bad dreams, being dear to humans, being dear to nonhumans, being protected by the gods, being unaffected by fire, poison, and sword, the ability to quickly concentrate the mind, a shining facial complexion, death without confusion, prompt rebirth in the *brahma* world [a favorable rebirth] if one does not achieve liberation. . . . [T]hese are the eleven welcomed benefits of loving kindness—mental liberation—which is followed,

developed, made much of, practiced, made a foundation, when it is familiar and well undertaken. (SD, 87)

Wondering just what it meant to practice something in this manner, the audience might have appreciated the *sūtra sannaya*'s repeated analogy to the hard work of farming, as when "practiced" was explained as that "which has been accomplished, as a plough is put down after use" (SD, 87–90). If the listeners also had doubts about just what was meant by mental freedom, they might well have learned the *sūtra sannaya*'s formulation that mental freedom meant freedom from the obstructions to liberation described as enemies: "if the mind which has reached mental liberation is freed from enemies such as the impediments, because of that, because of this loving kindness, the mind is freed from enemies" (SD, 87). If the preacher moved through the list of benefits of meditation on loving kindness with the help of the *sūtra sannaya*'s commentary, the audience would have experienced the contents of the Pāli *sutta* in an increasingly vivid manner. The *sūtra sannaya* contained comments on the benefits of "waking happily" and "not having bad dreams" that were suitable for inclusion in the monk's exposition: "If other people awake unhappily, tossing and constricting [their bodies] and feeling uneasy, [this] person awakes differently, comfortably, without movement, like an opening lotus . . . if [that person] dreams, she or he has appropriate dreams. [In the dream that person] is worshiping devotional memorials or listening to religious instruction. While other beings have nightmares like being thrown down a mountain or being oppressed by beasts of prey or being surrounded by thieves, this person doesn't have such nightmares" (SD, 87). Already intrigued by the idea that the power of meditation was great enough to bring ease even in the vulnerable moments of a night sleep, the audience might have been disposed to hear the preacher elaborate further on the benefits of meditation on loving kindness. Once again, if the preacher drew on his memory of the *sūtra sannaya*, the audience was likely to receive a rather detailed account of these positive outcomes, which included being prized by other humans and nonhumans alike. The benefit of being "dear to nonhumans" was likely to be compelling to an audience full of people who believed themselves to inhabit a world of diverse and powerful supernatural beings, and who already associated *The Discourse on the Benefits of Loving Kindness* with the protective powers of *paritta* recitation.[40] They were likely to hear about the monk Visākha in a form mediated by the Pāli *Visuddhimagga* and/or Saraṇaṃkara's *Sārārthasaṅgrahaya*,

[40] The many protective texts included in the British Library's Nevill Collection shows the complex and often threatening cosmology that informed the experiences of 18th century Lankan Buddhists. See Somadasa (1987).

since the *sūtra sannaya* guided monastic readers to those sources. The *sūtra sannaya* suggested a grand finale for the monastic preacher in its commentary on the benefit of being "unharmed by poison, fire, or sword." A monk who wanted to develop persuasive examples could take up the *sūtra sannaya*'s references to characters described in other texts and describe one or more of those characters: "It is said that fire [doesn't affect] the body of one living according to loving kindness (like the lay woman Uttarāya) or poison [one] like Cūḷasīva, who preached the *Saṃyutta* [*Nikāya*; a section of the Pāli *tipiṭaka*], or sword [one] like the novice Saṃkicca. [These things] don't have an effect, don't enter, don't disturb that person's body" (SD, 88–89). A trained preacher would have been likely to take up at least one of these characters in order to develop his message that meditative practice was appropriate to both monks and laity. He might have ended by connecting the sermon's discussion of proximate benefits of meditation on loving kindness to its ultimate benefits. This might have been accomplished by a return to the *sutta*'s initial theme of mental freedom and the use of loving kindness to reduce the defilements that delay one along the path to liberation.

Preaching from the Sannaya *on* The Discourse on the Standard's Tip

Because *The Discourse on the Standard's Tip* focuses intensely on the superiority of the Buddha's power over the power of the gods included within the Buddhist cosmology, it was a suitable topic for preaching whenever a monk wanted to emphasize the protective power provided by taking refuge in the Buddha and his teachings. At the beginning, the Buddha addresses a company of monks gathered in a monastery in Jeta's grove. He recounts an instance of divine battle in which Sakka, lord of the gods, addressed these gods living in the Tāvatiṃsa heaven saying, "If, sirs, going into battle you feel fearful, or stiffen with dread, or your hair stands on end, then you should look at the top of my battle standard. Whatever hair-raising fear or stiffening with dread you might experience will disappear as you look at the top of my standard" (SD, 109). Since the figure of Sakka would have been familiar to all but the youngest of the listening audience from a host of other stories, and since many of these stories depict Sakka as a sometimes humorous co-conspirator in the Buddha's own progress to liberation and in his attempts to teach others, the audience may well have expected an engaging story. As the preacher continued with the narrative using terms from the *sūtra sannaya* to translate the key elements of the Pāli *sutta*, he was likely to draw on a passage from the Sinhala commentary to intensify the drama of the narrative. In this passage, Sakka and his standard are described from the perspective of his watching subjects:

> The chariot of Sakka, king of the gods, was one hundred and fifty *yojana*s long.[41] From the middle of the chariot to its far end was fifty *yojana*s. From the middle of the chariot to its front was fifty *yojana*s. The [central] box was fifty *yojana*s. Doubling that measurement, they say you come up with three hundred *yojana*s. A white umbrella measuring three *yojana*s was raised up on top. A thousand horses were yoked [to the chariot], and that's not all regarding the rest of the accouterments. Its standard was two hundred and fifty *yojana*s high. When the wind hit the standard, it made a sound like that of the five types of instruments [as if saying], "look at this standard!" To those looking at that chariot, our king arrived and stood in the midst of a retinue like an upright pillar. Fear disappeared [as they thought], "why should we fear?" (SD, 110)

Drawing on this section of the *sūtra sannaya*, the preacher was able to create a vivid image of Sakka's strength, which would have led the audience to believe (perhaps with a certain pleasure derived from knowledge that in Pāli *sutta*s the Buddha always comes out ahead in the end) that Sakka was the main character of their sermon. This sense would have been further reinforced by the *sutta* itself, since Sakka's voice dominates the narrative for a time, with further instructions to his subjects. If the monk followed the *sūtra sannaya* to develop his exposition, he would have recounted Sakka's offer of alternative sources of solace for those who do not (presumably cannot, perhaps because of their vantage point) look at the top of his standard. The symptoms of fear are guaranteed to disappear for those looking at the top of battle standards belonging to Pajāpati, Varuna, and Isana (other gods in the Buddhist cosmology). The preacher would go on to indicate the change of voice in the Pāli *sutta* as the Buddha begins to set the stage for a specifically Buddhist challenge to Sakka's power. Thus the audience would hear the preacher's Sinhala version of the following challenge posed by the Buddha: "If that hair-raising fear, or stiffening with dread which occurs to those looking at the top of the divine king Sakka's standard—or the top of the divine king Pajāpati's standard, or the top of the divine king Varuna's standard, or the top of the divine king Isana's standard—doesn't disappear, what is the reason? Monks, Sakka, lord of the gods, is not without passion, not without hatred, not without delusion. He has fled, afraid, tense, trembling" (SD, 112). If the preacher chose to follow the guidelines of the *sūtra sannaya*, he would then provide the

[41] A *yojana* is equal to approximately seven miles.

audience with a vivid and accessible elaboration of the Buddha's statement, which is set out in the *sūtra sannaya*'s Sinhala commentary:

> the point is: if fear [felt by those looking at Sakka's standard] has been held at bay it doesn't remain so for long if they are looking at the standard of a Sakka who is disposed to flee, shaking, because he has not destroyed the defilements [mental impurities that impede progress toward liberation]. After describing the way Sakka, king of the gods and one of the four divine kings praised here, shook with fear and fled, what more could one say about the other three? Thus, by association with the statement that Sakka, king of the gods, trembled and fled, I have indeed said that the remaining three were disposed to flee, trembling with fear. (SD, 112–113)

The humorous image of powerful gods with celestial trappings fleeing the scene of battle and failing those with faith in them would have been made much of by a talented preacher. It is unlikely that the audience would have reached this point without hearing from the preacher that the defilements that weaken Sakka and his divine companions include passion, hatred, and delusion. The monk's exposition might well have emphasized the idea that if even the gods could be so weakened by their mental defilements, humans would do well to think about the ways that they too were weakened by these three negative mental states. The preacher was then likely to expound on the section of the Pāli *sutta* in which the Buddha goes on to set out an alternative to seeking refuge in Sakka and his companion gods. The *sutta* makes it clear that the battle that really matters is the battle for mental purity, and that devotion to the Buddha will cause all fear in this battle to disappear. At this point, the audience would have ceased to hear the voice of the now-humiliated figure of Sakka, and would begin to hear a popular Buddhist devotional refrain and meditative recollection [Pāli *buddhānusmṛti*] as the monk proclaimed the power of the Buddha's qualities, drawing on the words of the *sutta* presented in the *sūtra sannaya*.

> If, monks, you are fearful, overwhelmed by hair-raising fear when you are in the forest, at the foot of a tree or in an empty building, at that time you should remember me thus: he is fortunate, an *arahant*, perfectly enlightened, endowed with wisdom and virtue, well-gone one, knower of the world, unrivaled, guide of people who must be trained, teacher to gods and men, Buddha, fortunate one. (SD, 113)

The *sūtra sannaya* goes on to give an explanation for each epithet of the Buddha listed in this quotation. Any of these explanations would have been appropriate for the preacher's exposition, but the audience's listening experience would have varied somewhat depending on which portions of the *sūtra sannaya* the preacher chose to emphasize from the following section of the Sinhala commentary. The words taken from the Pāli *sutta* are in bold.

> ***Arahant***, an *arahant*; because he doesn't do improper things in private, because he is worthy of things like the four requisites, because he has destroyed the enemies, the defilements. . . . **well-gone one** [Pāli **sugato**], called *sugato* because of speaking well and having gone well, and because of having gone to *nirvāṇa*, which is termed a good place, and because of having a good journey. . . . **guide of people who must be trained**, because of establishing malleable people in the refuges, moral conduct, etc. and training [them]. **teacher for gods and men**, because he gives instruction in the various appropriate ways with compassion for his world and other [worlds], for gods and men. . . . **fortunate one** [Pāli **bhagavā**], called *bhagavā* because he has destroyed all of the defilements such as passion and because he possesses merit accomplished through the perfections such as generosity and moral conduct. (SD, 113)

Creative etymology takes a central role in the commentary's elucidation of the Buddha's epithets, and would have allowed the preacher to develop a line of analysis that included both complex but sonorous play with language and very straightforward description. Many members of the listening audience would not have understood the word play but would have enjoyed the play of sound. They might also have caught just enough of the sense to understand that the preacher was unpacking the *sutta* in what appeared to be a learned manner. A few highly educated participants in the event might have enjoyed the fact that the preacher's exegesis of *arahant* played on the Pāli word for "private" (*rahas*) as well as the Pāli verb *arahati* (to be worthy of) and the Pāli noun *arī* (enemy). Those members of the audience would also have been able to notice the way the preacher glossed *sugato* with several uses of the root *gam* (to go), for which the past participle is *gato*, here combined with the prefix *su-*, meaning "good." It is likely that the monk's exposition would have taken up at least one of the epithets for elaboration in more accessible terms, still drawing on details included in the *sūtra sannaya* commentary. Thus the entire audience might have heard the joke about Sakka's cowardice turn into a discussion of the Buddha's absence of defilements. The monk could also have expounded on the "good trip" to *nirvāṇa* characteristic of an enlightened person or the fact that a liberated person (*arhant*) is someone who has destroyed the most powerful enemies—the mental defilements that caused Sakka's downfall.

The power of a preaching performance of this *sutta* would have been greatly enhanced because the Buddha's epithets (known as the *iti pi so gathā* or " the verses saying what he [the Buddha] is like") have a long history as a focus for meditation practice and as part of a group of chants suitable for devotional recollection of the Buddha.[42] By at least the eighteenth or early nineteenth century they were also used as a protective verse.[43] At this point in the sermon, because of the familiarity of these verses, the entire audience might have been drawn fully into the preaching event, perhaps reciting the Buddha's epithets to themselves. With this momentum, the audience would have entered the final moments of the sermon as the preacher recounted the Buddha's exhortation to recollect the teaching if they do not recollect him, and to recollect the monastic community if not the teaching. At this point in the *sutta*, in a return to the first frame of the narrative, the Buddha declares that any of these three refuges (the Triple Gem) will vanquish hair-raising fear and paralysis. The audience listening to the Buddha's words on the value of recollecting the Triple Gem would have once again been drawn into the preaching directly, since the Buddha's declaration includes the standard epithets appropriate to each refuge, epithets that were also commonly used in devotional recitation.

> **In the forest, at the base of a tree, in an empty place, monks, recollect the Buddha; your fear would disappear.**
>
> **If you should not recollect the Buddha, best of the world, bull of men, then you should remember the *dhamma*, well taught and leading out [of the cycle of rebirth].**
>
> **If you should not recollect the *dhamma*, well taught and leading out [of the cycle of rebirth], then you should recollect the *saṃgha*, an unrivaled field of merit.** (SD, 116)

The conclusion of the *sūtra sannaya* written for *The Discourse on the Standard's Tip* gave the preacher one last tool with which to further reinforce the contrast between Sakka and the Buddha. The Pāli *sutta*'s section on recollection of the monastic community ends with a summary statement that links the efficacy of recollecting the monastic community to the character of the Buddha by replacing the *sutta*'s initial identification of Sakka's power and that of the other gods with an identification of the Buddha's power and that of the monastic community.

> **Monks, the hair-raising fear or paralysis that arises will disappear for those recollecting the monastic community. Why? The Buddha, monks, an *arahant*, perfectly enlightened, without passion, hatred and delusion, fearless, unparalyzed, courageous didn't flee.** (SD, 115)

The audience might have heard the preacher drawing on the *sūtra sannaya* to emphasize the fact that, in the course of the preaching event,

[42] See, for instance, Vm 7.

[43] Jonathan Walters, personal communication. In personal communication Charles Hallisey has suggested still earlier use.

the Buddha had come to speak as ***sugato***, in Sakka's place (SD, 113). By the end of an exposition based on the *sūtra sannaya*, the monk's listeners would have been left with no uncertainty about the fact that the Buddha had redefined the terms of power, replaced Sakka as refuge and overtaken Sakka's place at the head of his own retinue.

A NEW BUDDHIST TEXTUAL COMMUNITY

The changes in monastic preaching brought about by the use of *sūtra sannaya*s in monastic education had far-reaching effects on the Buddhist community of eighteenth-century Lanka, extending the impact of the Siyam Nikāya's educational institutions beyond a narrow community of educated monastics. Ties between the monks of the Siyam Nikāya and lay Buddhist communities were inevitably strengthened by the presence of trained monastic preachers prepared to devote themselves to the education of local lay Buddhists. At the same time, because these monks were able to preach on the basis of valued texts from the Pāli *tipiṭaka* and to demonstrate their knowledge of commentarial traditions in Pāli and Sinhala, it is likely that they were received by the lay Buddhist community with greater respect than might otherwise have been the case.

In addition, the popularity of the new *sūtra sannaya*s and their simultaneous use in preaching and monastic education helped to create a new Buddhist textual community in Lanka. This community encompassed both the monastic community of the early Siyam Nikāya and the lay community; the two were firmly linked by their shared exposure to textual forms like the *sūtra sannaya*s. Because the *sūtra sannaya*s were used in monastic education and in Buddhist preaching, they drew monks and laity together as participants in a shared "thought world" created by the sounds, stories, images, and interpretive emphases set forth in these commentaries. Members of the new textual community thus shared a textualized point of orientation for action and reflection, even as such action and reflection took diverse forms. In other words, the development of new educational institutions and practices by and for the monks of the early Siyam Nikāya should not be seen as an occurrence that simply widened the gap between lay people and monastics in eighteenth-century Lanka. Indeed, the Siyam Nikāya educational institutions and practices helped to assure that subsequent struggles for institutional and interpretive authority across the Lankan Buddhist community would occur against the backdrop of shared views on textual authority and desirable knowledge.

This new textual community in which lay Buddhists and monastics developed understandings of Buddhist teachings and desirable practice oriented by a shared collection of texts was one that encompassed men and women at all levels of literacy. Since the contents of the *sūtra sannayas* formed the basis for expositions of authoritative teaching accessible to all Buddhists, their experiences of textuality and textual authority differed much less in relation to literacy than one might initially expect. The history of *sūtra sannaya* use in eighteenth-century Siyam Nikāya institutions thus makes it much more difficult to sustain the view that verbal texts were relatively unimportant in educating the majority of Lankan Buddhists about Buddhist teachings. Such a view is articulated clearly by Holt in his discussion of temple wall paintings in the Kandyan Kingdom:

> The selection of themes expressed in these paintings formed a kind of canon of its own, or a visual orthodoxy. By virtue of their very arrangement in temples, they comprised a visual liturgy for a classical Theravāda Buddhist world view. These paintings provided the means by which a visual understanding of Buddhism could be achieved, without the intervention of sermons preached by monks or the authoritativeness of an ancient language (Pali) in largely undistributed hallowed texts that very few (only learned monks) could understand.
>
> The didactic importance of temple wall paintings as a means of propagating a normative religious world view is further underscored when we consider that most Sinhalese Buddhists of the eighteenth century could not read, let alone decipher (when they heard), the Pali verses that comprised sacred literature or were chanted on ritual occasions. It is true that a considerable efflorescence of Pali literature occurred during the reign of Kīrti Śrī, owing to the notable efforts of the venerable monastic scholar, Välivița Saranaṃkara. But the meaning and significance of these religious treatises were limited to a small, albeit important, circle of monastic scholars, especially in the latter part of the nineteenth century. The fact of the matter is that most Sinhalese Buddhists, especially women, in the eighteenth century did not read. And if they did read, they read Sinhala, and probably not Pali. (1996, 94)

Holt's work has rightly been celebrated for its claims that the visual arts were an important didactic medium in Theravādin cultures before the rise of printing and wide-scale literacy. However, when examined with closer attention to the nature of educational practices and patterns of textual transmission in eighteenth-century Lanka, it is clear that these arguments for the primacy of paintings in the development of religious understanding are overstated.

At least in the context of Lankan Buddhist communities during the latter half of the eighteenth century (by which time the Siyam Nikāya educational institutions had become well established and had affected several generations of monastic students), illiterate Buddhists or those only literate in Sinhala were exposed to a substantial amount of text-based religious teaching as it was mediated through oral exposition. Through preaching (and, presumably, through less formal conversation about which we know almost nothing), the contents of texts studied by monks in the Siyam Nikāya educational centers reached a larger Buddhist audience. Many of these texts were made still more accessible by translations or commentaries written in Sinhala. As I have already shown, enough evidence exists to analyze this process quite clearly with respect to the *sūtra sannaya*s. Other textual forms, however, like those collected in monastic handbooks, almost certainly helped to shape understandings of Buddhist devotion, meditation, and ethics shared by monks and laity alike. Although only a small circle of educated elites gained the skills to appreciate the aesthetic subtleties and conceptual distinctions characteristic of texts studied by the more advanced students, a large community shared a foundational access to narratives, injunctions, and didactic images found in genres like the *sūtra sannaya*s. Even when audiences did not understand all the elements of preaching evocative more of confidence than of wisdom, they participated in the larger textual community for which experiences of sermonic form and content were defined by the body of texts studied in the educational institutions of the early Siyam Nikāya. If large numbers of Buddhists appreciated the "visual liturgy" of temple paintings, they could only have done so in the context of an aural-oral memory that helped to constitute didactic expectations, providing the background necessary for the interpretation of rich visual images.[44]

[44] It is not impossible that such visual texts functioned in many ways on the model of royal inscriptions, that is, as public signs of a patron's prestige, merit, and compassion rather than as didactic tools.

CHAPTER SEVEN

"Let Us Serve Wisdom"

THE SIMULTANEOUS formation of the Siyam Nikāya, a systematization of monastic education, and the new centrality accorded to the *sūtra sannaya* commentaries in monastic educational practice made a considerable impact on Lankan Buddhism.[1] The complexity and extent of this impact has until now been doubly hidden: by scholarly treatments of "traditional" Buddhism, and by eighteenth-century Lankan narratives that depict the rise of the Siyam Nikāya within a decline-and-revival framework. Throughout preceding chapters I have attempted to extricate my analysis from this double bind by approaching the Siyam Nikāya's formation from several perspectives simultaneously.

Against the historical backdrop sketched in chapter 2, chapter 3 described the educational system created by and for Siyam Nikāya monastics. There I argued that educational institutions, and the educational practices developed for use within them, created a monastic order oriented by a set of texts and interpretive strategies remarkably standardized for a pre-print context. The same chapter broached questions about the relationship between education and monastic identity, and about the place of monastic learning in a culture characterized by strong links between performance and social prestige. Focusing on the Siyam Nikāya's formative period, I have suggested a variety of answers throughout chapters 4, 5, and 6 by examining a a larger set of interconnected activities that occurred in eighteenth-century Lankan Buddhism. These chapters have argued, for instance, that commentarial practice and the articulation of a new discourse on monasticism both played a role in the construction of monastic lineage; that systematized education shaped collective identity while providing occasions for resistant interpretation; that Buddhist education was critical to public performance and the accumulation of symbolic capital; and that the public activities of monks and kings together created and sustained new expectations with regard to desirable knowledge and devotional activity.

In all cases I have attempted to historicize the composition, transmission, and reception of texts, placing these practices within a broad sphere of meaningful, though not always intentional, action. Although it grants a powerful role to texts as constitutive of identity and guides to

[1] The quotation in the title is from *Mahāmaṅgala Sūtra Sannaya* (Devānanda1894, iv).

conduct, this study offers plentiful reminders that the educational institutions and practices of the early Siyam Nikāya were not hegemonic or totalizing in their impact on Lankan Buddhism. Indeed, as the nineteenth-century history of Lanka shows very clearly, the creation of a new Buddhist textual community during the last two-thirds of the eighteenth century did not inhibit diverse institutional responses to the Siyam Nikāya's hierarchy and administrative system. It is important to note, however, that the eighteenth-century transformation of Lankan Buddhism continued to shape nineteenth-century Buddhist practice, even as emergent monastic orders and debates within the monastic community challenged the authority of Siyam Nikāya monks in many ways.

What I have called the eighteenth-century reformulation or transformation of Lankan Buddhism is evident in two aspects of Buddhist practice. First, as a result of the three interdependent shifts that took place in Lankan Buddhism at this time, lay and monastic understandings of Buddhist discipline and devotion came to be shaped by a new collection of texts whose content was made accessible through reading, preaching, and listening. Second, as a result of their encounters with this new collection of texts, Buddhist attitudes toward textual authority underwent a significant change.

Between the early fourteenth century and the middle of the eighteenth century, ideas from the authoritative Pāli *tipiṭaka* most often reached Lankan Buddhists through two types of texts. The first included poetic works in Pāli, Sanskrit, and Sinhala that drew on ideas found in the *tipiṭaka* for inspiration but were otherwise quite autonomous. The second was compilations of preaching narratives written in Sinhala. These drew on *tipiṭaka* texts and their commentaries largely through processes of interpolation, translation, and paraphrase. Although Pāli *tipiṭaka* texts were clearly preserved during this period, they by no means dominated the direct textual experience of readers and listeners. One might say, taking terms from the Latin literary context, that most audiences between the early fourteenth century and the middle of the eighteenth century encountered only the *res* of the Pāli *tipiṭaka* rather than these texts *verbaliter*. This situation changed substantially as the result of the Siyam Nikāya's rise and the educational practices developed for the order's monks.

Beginning in 1753, in the educational centers discussed in chapter 3, Lankan monks engaged in the systematic and significantly standardized study of Pāli texts. These monks were, as I have shown, intent on the study of Pāli grammar and early commentaries written for texts from the *tipiṭaka*. Moreover, the translation of texts from the *tipiṭaka*, and a few other early and authoritative Pāli texts (like *Milindapañha* and *Visuddhimagga*), into Sinhala became a central task for monastic students.

Through the composition of primary translations in commentarial form as well as through secondary translations, foundational Pāli authorities were made accessible in Pāli and in Sinhala. At the same time, the study of Pāli and the transmission of authoritative Pāli texts became central to the identification of proper, desirable monasticism to a degree unprecedented since the thirteenth century. More urgently than at any time since the Daṁbadeṇi period, monks needed to display their command of Pāli textual traditions. Popular within the Siyam Nikāya's educational institutions, the *sūtra sannaya*s created a new type of access to the Pāli *tipiṭaka* for lay and monastic Buddhists. As a result of their importance in the monastic curriculum of the early Siyam Nikāya, the *sūtra sannaya*s helped to determine the nature of Pāli study throughout the nineteenth century and into the twentieth. For the first time in several centuries, through the *sūtra sannaya*s, texts from the *sutta* division of the Pāli *tipiṭaka* were "authorized . . . as objects of serious study" (Irvine 1994, 15), study that was expected to engage the *sutta*s word for word and to incorporate them into bilingual preaching practices. This attitude to the Pāli *sutta*s—like the other aspects of the Siyam Nikāya's curriculum described in chapter 3—continued to influence monastic education during the subsequent two centuries. And, as a result, it influenced the rise of "Protestant Buddhism" as well.

It is now commonly accepted that the combined forces of colonial administrators, Indologists, and Christian missionaries "constructed" "Buddhism" as an object of discourse and a focus of study in ways that importantly shaped local Asians' understandings of their own religious practices. As Philip Almond puts it in his study of "the British discovery of Buddhism," "what we are witnessing in the period from the later part of the eighteenth century to the beginning of the Victorian period in the latter half of the 1830s is the *creation* of Buddhism. It *becomes* an object, is constituted as such; it takes form as an entity that 'exists' over against the various cultures which can now be perceived as instancing it, manifesting it, in an enormous variety of ways. During the first four decades of the nineteenth century, we see the halting yet progressive emergence of a taxonomic object" (1988, 12, author's emphasis). Moreover, according to Almond, the emergence of Buddhism as a "taxonomic object" went hand-in-hand with a "textual reification of Buddhism." The understanding of Buddhism that emerged from the study of Buddhist texts came to be seen as the true or essential Buddhism: "Defined, classified, and understood as a textual object, its contemporary manifestations were seen in the light of this, as more or less adequate representations, reflections, images of it, but no longer the thing itself" (25).

For those interested in the Theravāda, this textual object was, by the late nineteenth century, composed of a collection of Pāli texts. Of these, the most important were the *tipiṭaka*, Buddhaghosa's *Visuddhimagga*, and the commentaries composed for the *tipiṭaka* during the fifth century of the common era. Such texts were edited and translated, often by scholars associated with the Pali Text Society. The work of Euro-American scholars typically privileged Buddhist "classical" traditions and the "rational" aspects of Buddhism. These ideas were, at times, appropriated by local elites. The result, given additional impetus by the need some Lankan Buddhists felt to respond to and to defend central Buddhist teachings in the face of Protestant missionary activities, was a new orientation within the Lankan Buddhist community (or at least in its elite, urban circles). This new orientation is often identified as "Protestant Buddhism," a term coined by Gananath Obeyesekere (1970).[2] Following Gombrich, Protestant Buddhism may be defined in terms of three characteristics. "It tends to fundamentalism, despising tradition; it claims that Buddhism is 'scientific', 'rational', 'not a religion', etc. and it depends on English concepts, even when expressed in Sinhala. The fundamentalism comes direct from the Protestant missionaries, the claims of rationalism from their opponents, the English cast of thought from both. The fundamentalism also received an impetus from western scholarship, which began to make the Pali texts more accessible" (1988, 195). Although the notion of Protestant Buddhism has greatly enlivened histories of religious identity and practice in nineteenth- and twentieth-century Lanka, it has come to obscure as much as it reveals. Analyses of this new Buddhist orientation have emphasized changes in Lankan Buddhism *in response to* a variety of eighteenth- and nineteenth-century Euro-American forces. They have, however, rarely sought to understand the local conditions that disposed Lankan Buddhists to respond in the ways they did.[3] Here I briefly probe one aspect of Lankan Buddhist responses, focusing on the emergence of what Gombrich calls "fundamentalism": the growing tendency, from the late nineteenth century onward, for Lankan Buddhists to focus their attention on the texts of the Pāli *tipiṭaka* as the repository of essential Buddhist teachings and as the proper focus of religious education. Looking at the history of the *sūtra sannaya*s' use from the time of the early Siyam Nikāya into the nineteenth century, we see that Protestant Buddhist approaches to Buddhist

[2] For a critical account of this term, with special attention to the view of Protestant Christianity on which it draws, see Holt (1990). Another response to arguments for Protestant Buddhism that focuses particularly on questions about continuity and change in monastic educational and lay devotional practices appears in Blackburn (n.d.a).

[3] See Gombrich and Obeyesekere (1988), Obeyesekere (1970) and Prothero (1996). Malalgoda's study (1976) is a striking exception; his detailed discussions of monastic organization and debate help to illuminate local patterns of response.

texts are not primarily the effect of Orientalist textual predilections and bookish Protestantism.

In suggesting this I am in sympathy with, and indebted to, Hallisey's analysis of the relationship between Theravādin attitudes toward texts and the approach to Buddhist texts taken by European Orientalists. Hallisey suggests that Orientalist tendencies to emphasize Pāli texts over those written in local languages were consistent with the way that local-language commentaries and translations were understood in the Lankan Theravāda. Such commentaries and translations consistently drew attention from the moments of composition to earlier moments in the textual tradition, encouraging "their users to approach them as provisional entrées to the 'more authoritative' texts of the Pali canon" (1995, 44). European preoccupations with *tipiṭaka*-focused essences and origins existed in a "productive 'elective affinity' " with Theravādin ideas that most texts composed and preserved were valuable as a means of access to the words and ideas of the Pāli *tipiṭaka* but quite unimportant otherwise (42–43). In other words, European scholars were encouraged to privilege Pāli texts by the approach to Pāli texts found in the Buddhist sources that they studied.

Looked at from the point of view of local Asian responses to Orientalist scholarship, one might develop this point further by suggesting that the Theravādin disposition to understand composition and transmission in terms of access to an older *tipiṭaka* tradition increased the likelihood of a positive local response to the Orientalist fascination with the *tipiṭaka*. Because of this, the "intercultural mimesis" (Hallisey 1995, 33) that characterized the beginnings of Buddhist studies, also shaped later Lankan Buddhist reactions to European scholarship on Buddhism. It disposed local Buddhists to make such scholarly emphases part of their own self-understanding as Buddhist practitioners. The possibilities for this two-stage mimetic process had much to do with the educational activities that characterized the rise of the Siyam Nikāya.

It is striking that when local Buddhist elites in Lanka first began to show signs that they accepted the study of Pāli texts as the cornerstone of proper, "modern" Buddhist practice, many of them made use of the *sūtra sannaya* form to express their "fundamentalism." The history of printed Buddhist texts in the late nineteenth and early twentieth centuries is instructive in this regard. Among the printed Buddhist texts published by local presses, *sūtra sannaya*s were a strong presence. Printing was most often paid for by lay Buddhists, but the editions themselves were typically the work of monastic scholars. This was true not only of the print edition of *Sārārthadīpanī* (1891) that I have used throughout this study, but also of *sūtra sannaya*s for *Mahāparinibbānasutta* (Paññānanda 1887), *Mahāsatipaṭṭhānasutta* (W. D. Appuhāmi and K. Appuhāmi 1883), *Āḷavakasutta* (Kurē 1897; P. Appuhāmi 1926), *Mahā-maṅgalasutta* (Devānanda 1894), *Dhammacakkappavattanasutta* (Silva 1887; Khemānanda and Indajoti 1915), *Mallikovādasutta* (n.d.), *Mahāsamayasutta* (Prērā 1891), and *Saptasūriyodgamanasutta* (A. D. Appuhāmi 1898), for instance. The idea often associated with "Protestant Buddhism" that all Buddhists, lay and monastic, should engage texts from the Pāli *tipiṭaka* on the path to liberation is expressed quite clearly by the layman who paid for publication of a *sūtra sannaya* for *Mahāparinibbānasutta*: "this section of the teaching should be diligently engaged, certainly with reverence and respect, by all of us Buddhists, lay and monastic, through study and memorization" (Paññānanda 1887, i–ii). His perspective was echoed, somewhat more poetically, by the laymen who made possible publication of *Mahāmaṅgalasutta*'s *sūtra sannaya*: "Thus, while everyone reflects on the process of developing our world and Buddhist dispensation, let us all remember with compassion the well-being of gods and men and the end [goal] like someone trying to bring the attainment of *nirvāṇa* within his grasp. At the same time let us take up and study various texts; having illuminated the shade of ignorance, let us serve wisdom" (Devānanda 1894, iv).

Among the earliest local responses to the highly textualized "construction" of Buddhism in Europe and England was the return to the *sūtra sannaya* commentarial genre first popularized by the monks of the early Siyam Nikāya as a means of accessing the authoritative texts of the Theravāda. Thus a textual form popularized by Siyam Nikāya monks was drawn into new types of Buddhist practice characteristic of the late nineteenth and early twentieth centuries. Under the shared control of lay and monastic Buddhists, the *sūtra sannaya*s came to influence the private reading practices of "modern" Lankan Buddhists as well as the public sermons preached by educated monks. As Lankan Buddhists moved from a manuscript culture to print-era textuality, the effects of Siyam Nikāya-style educated monasticism continued. The texts privileged by Siyam Nikāya monastics, and the attitudes toward textual authority shaped by the Siyam Nikāya, remained a force in Lankan Buddhist life long after the formative years of the order on which this study has focused. This was the case despite the facts that the social organization of monasticism became increasingly diverse in nineteenth-century Lanka with the rise of the Amarapura and Ramañña Nikāyas, and that Lankan Buddhism was increasingly cross-cut by caste and class.[4]

Looking at the relationship between events in eighteenth-century

[4] My comments in this regard are necessarily preliminary. It is not clear, for instance, to what extent printed *sūtra sannaya*s used in the southern coastal regions were used in the island's interior, or how widely the texts of each print run were distributed. An analysis of caste and *nikāya* affiliations for lay patrons and monastic editors would be revealing.

Lankan Buddhism and those that took place in the nineteenth and early twentieth centuries thus offers further evidence of the creative relationship between shifting forms of monastic organization, institutionalized education, and textual practices. As I have shown in several ways throughout this study, the rise of the Siyam Nikāya made possible a series of events that led to a redefinition of desirable Buddhist knowledge and to the establishment of new institutional supports for the development and spread of this desirable form of knowledge. Through this congeries of events—some intentional and others not—occurred a decided shift in the way that participation in the Buddhist *sāsana* was understood. The emergence of a new textual community in eighteenth-century Lanka was made possible by these events. In turn, it helped to sustain attention to the texts, languages, and understandings of monasticism that were articulated during the early years of the Siyam Nikāya. Local elites—both lay people and monastics—participated in the "invention of tradition" (Hobsbawm and Ranger 1983) made possible by the Siyam Nikāya's rise. The claims made by *Saṃgharājavata*'s author—our poet from the first pages of this study—were historically quite particular. Rooted in assumptions about language, learning, and desirable monasticism that had begun to crystallize by the 1780s, the poet's images remind us that educational practices were (and are) a central arena in which the "contentious traditions" (Mani 1990) of Lankan monasticism were vaunted, defended, and made manifest.

APPENDIX A

Contents of the Monastic Handbook Attributed to Saraṇaṃkara

TITLES of Pāli works use Sinhala form, in congruence with Sannasgala's usage (1964, 476). Longer descriptions of most of these selections may be found in Somadasa (1987).

Anuśāsanā Vaṭṭōruva: an advisory letter composed by Saraṇaṃkara
Maitribhāvanā Gāthā Saha Ehi Anusas: a set of Pāli verses about meditation on loving kindness plus further instruction
Heraṇasikha Ema Vinisa Hā Ema Gäṭapadaya: a condensation of rules for a novice monk with explanation and a word commentary
Navamahāphala: an account of the fruits of Buddhist practice
Akkodhanena Gāthā Yana Vyākhyānaya: a Sinhala translation of Pāli verses about anger from the *Dhammapada*, with an accompanying Sinhala explanation
Sekhiyāpela Hā Ehi Padārtha: minor rules of good conduct for monks taken from the Pāli *Vinaya*, along with a Sinhala commentary
Catupārisuddhisīlaya = *Satarasaṃvara Sīlaya*: a discussion of four areas in which a monk should attend to the purification of his conduct. These are: Prātimokṣa Saṃvarasīlaya, Indriya Saṃvarasīlaya, Ājīva Saṃvarasīlaya, and Paccaya-sannisita Saṃvarasīlaya
Käli Sannaya: a Sinhala paraphrase of difficult Pāli terms used in the Pāli *Vinaya*'s Kālika sections that discuss the diet, medicines, and so on appropriate to a monk
Dinacariyāva: a Sinhala prose discussion of monks' daily duties compiled from the Pāli *Vinaya*
Sikhakaraṇiya: a Sinhala work based on the Pāli *Vinaya* that prescribes the way to wear robes, beg for alms, eat, and preach
Dhutāṃgaya: a Sinhala discussion of ascetic practices appropriate for monks taken from the Pāli *Visuddhimagga* or *Milindapañha*
Pasvikuṃgāthā Hā Sannaya: Pāli verses on the five impediments to monastic training precepts, plus a commentary in Sinhala
Dasadhammasūtra Hā Sannaya: the Pāli *Dasadhammasutta*—containing topics for monastic reflection—plus a Sinhala commentary
Mulsikha: a Pāli verse summary of the *Vinaya* written in Pāli

Sūtisyodhayingē Vaga: a Pāli extract on the thirty-four forces that destroy *sīla*

Dasasīlaya: forty-eight Pāli verses on the precepts to be observed by a novice monk

Navaguṇa Sannaya: a Sinhala translation of Pāli stanzas used to describe the Buddha, taken from *Visuddhimagga* or *Pūjāvaliya*

Abhidharma Kamaṭahana: a short meditation treatise in Sinhala and Pāli based on sections of the Pāli *Abhidhamma*

Asū Mahā Śrāvakanāma: Pāli verses on the eighty chief followers of the Buddha

Navalokottara Saṃgraha: a Sinhala discussion of a portion of the Pāli *Abhidhamma*

Apara Jinapaṃjaraya: Pāli verses on the virtues of the Triple Gem, used as a *paritta*

Satipaṭṭhāna Sūtraya: a Pāli *sutta* on the foundations of mindfulness

Solospūjā: Pāli verses on different sorts of offerings

Aṣṭa Duṣṭakṣana: an account of the eight terrible periods in which it is impossible to create merit

Saṃghavandanā: Pāli verses of homage to the monastic community

Detiskuṇu Koṭasa: a Sinhala paraphrase of discussions of the perishable and unclean nature of the body, taken from the Pāli *Satipaṭṭhānasutta* and *Visudhimagga*

Bhavavirati Gāthā: twelve verses in Pāli on the uncertainty of movement from one existence to another

Pirita: protective texts in Pāli taken from the *Suttapiṭaka*

Paṭicca Samuppāda: a Pāli discourse on codependent orgination

Satara Kamaṭahana Hā Ehi Sannaya: four forms of meditation discussed in the *Visuddhimagga*, presented through thirty Pāli verses: meditation on the Buddha's virtues, on friendship to all, on the impurity of the body and on the omnipresence of death

Āhara Pratikulaya: a Sinhala discussion of the disgusting nature of food

Kusītavastu: probably a Sinhala account of the grounds for indolence based on the *Kusīta Sutta*

Pañcadharma: a Pāli text from the *Aṅguttara Nikāya* that discusses the five factors involved in a monk abandoning or maintaining a connection to Buddhist teachings and to the *sāsana*

Mittāmitta Jātaka: a Pāli prose and verse account of the benefits of friendship

Jayamaṅgala Gāthā: Pāli verses used as a *paritta*

Damsakpävatumsūtra Sannaya: the Pāli *Dhammacakkappavattanasutta* plus a Sinhala commentary

Bodhi Vandanā: verses in Pāli to honor the trees under which past *buddhas* attained enlightenment

Buddha Vandanā: Pāli verses to honor the Buddha
Vandanā Gāthā: a collection of Pāli devotional verses
Pārājikādi Saṅgraha: a collection of major rules from the Pāli *Vinaya*, explained in Sinhala
Catusampajañña: a text in Sinhala based on the *Vibhaṅgāṭṭhakathā*, which describes the way to perform simple daily tasks in a meditative manner
Prātimokṣa Saṃvaraśīlaya: an exposition on this theme in Sinhala; see Satarasaṃvarasīlaya above
Sārasūtraya: a non-canonical Pāli *sutta* in which body, life, and wealth are described as *asāra*/without value, and the observance of certain monastic disciplines are described as *sāra*/valuable
Saraṇagamana Sūtraya: a part of the Pāli *paritta* collection in which refuge in the Triple Gem is described = *Going for Refuge*
Kaṭhīnadānānumodanā: a Pāli formula for the expression of thanks used when monastic requisites are offered after the rains retreat
Aṣṭapariṣkāradānaya: a Sinhala formula appropriate to the receipt of the eight monastic requisites
Sucidānānumodanā: a Pāli formula of thanks appropriate to the receipt of a pure gift
Kāyabandhanānumodanā: a Pāli formula of thanks appropriate in response to the gift of a waistband for monastic robes
Āvāsadīpagandhadānānumodanā: a Pāli formula of thanks appropriate in response to the gift of lamps and candles to be used in the monastic dwelling place
Yāgaggidānānumodanā: a Pāli formula of thanks appropriate in response to a meritorious gift
Tāmbūladānānumodanā: a Pāli formula of thanks appropriate in response to the gift of betel
Dähäṭi Dānānumodanā: a Pāli formula of thanks appropriate in response to the gift of toothpicks
Chattadānānumodanā: a Pāli formula of thanks appropriate in response to the gift of an umbrella
Dussadānānumodanā: a Pāli formula of thanks appropriate in response to the gift of garments
Parissadānānumodanā: a Pāli formula of thanks appropriate in reponse to the gift of a water strainer
Cīvaradānānumodanā: a Pāli formula of thanks appropriate in response to the gift of outer robes
Pupphadānānumodanā: a Pāli formula of thanks appropriate in response to the gift of flowers
Dasamahāyodhayo: verses in Sinhala on the ten challenges to moral conduct

Pasvisimahabhaya: verses in Sinhala on the twenty-five sources of fear

Dasabodhi: a brief passage on the last ten *bodhisattva* lives of Gotama Buddha

Aṭavisi Budungē Nam Hā Mahābodhi: a Sinhala description of the twenty-eight previous *buddhas* and their trees of enlightenment

Elusilō: One hundred Sinhala verses in praise of the Buddha, composed in the fifteenth century

APPENDIX B

Level Four Subject Areas and Texts

Grammar

Students were expected to read Pāli texts, to compose Sinhala commentaries on them, and to create new prose and verse compositions in Pāli. The ability to compose poetic works in Sinhala, often following Sanskrit poetic conventions, was also prized. In addition, students studied traditional sciences—including astrology and medicine—for which knowledge of Sanskrit was essential. Works on grammar for all three languages were therefore indispensable. Among them, Sannasgala singles out *Bālāvatāra* (a Pāli grammar composed in Lanka during the thirteenth or fourteenth century and indebted to the Pāli grammarian Kaccāyana) as particularly important to Pāli studies, as well as *Padasādhanaya* (a twelfth-century text containing rules of the Moggallāna grammar set out systematically with examples) and *Pāli-Siṃhala Artha Kathana*, a list of five hundred Pāli words glossed with Sinhala equivalents and explanations of verbal roots for verbal forms. Several works by Rājaguru Baṇḍāra also appear to have been important, including *Suthīramukhamaṇḍanaya* (a Sanskrit grammar written in Pāli), plus *Kārakapuppha* (a Sinhala explanation of Pāli grammar) and *Ākhyāta Rūpamālāva* (a work on Pāli verbal conjugation) (Sannasgala 1964, 479–82; Godakumbura 1955, 315–317; Norman 1983, 163–165, Vijayaśirivardhana 1989, 148). For Sinhala, the most important work was Saraṇaṃkara's Sinhala commentary for *Sidatsaṇgarāva*, a thirteenth-century work on grammar influenced by the poetic usage of the day (Godakumbura 1955, 319; Sannasgala 1964, 495). *Amāvatura* and *Butsaraṇa* were also used as guides to proper Sinhala usage (Vijayaśirivardhana 1989, 147).

Poetic Theory and Composition

Model texts for Pāli compositions included *Bodhivaṃsa*, *Hatthavanagalavihāravaṃsa*, *Anāgatavaṃsa*, and Saraṇaṃkara's Pāli *Muniguṇālaṇkāraya*, plus the *Abhisambodhi Alaṃkāra* (Sannasgala 1964, 491–492; Vijayaśirivardhana 1995, 148). Verse compositions in Sinhala were almost always modeled on works composed before the Mahanūvara period, according to Vijayaśirivardhana (1989, 148). In addition, Baṇḍāra's *Vṛttāvatāraya,* a handbook on verse composition written in Sinhala served as a general guide (Sannasgala 1964, 486). An important part of developing skill in poetics was the consultation of works containing vocabulary appropriate for ornate verse composition. Lexicons, or *nighaṇḍu*s, written before and during the eighteenth century were used for this purpose (Vijayaśirivardhana 1989, 148). These typically gave Sinhala synonyms for Sanskrit words, enabling students to compose Sinhala poetry in accordance with Sanskrit conventions. New "treasuries" of words were compiled containing vocabulary in Sinhala and Pāli suitable for poetry (Sannasgala 1964, 497).

Prose Composition

Prose compositions were heavily weighted toward the production of Sinhala commentaries for Pāli texts, of Sinhala compendia based on Pāli prose texts, and of translations for Pāli prose texts. *Visuddhimagga* was an important work for Siyam Nikāya students, as is clear from selections from it or references to it in compendia and commentaries. That Saraṇaṃkara's compendium *Sārārthasaṅgrahaya* was a model text is clear from the compendium called *Saddharmāvavāda,* subsequently composed by his student Buddharakkhita. *Sārārthadīpanī,* a collection of Sinhala commentaries for Pāli *suttas,* served as the model for subsequent *sūtra sannaya* compositions. Other Sinhala commentaries took Poḷonnaruva- and Daṁbadeṇi-period compositions as their model, such as *Dhammapada Sannaya,* a renowned Sinhala commentary on the Pāli *Dhammapada,* composed no later than the thirteenth century.

Protective Techniques and Meditation

In addition to learning Pāli *paritta* texts that could be recited to deter dangerous human and superhuman forces, it is likely that many students studied astrological works and those containing guidelines for making offerings to gods and demons (Sannasgala 1964, 498–501). Sannasgala notes that Sinhala works used at this time for astrology included *Daśāsaṅgrahaya* and a variety of small manuscripts enumerating the lunar mansions (501). The manuscripts collected in the British Library's Nevill Collection indicate the breadth of topics studied as protective techniques. (Somadasa 1995, esp. 106–109). These included divination, the study of physiognomy, and the memorization of words and verses that could be recited in order to control threats to one's wellbeing. There are references to the use of traditional Lankan books that belong to the monastic lineages at Asgiri, Hanguranketa, and Bambaragala Vihārayas (and the latter was a special dwelling place for meditative monks during this period). However, there is little evidence regarding what books these were. At Hanguranketa and Degaldoruvē Vihārayas, books were better protected and include *Vimuktimārgaya* and *Vimuktisaṅgrahaya* plus two books incorporating tantric practices. There is evidence that some books on meditation included medical, *yōga*, and *mantra* texts also to cope with practitioners' problems (Sannasgala 1964, 501).

Medicine

There is ample evidence that in many cultural contexts monks served as repositories of medical knowledge and also as practitioners. That some Siyam Nikāya monks studied medicine is suggested by the proliferation of Sinhala commentaries written for Sanskrit and Pāli medical texts. For instance, Rājaguru Baṇḍāra composed a Sinhala *sannaya* on the Sanskrit medical text *Sārasaṃkṣepa* (Sannasgala 1964, 486). *Sannaya*s were also written for *Śataślokaya* (Sanskrit verses on medical treatment) and the medical treatises called *Bhaiṣajyakalpaya*, *Ariṣṭaśatakaya*, *Yogaśatakaya*, *Guṇa Pāthāya*, *Auṣdhaguṇapāthāya*, and *Vaidyājārā* (498–500). Medical lexicons were also compiled that provided Sinhala synonyms for Sanskrit technical terms (499). A thirteenth-century Pāli treatise on medicine, called *Bhesajjamañjusā*, was given a new Sinhala commentary by Saraṇaṃkara (501).

Visual Arts

Although members of the artisan caste (Sinhala *navandanna*) were not eligible for higher ordination within the Siyam Nikāya because of the order's caste exclusivity, they sometimes took novitiate ordination. Such novice monks are likely to have combined the first stages of a monastic education with an artist's apprenticeship and the study of three Sanskrit texts. These texts—*Rūpāvaliya, Sāriputra*, and *Vaijayantaya*—prescribed the rules for depicting set characters in temple paintings. Novice monk-artists were responsible for some of the paintings done at royal behest in the temples built or restored after 1753, such as Degaldoruvē Vihāraya and Ridī Vihāraya (Gatellier 1991, 55–56).

Pāli Tipiṭaka and Commentaries

Some of the best evidence for the place of Pāli *tipiṭaka* texts and commentaries at level four of the curriculum is the first monastic regulation composed for the Siyam Nikāya and promulgated in 1753, which shows that this aspect of education was heavily indebted to thirteenth-century ideas about proper monastic learning. Although the monastic handbooks used by students at a lower level contained selections or condensations from the Pāli *Vinaya* (often translated or commented upon in Sinhala), more advanced students studied larger parts of the *Vinaya* directly. As part of the preparations made to leave a dependent student-teacher relationship after a minimum of five years (marked by the monastic title *Niśrayamukta*), they were expected to study the monastic rules of discipline for monks and nuns (the *Bhikkhu-* and *Bhikkhunī-pāṭimokkha*) in conjunction with *Kaṅkhāvitaranī* (Buddhaghosa's commentary on the Pāṭimokkha). In order to receive the higher monastic title of *Sthavira*, monks were expected to learn the *Mahā-* and *Cūla-vibhaṅga* sections of the *Vinaya*, as well as its Khandaka-vatta. At this time also, monks were expected to study one of the four *nikāya*s from the *sutta* portion of the *tipiṭaka*. All of these *tipiṭaka* texts were to be studied with commentaries (Ratnapala 1971, 143–145, 288–290). It is likely that these commentaries included early Pāli commentaries and later Sinhala explanations and glosses. The term used for commentaries is *ṭīkā*, which in Sinhala most often means "commentarial texts" rather than "Pāli sub-commentaries." (See Sorata 1970, s.v.) The manuscript data reproduced in Appendix C strongly suggests that most monks were familiar only with sections of the *Suttapiṭaka*, since much of its contents circulated in smaller manuscripts.

APPENDIX C

Siyam Nikāya Temple Manuscript Collections

Saṃgharāja Pansala, Malvatu Vihāraya

The collection of manuscripts held in the Saṃgharāja Pansala of the Malvatu Vihāraya includes works said to have been used by the eponymous Saṃgharāja Saraṇaṃkara and his students. Some of these texts have always been held in the Malvatu Vihāraya, which was one of the key temples for Siyam Nikāya monks. Other texts were previously held at Gaḍaladeṇiyē Saddhamatilaka Rajamahavihāraya, which was also an important educational center. The titles are taken from the handlist of manuscripts held by the incumbent of Saṃgharāja Pansala. For further details see Blackburn (2001).

Aṅguttara Nikāya, Apadāna, Buddhavaṃsaya, Ittivuttaka, Abhidhamma mūla ṭīkā, Abhidānapradīpikā, Kaccāyana Sannaya, Gaḍaladeṇiya Sannaya, Gihi Vinaya, Catubhāṇavāra Pāli, Cariyapiṭaka Aṭṭhakathā, Cullavagga Pāli, Jātaka Aṭṭhakathā Sannaya, Dhātuvaṃsaya, Dīgha Nikāya, Dhammasaṅgani Prakaraṇaya, Vibhaṅga, Kathāvastu, Dhammapradīpikā, Mahakappinarāja Kathā, Pañcikāpradīpiya, Pālimuttakavinayavinicchaya, Parivāra Pāli, Pācittiya Pāli, Pirinivan Hela, Puggalapaññati, Dhātupaṭhā, Bālāvatāraya, Bālāvatārasugaṅdhisāra, Tunliṅgurūpamālāva, Butsaraṇa, Saṃghasaraṇa, Buddhavaṃsa Aṭṭhakathā, Brahmajālasutta Sannaya, Bhesajamañjusā, Majjhima Nikāya Aṭṭhakathā, Madhuraṭṭhapakāsiṇī, Mahāniddesa Pāli, Mahāniddesa Pāli Aṭṭhakathā, Mahāvagga Pāli, Mogalyāyana Vyākarana, Vimānavatthu Aṭṭhakathā, Bimbavannaṇā, Muniguṇālaṅkāraya, Sīmā Vaṇṇanā, Lakdiva Vidiya, Daṁbadeṇi Sannaya, Satipaṭṭhānasutta, Satipaṭṭhāna Sūtra Sannaya, Saptasuriyodgamana Sūtra Sannaya, Samantapāsādikā, Sārārthadīpanī, Sikhavalaṅda, Dhammamātika, Sutta Nipāta, Sulu Umandāva, Sulu Rājavaṃsaya, Daḷadā Pūjāvaliya, Saṃgharājasādhucariyāva, a *Jātaka* collection, *Visuddhimagga Sannaya, Visuddhimagga Pāli, Visuddhimagga ṭīkā, Mahāsatipaṭṭhānasutta, Paṭisambhidā Aṭṭhakathā, Khuddakapāṭhā Aṭṭhakathā, Cariyapiṭaka Pāli, Cariyapiṭaka Aṭṭhakathā, Jātaka Aṭṭhakathā.*

A manuscript library at Pādeniya Rajamahavihāraya was constructed during the reign of Kīrtī Śrī Rājasiṃha, and the temple became a monastic center for monks in the Sat Kōralē district. Once again the titles are taken from the handlist of manuscripts held by the incumbent. See also Blackburn (2001).

Bālāvatāra, *Bālāvatāra Sannaya*, *Dhammapradīpikā*, *Gihi Vinaya*, *Brahmajāla Sūtraya*, *Mahāsatipaṭṭhāna Sūtraya*, *Dhammacakkappavattana Sūtraya*, *Devadā* (*Devadatta*) *Sūtraya*, *Girimānānda Sūtraya*, *Sugāṇḍisāra Gätapada*, *Brahmajāla Sūtra Sannaya*, *Sārārthasaṅgrahaya*, *Śīla Paricchedaya*, *Saṃkhyanāya*, *Dahamsoṅda Kathāvastu*, *Brahmajāla Sūtra Vaṇṇanā*, *Pretakathāvastu*, *Bhikṣu-prātimokṣa Sannaya*, *Todeyya Sūtraya*, *Dhammacakkappavattana Sūtra Sannaya*, *Pañcanivāraṇa Nidesaya*, *Brahmajāla Sūtra Vaṇṇanā*, *Brahmapūjāvaliya*, *Uposatha Sūtra Sannaya*, *Ratnamālicaitya Vaṇṇanā*, *Damsakpävatum* (*Dhammacakkappavattana*) *Sūtra Sannaya*, *Kaṭhinānisaṃsaya*, *Dakkhiṇāvibhaṅga Sūtraya*, *Aggikhandopama Sūtraya*, *Thūpavaṃśaya*, *Abhidānapradīpikā*, *Anāgatavaṃsaya*, *Saddhamopaya*, *Saptasuriyodgamana Sūtraya*, *Dhammapada Sannaya*, *Mahāparinibbānasutta*, *Mahāsupina Jātakaya*, *Abhidharmārtha Kamaṭahana*, *Mulsikha*, *Yōgaratnākaraya*, *Basvana Purāṇabaṇavastuva*, a *paritta* collection, *Saṃyutta Nikāya*, *Saṃskṛtaliṅgavi Saṅgahavargaya*, *Visakhavattīya*, *Pansiyapanasjātaka*, *Khuddhaka Nikāya*, *Dhampiya Aṭuvā*, *Majjhima Nikāya*, *Pūjāvaliya*, *Aṅguttara Nikāya*, *Vinayapiṭaka*, *Moggalāna Sutta*, *Aggikhandopama Sūtraya*, *Kusala Sūtra Desanāva*, *Saccavibhaṅga Sūtraya*, *Kusala Sūtraya*, *Vammika Sūtraya*, *Ātānāṭiya Sūtraya*, *Visuddhimagga Śilanirdeśaya*, *Pātimokkha Sannaya*, *Pāli Nighaṇḍuva*, *Bhikṣu-bhikṣunī-prātimokṣaya*, *Sikhavalaṅdavinisa*, *Abhidharma* manuscript, *Anāgatavaṃsa Desanāva*, *Nighaṇḍu Sannaya*, *Mahasudassana Sūtrārthavyākhyānaya*, *Vinayasaṅgaha*, *Kōsalabimbiya Vaṇṇanā*, *Päraṇivyākarana*, *Raṭṭhapāla Sūtraya*, *Saleyya Sūtraya*, *Vimānavatthu Vaṇṇanā*, *Dhajagga Sūtraya*, *Saleyya Sūtrārthavyākhyānaya*, *Saddhamaratnākāraya*, *Buddhavaṃsaya*, *Bālāvatāravyākhyāva*, *Cūlakammavibhaṅga Sūtraya*, *Hatthavanagalavaṃsaya*, *Subhasutta*, *Cakkavattisīhanāda Sūtraya*, *Saddhammālaṅkāraya*, *Culavaggaya*, *Dhammasaṅgani Prakaraṇaya*, *Vuttodaya*, *Milindapañha Pāli*, *Aṅguttara Nikāyēpañcakanikāya*, *Mahābodhivaṃsaya*, *Mettā Vaṇṇanā*, *Pārājika Pāli*, *Pācittiya* manuscript, *Sīmābhandana Māntraya*, *Buduguṇa Vaṇṇanā*, *Devadūta Sūtraya*, *Aṭṭhasālinī*, *Vinayakamma* manuscript, *Saptabojjhaṅga*, *Sāranaṃveda* manuscript, *Sārārthaviśaveda* manuscript, *Sāravaṅgaveda* manuscript, *Māntra* manuscript, *Butsaraṇa*, *Pādeṇi Vihāra Katikāvata*, *Daḷada Pūjāvaliya*.

Ridī Vihāraya

Ridī Vihāraya was an important temple for Siyam Nikāya monks, since the incumbent of the *vihāraya* also consistently held high office in the Malvatu Vihāraya administrative division of the Siyam Nikāya. The first incumbent during the period with which I am concerned was Saraṇaṃkara's chief student, Tibboṭuvāvē Buddharakkhita. The list of manuscripts is taken from a typed list compiled by the Government Religious Affairs Department and now held securely at Ridī Vihāraya. For further details see Blackburn (2001).

Abhidhamma, Abhidharmārthasaṅgrahaya, Abhidāna Sannaya, Anāgatavaṃsaya, Aṅguttara Nikāya Aṭṭhakathā, Umandava, Brahmasīrinighaṇḍuva, Kurudharmajātakaya, Kaccāyana, Cullaniddesa, Cariyapiṭakaya, a *Jātaka* collection, *Thūpavaṃsa* (*Pāli*), *Dhammacakkappavattanasutta, Dakṣiṇāvibhaṅgasutta, Dīgha Nikāya, Dhamma Upasaṅgrahaya, Dhammasaṇgani Prakāsaṇaya, Dhammapradīpikāva, Parabhāvasutta, Paṭiccasamuppādasutta, Pāṭimokkha, Dasuttarasutta, Pālimuttaka-vinayavinicchaya, Pāli Nighaṇḍuva, Pāli Vyākarana,* a *paritta* collection, *Pūjāvaliya, Petavatthu, Bālāvatāra ṭīkā, Bālāvatāra, Butsaraṇa, Buddhavaṃsaya, Anāgatavaṃsaya, Brahmajālasutta, Manorathapūranī, Prapañcasūdanī, Rasavāhinī, Vammikasutta, Vinayasaṅgraha ṭīkā, Kaṅkhavitāranī,* (*Vinaya*) *Sārārthadīpanī, Satipaṭṭhānasutta, Satipaṭṭhāna Sūtra Sannaya,* an abbreviated grammar, *Saṃyutta Nikāya* (partial), *Saṃghasaraṇa, Saddhammaratnāvaliya, Saddhamālaṅkāraya, Sumaṅgalavilāsanī.*

Mulkirigala Rajamahavihāraya

Mulkirigala Rajamahavihāraya in Rūhunu was the center of monastic education in the maritimes during this period and became the home monastery of an influential lineage within the Siyam Nikāya. The list of manuscripts is taken from the catalogue made by Somadasa on the basis of temple visits and questionaires. See Somadasa (1959/1964).

Aggikkhandopamasutta, Aṅguttara Nikāya, Anguttara Nikāya Aṭṭhakathā, Angulimāla Sūtra Sannaya, Anāgatavaṃsa (Sinhala), *Abhidhammāṭṭhasaṅgaha Sannaya, Abhidānapradīpikā Sannaya/Niggaṇḍu Sannaya, Amarakośa, Āḷavaka Sūtra Sannaya, Āsīvisopamasutta, Itivuttaka Aṭṭhakathā/Paramātthadīpanī, Udāna, Upāsakajanālaṅkarāya* (Sinhala), *Uposathasutta, Elū Attanagalu Vaṃsaya, Elū Umandava, Ekkhara Kosa* (Pāli), *Kaccāyana Sannaya, Kaṭhīnānisaṃsaya, Kathāvatthu/Kathāvatthuppakaraṇa, Kavmini Koňḍola, Kasībhāradvāja Sūtra Sannaya, Kālakārāma Sutta Sannaya, Kurudharma Jātakaya, Khuddaka Nikāya Aṭṭhakathā, Khuddasikkhā, Khuddasikkhā ṭīkā, Girā Sandeśaya, Girimānanda Sūtra Sannaya, Catubhāṇavāra Pāli, Cariyapiṭaka, Cundovāda Sūtra Sannaya, Cullaniddesa* (Pāli), *Cullavaṃsaya* (Sinhala), *Cullavagga* (Pāli), *Cūlahatthipadopama Sūtra Sannaya, Jātaka Aṭṭhakathā, Pansiyapanasjātakā, Tissamahavehera Dhātukathāva, Theragāthā, Theragāthā Aṭṭhakathā, Therīgāthā Aṭṭhakathā, Dakkhiṇāvibhaṅga Sūtra Sannaya, Dantakuṭumbika Kathāva, Dahaṃ Saraṇa, Dahamsoňḍa Vata, Dāṭhāvaṃsaya Sannaya, Dīgha Nikāya, Dīgha*

Nikāya Aṭṭhakathā, Dūta Jātakaya, Devadūta Sutta Pada-äṇuma, Devadūta Sūtra Sannaya, Dhammacakkappavattana Sūtra Sannaya, Dhammapāda, Dhammapāda Aṭṭhakathā, Dhammapāda Vaṇṇanā, Dhammapāda Sannaya, Dharmapradīpikāva, Dhātu Kathāppakaraṇa, Nagaravindeyya Sutta, Navagraha Śāntiya, Nāmapadamālā, Nītibandhana Sannaya/Kulavādaya, Paṭisambhidāmagga, Paṭṭhāna Pāli/Paṭṭhānapakaraṇa, Pada Sādhana, Pada Sādhana Sannaya, Parivāra Pāli, Pācittiya Pāli, Pātimokkha Aṭṭhakathā, Pātimokkha Sannaya, Pārājikā Pāli, Pālimuttaka Vinayavinicchaya Saṇgaha, Puggalapaññatippakaraṇa, Pūjāvaliya, Bālapaṇḍita Sūtra Sannaya, Lakkhaṇa Sutta, Bālāvatāraya, Bālāvatāra Gaḍaladeṇi Sannaya, Buddhavaṃsaya (Pāli), *Buddhavaṃsa Aṭṭhakathā, Bodhivaṃsa/Mahābodhivaṃsa, Bodhivaṃsaya* (Sinhala), *Bodhivaṃsa Parikathā, Bodhivaṃsa Sannaya, Brahmajāla Sutta, Brahmajāla Sūtra Sannaya, Brahmāyu Sūtra Sannaya, Makhādeva Jātakaya, Maṅgala Sutta Aṭṭhakathā, Majjhima Nikāya, Majjhima Nikāya Aṭṭhakathā, Mahāvaṃsa* (Pāli), *Mahāvaṃsaya* (Sinhala), *Mahāvagga Pāli, Mahāsudassana Sutta, Mādhava Nidana, Milindapraśnaya* (Sinhala), *Moggallāyana Pancikā Pradīpaya, Moggallāyana Sannaya, Yōgadāraṇaya, Yōgaratnākaraya, Yōga Śatakaya, Yōga Sāraya, Raṭṭhapāla Sūtra Sannaya, Rasavāhinī, Rūpamāla, Rōga Lakṣaṇa, Vaṭṭōruveda Pota, Varayoga Sāraya, Vinayavinicchaya, Vibhaṅgappakaraṇa, Vimānavatthuppakaraṇa Aṭṭhakathā, Visuddhimagga, Visuddhimagga Mahasannaya, Vessantara Jātakaya* (Sinhala), *Śrī Saddharmāvavāda Saṅgrahaya, Saṃyutta Nikāya, Saṃyutta Nikāya Aṭṭhakathā, Satipaṭṭhāna Sutta, Satipaṭṭhāna Sūtra Sannaya, Saptasuriyodgamana Sutta, Sattasuriyuggamana Sūtra Sannaya, Saddharmaratnākaraya, Saddharmaratnāvaliya, Samantapāsādikā, Samantapāsādikā Navaṭīkā, Sarasavati Nighaṇḍu, Sādhucaritodaya, Sāra Saṃkṣepa, Sārārtha Saṅgrahaya, Säḷa Lihiṇi Sandeśaya, Sigalovāda Sutta, Sigalovāda Sūtra Sannaya, Siddhausadha Nighaṇḍu Sannaya, Sīla Paricchedaya, Sutta Nipāta Aṭṭhakathā, Sutta Nipāta Sannaya, Subha Sūtra Sannaya.*

APPENDIX D

List of Manuscripts Brought from Siam in 1756

LISTED IN Vijayavardhana and Mīgaskumbura 1993, 100–102.[1]

Sumaṅgalavilāsinī Aṭṭhakathāsuttapiṭaka, Paṭhama Samantapāsādikādi Pañca Vinayaṭṭhakathā, Moggalānapakaraṇa, Aṭṭhakathāvinayasaṭīkā, Vimativinodanī, Rūpasiddhi, Bālappabodhisaṭīkā, Bālāvatārasaṭīkā, Saddasārasaṭīkā, Saddabindupakaraṇa, Kaccāyanapakaraṇa, Sampiṇḍamahānidānapakaraṇa, Vimānavatthupakaraṇa, Petavatthupakaraṇa, Cakkavāḷadīpanīpakaraṇa, Sotabbamālinīpakaraṇa, Soḷaskīmahānidāna, Lokadīpaka, Lokavināsa, Jambūpati Sutta, Theragāthā-Therīgāthā-pakaraṇa, Anuṭīkāsaṃgahapakaraṇa, Mahāvaṃsapakaraṇa, Majjhima Nikāya Pakaraṇa Papañcasūdanī, Aṅguttara Nikāya-Manorathapūraṇī, Sammohavinodanī, Vajirabuddhi-Ṭīkāpakaraṇa, Nettipakaraṇa, Cūlavagga, Mahāvagga, Parivāra, Aṭṭhakathāmātikāpakaraṇa, Vinayavinicchaya, Ṭīkāsaṅgaha, Vibhaṅgapakaraṇa, Anuṭīkāsaṅgaha, Dhutaṅga, Kaṅkhāvitaraṇī, Pañcappakaraṇa-aṭṭhakathā-Paramatthadīpanī, Sīlakhandhavagga, Mahāvagga, Pātika ṭīkā, Paramatthavinicchaya, Saccasaṃkhepa, Paramatthappakāsinīsaṃkhepa, Ṭīkāsaṃkhepa, Paramatthamañjūsāṭīkā-Visuddhimagga, Ṭīkāparamatthavinicchaya, Ṭīkākhuddakasikkhā, Aṭṭhakathātheragāthā, Sāratthajālinī, Ṭīkāpetavatthu, Ṭīkāsuttanipāta, Ṭīkācariyāpiṭaka, Ṭīkānettipakaraṇa, Ṭīkā-aṭṭhakathāpaṭisambhidāmagga, Ṭīkā-itivuttaka, Aṭṭhakathācūḷaniddesa, Pālibuddhavaṃsa, Ṭīkābuddhavaṃsa, Pāli-anāgatavaṃsa, Ṭīkā-anāgatavaṃsa, Ṭīkāmilindapañha, Ṭīkāmadhurasavāhinī, Ṭīkāvinayavinicchaya, Yamakapakaraṇa, Buddhasihiṅganidāna aṭṭhakathā-udāna, aṭṭhakathā-anāgatavaṃsa.

[1]For a discussion of these texts see von Hinüber (1988).

Glossary

adigār one of two chief administrative officers of the Kandyan Kingdom

anunāyaka deputy supreme chief monk, a position in the monastic hierarchy created in 1753

Anuśāsanā Vaṭṭōruva early letter of monastic instruction by Saraṇaṃkara

āsana deke baṇa "two-seated preaching"; a style of preaching in which two monks participate, using Pāli and Sinhala

aṣṭaka verses of eight syllables, a prestigious poetic form used for poems of praise and protection

baṇa pot also *baṇa daham pot* (sing. *pota*); monastic handbooks

Butsaraṇa the title of a thirteenth-century text that elaborates the life and virtues of the Buddha

Cūlavaṃsa the later sections of the *Mahāvaṃsa*, a royal-monastic history composed in Pāli in serial form and including eighteenth century chapters authored by Tibboṭuvāvē Buddharakkhita

dhamma Buddhist teachings

dhūtāṅga ascetic practice that may be adopted as part of intense meditation

dinacariyāva an account of the daily duties appropriate to a monk

disāva administrator of outlying regions of the Kandyan Kingdom

gaṇinnānse the term applied to eighteenth-century members of the monastic community who did not receive novitiate and higher ordination, sometimes used to describe novice monks in the absence of higher ordination rituals

ganthadhura (Sinhala *granthadhura*) the responsibility to study and preserve texts

katikāvata monastic regulations promulgated by kings with the support of monastic leaders

mahānāyaka supreme chief monk, a position in the monastic hierarchy created in 1753

mahāthera senior monk or monastic elder of twenty years' standing in the community

Mahāvaṃsa a fifth-century royal-monastic history composed in Pāli and continued in serial form (see also *Cūlavaṃsa*)

māra/Māra non-human figure associated with death and the attempt to distract *buddha*s on the path to enlightenment

Milindapañha authoritative non-*tipiṭaka* text composed in Pāli between the second century B.C.E. and the fifth century C.E., and translated into Sinhala as *Siṃhala Milindapraśnaya* in the eighteenth century

mūla fraternity of monks, led by a *mahāthera*

nāyaka monastic honorific, used for district chief monks in the monastic hierarchy created in 1753

nibbāna (Sanskrit *nirvāṇa*) ultimate goal of Buddhist practice

nidāna kathā introductory story used especially for *sutta* and *jātaka* texts

nikāya "group, collection"; collection of *sutta* texts from the Pāli *tipiṭaka*, or a group of monasteries under single leadership

Nikāyasaṅgraha a fourteenth-century historical text detailing events related to the success and decline of Buddhist teachings

nirutti (Sanskrit *nirukti*) etymological interpretation

nirvāṇa see *nibbāna*

nissaya "support, foundation"; the period in which a monastic student is dependent on his preceptor, usually five years after higher ordination

Niyamakanda a monastic educational center near the city of Kandy, founded in the mid-eighteenth century for students associated with Välivița Saraṇaṃkara

paritta protective texts from the *tipiṭaka*

pariyatti learning, one of the three aspects of the *sāsana*

paṭipatti conduct or practice, one of the three aspects of the *sāsana*

paṭivedha realization or attainment, one of the three aspects of the *sāsana*

raṭērāla an administrator in charge of one of the districts closest to the royal capital in Kandy

Rājaguru Baṇḍāra an erudite eighteenth-century monk who became a layman but who served as royal tutor to the Kandyan court and composed texts important to the Siyam Nikāya's curriculum

samaṇa renouncer

sāmaṇera piriveṇa educational center for novice monks

saṃgha Buddhist monastic community

saṃgharāja leader of the Buddhist monastic community, highest position in the monastic hierarchy created in 1753

Saṃgharājasādhucariyāva prose biography of Välivița Saraṇaṃkara, composed in the late eighteenth century

Saṃgharājavata verse biography of Välivița Saraṇaṃkara, composed in the late eighteenth century

sannasa official deeds or grants regarding land or land-based resources *sannaya* commentary composed in Sinhala for works originally written in Pāli or Sanskrit

Sārārthadīpanī model *sūtra sannaya* composed by Välivița Saraṇaṃkara in the mid-eighteenth century

sāsana Buddhist teachings and the institutions that sustain them

śāstra technical learning, such as grammar, prosody, medical science, and astrology

śataka Sanskrit poem one hundred verses long

śataka pot books containing collections of *śataka*s

sekhiyāva minor rules for monastic conduct

sīla virtue

Silvat Samāgama a group of peripatetic monastic teachers and students formed around Välivița Saraṇaṃkara

śloka Sanskrit couplet

sūtra sannaya commentary written in Sinhala for Pāli *sutta*s

sutta discourse attributed to the Buddha and contained in the *sutta piṭaka* section of the Pāli *tipiṭaka*

thera senior monk or monastic elder of ten years' standing in the community

Theravāda tradition of Buddhism followed in Sri Lanka and large parts of Southeast Asia

tipiṭaka "three baskets"; the authoritative Pāli texts of the Theravāda

upasaṃgharāja deputy leader of the monastic community, the second highest position in the monastic hierarchy created in 1753

upasampadā higher ordination ritual for monastics

vaṃsa lineage text or chronicle

vihārādhipati abbot or incumbent of a Buddhist temple

vihāraya (Pāli *vihāra)* a temple with monastic residences

Vimānavatthu collection of Pāli stories about meritorious Buddhists, translated into Sinhala in the eighteenth century as *Vimānavastuprakaraṇaya*

Vinaya monastic disciplinary rules contained in the *tipiṭaka*

vipasanādhura (Sinhala *vidarśanādhura*) the responsibility to meditate

Visuddhimagga normative compendium of Buddhist teachings complied in the fifth century C.E.

References

Adikaram, E. W. 1946. *Early History of Buddhism in Ceylon.* Migoda, Sri Lanka: D. S. Puswella.

Adikāri, Abhayaratna. 1991. *Śrī Laṃkāvē Sambhāvya Adhyāpanaya Saha Mahasagana.* Colombo: S. Godhagē saha Sahōdarayō.

Ahearn, Laura M. Forthcoming. *Invitations to Love: Literacy, Love Letters, and Social Change in Nepal.* Ann Arbor: University of Michigan Press.

Allon, Mark. 1997. *Style and Function.* Studia Philologica, Buddhica Monograph Series 12. Tokyo: International Institute for Buddhist Studies of the International College for Advanced Buddhist Studies.

Almond, Philip C. 1988. *The British Discovery of Buddhism.* Cambridge: Cambridge University Press.

Amaramoli, Vēragodha, ed. 1956. *Śrī Saddharmāvavāda Saṃgrahaya.* Colombo: Sīmāsahita Ratnākara Mudraṇālaya.

Amaravaṃśa, Akuraṭiyē. 1995. "Välivița Saṃgharāja Māhimiyangēn Dakuṇu Paḷātaṭa Sidu vū Dharma Śāstriya hā Sāsanika Sēvāva." In *Välivița Saraṇaṃkara Saṃgharāja Praṇāmaya,* edited by Kandhakkulamē Dharmakīrti and Tārūlē Dhammaratana. Colombo: Madhyama Saṃskṛtika Aramudala.

Ānānda Maitreya, Baḷangoḍa. 1996. *Budubava Patana.* Dehivela, Sri Lanka: Srīdevī Printers.

Anderson, Benedict. 1991. *Imagined Communities.* London: Verso.

Appuhāmi, A. D. 1898. *Saptasūriyodgamana Sūtraya.* Peliyagoḍa, Sri Lanka: Sevyaśrī Yantrālaya.

Appuhāmi, Pēdrikkurē, pub. 1926. *Āḷavaka Sūtraya.* Colombo: Sudarśana Yantrālaya.

Appuhāmi, W.D.L. and K.E.J. Prērā Appuhāmi, pub. 1883. *Mahāsatipaṭṭhāna Sūtraya.* Colombo: Śāstrāloka Yantrālaya.

Arasaratnam, S. 1996. *Ceylon and the Dutch.* Adershot, Great Britain: Variorum.

Aung Thwin, Michael. 1979. "The Role of *Sasana* Reform in Burmese History." *Journal of Asian Studies* 38.4:671–688.

———. 1985. *Pagan.* Honolulu: University of Hawai'i Press.

Basso, Keith. 1974. "The Ethnography of Writing." In *Explorations in the Ethnography of Speaking,* edited by Richard Bauman and Joel Sherzer. Cambridge: Cambridge University Press.

Bechert, Heinz, ed. 1969. *Singhalesische Handschriften, Part 1.* Wiesbaden: Franz Steiner Verlag.

———. 1977. "Mahāyāna Literature in Sri Lanka: The Early Phase." In *Prajñāpāramitā and Related Systems. Studies in Honour of Edward Conze,* edited by L. Lancaster. Berkeley and Los Angeles: University of California Press.

———. 1988. *Buddhismus, Staat und Gesellschaft in den Ländern Theravāda-*

Buddhismus. 3 vols. Göttingen: Seminars für Indologie und Buddhismuskunde der Universität Göttingen.
———. 1991. *The Dating of the Historical Buddha*. Göttingen: Vandenhoeck and Ruprecht.
———, ed. 1997. *Singhalesische Handschriften*. Part 2. Stuttgart: Franz Steiner Verlag.
Bizot, François. 1976. *Le figuier à cinq branches*. Paris: École Française d'Extrême-Orient.
Blackburn, Anne M. 1996. "The Play of the Teaching in the Life of the *Sāsana*." Ph.D. dissertation, University of Chicago.
———. 1999a. "Looking for the Vinaya: Monastic Discipline in the Practical Canons of the Theravāda." *Journal of the International Association of Buddhist Studies* 22.2:281–309.
———. 1999b. Magic in the Monastery. *History of Religions* 38.4:354–372.
———. 2001. "Notes on Sri Lankan Temple Manuscript Collections." *Journal of the Pali Text Society* 27.
———. n.d.a. "Crossing the Watershed: Buddhist Education, Devotion, and Communities in Nineteenth-Century Sri Lanka." Under review.
———. n.d.b. "Localizing Lineage: Importing Higher Ordination in Theravādin South and Southeast Asia." Under review.
Bond, George D. 1982. *The Word of the Buddha*. Colombo: M. D. Gunasena.
Boyarin, Jonathan, ed. 1993. *The Ethnography of Reading*. Berkeley and Los Angeles: University of California Press.
Breckenridge, Carol, and Peter van der Veer, eds. 1993. *Orientalism and the Postcolonial Predicament*. Philadelphia: University of Pennsylvania Press.
Buddhadatta, Polvattē. 1950. *Samīpātītayehi Bauddhācāryayō*. Koṭahena: Koṭahēne Sāhitya Yantrālaya.
Bynum, Caroline Walker. 1992. *Fragmentation and Redemption*. New York: Zone Books.
Cantor, Norman. 1973. *The Meaning of the Middle Ages*. Boston: Allyn and Bacon.
Carrithers, Michael. 1979a. "The Modern Ascetics of Lanka and the Pattern of Change in Buddhism." *Man* (n.s.) 14:294–310.
———. 1979b. "The Social Organization of the Sinhalese Sangha in an Historical Perspective." In *Contributions to South Asian Studies,* edited by Gopal Krishna. Delhi: Oxford University Press.
———. 1983a. *The Forest Monks of Sri Lanka*. London: Oxford University Press.
———. 1983b. *The Buddha*. London: Oxford University Press.
Carruthers, Mary. 1990. *The Book of Memory*. Cambridge: Cambridge University Press.
Carter, John Ross. 1978. *Dhamma*. Tokyo: Hokuseido Press.
Chutiwongs, Nandana, et al. 1990. *Paintings of Sri Lanka, Padeniya*. Colombo: Centenary Publications.
Clanchy, Michael. 1979. *From Memory to Written Record*. Cambridge: Harvard University Press.
———. 1983. Review of *The Implications of Literacy* by Brian Stock. *Canadian Journal of History* 18.3:403–404.

Codrington, H. W. 1945. "A Letter from the Court of Siam, 1756." *Journal of the Ceylon Branch of the Royal Asiatic Society* 36.99:97–99.

Coedès. G. 1915. "Note sur les ouvrages palis composés en pays thai." *Bulletin de l'École Française d'Extrême-Orient.* 15.3:39–46.

Cohn, Bernard S. 1996. "The Command of Language and the Language of Command." In *Colonialism and Its Forms of Knowledge.* Princeton: Princeton University Press.

Collins, Steven. 1990. "On the Very Idea of the Pali Canon." *Journal of the Pali Text Society* 15:89–126.

———. 1992a. "Notes on Some Oral Aspects of Pali Literature." *Indo-Iranian Journal* 35.2–3:121–135.

———. 1992b. *Selfless Persons.* Cambridge: Cambridge University Press.

———. 1998. *Nirvana and Other Buddhist Felicities.* Cambridge: Cambridge University Press.

———. n.d. *Pali Literature.* Manuscript.

Coomaraswamy, Ananda. 1956. *Medieval Sinhalese Art.* New York: Pantheon Books.

Copeland, Rita. 1991. *Rhetoric, Hermeneutics, and Translation in the Middle Ages.* Cambridge: Cambridge University Press.

Copleston, Reginald Stephen. 1984. *Buddhism Primitive and Present in Magadha and in Ceylon.* 2nd ed. New Delhi: Asian Educational Services.

Cūlavaṃsa. See *Mahāvaṃsa.*

Dagenais, John. 1994. *The Ethics of Reading in Manuscript Culture.* Princeton: Princeton University Press.

Davis, Richard. 1997. *Lives of Indian Images.* Princeton: Princeton University Press.

d'Avray, D. L. 1985. *The Preaching of the Friars.* Oxford: Clarendon Press.

de Certeau, Michel. 1984. *The Practice of Everyday Life.* Translated by Steven Randall. Berkeley and Los Angeles: University of California Press.

de Silva, C. R. 1992. *Sri Lanka: A History.* New Delhi: Vikas.

de Silva, K. M. 1981. *A History of Sri Lanka.* Delhi: Oxford University Press.

de Silva, Lily. 1983. *Paritta.* Colombo: Department of Government Printing.

Devānanda, Hōkandara, ed. 1894. *Mahāmaṅgala Sūtraya.* Colombo: Laṅkābhinava Visṛtayantrālaya.

Dewaraja, Lorna. 1988. *The Kandyan Kingdom of Sri Lanka 1707–1782.* Colombo: Lake House.

———. 1994. *The Muslims of Sri Lanka.* Colombo: Lanka Islamic Foundation.

Dhammānanda, Nāvullē, ed. 1969. *Madhyama Laṅkā Purāvṛtta.* Colombo: M. D. Gunasena.

Dhammaratana, Kirindigallē. 1995. "Välivița Saṃgharāja Māhimiyan nisā vū Adhyāpanaya (Siṃhala, Pāli hā Dharma Grantha)." In *Välivița Saraṇaṃkara Saṃgharāja Praṇāmaya,* edited by Kandhakkulamē Dharmakīrti and Tärūlē Dhammaratana. Colombo: Madhyama Saṃskṛtika Aramudala.

Dhammarakkhita, Kulugamana. 1995. "The Revival of Buddhism under Velivita Saranankara Sangharaja." In *Välivița Saraṇaṃkara Saṃgharāja Praṇāmaya,* edited by Kandhakkulamē Dharmakīrti and Tärūlē Dhammaratana. Colombo: Madhyama Saṃskṛtika Aramudala.

Dhammatilaka, Obēgoḍa. 1995. "Välivița Saraṇaṃkara Samgharāja Māhimiyangēn Ūva Vellassē Pätira Giya Sanga Parapura hā Dharma Śāstrālōkaya." In *Välivița Saraṇaṃkara Saṃgharāja Praṇāmaya*, edited by Kandhakulamē Dharmakīrti and Tärūlē Dhammaratana. Colombo: Madhyama Saṃskṛtika Aramudala.

Dharmadasa, K.N.O. 1976. "The Sinhala-Buddhist Identity and the Nayakkar Dynasty in the Politics of the Kandyan Kingdom, 1739–1815." *Ceylon Journal of Historical and Social Studies* n.s. 6.1:1–23.

———. 1991. "The Gaṇinnānsē: A Peculiar Development of the Sangha in Eighteenth Century Sri Lanka." In *Studies in Buddhism and Culture in Honour of Professor Dr. Egaku Mayeda on His Sixty-fifth Birthday*. Tokyo: Sankibo Busshorin.

Dharmakīrti, Kandhakkulamē, and Tärūlē Dhammaratana, eds. 1995. *Välivița Saraṇaṃkara Saṃgharāja Praṇāmaya.* Colombo: Madhyama Saṃskṛtika Aramudala.

Duncan, James S. 1990. *The City as Text.* Cambridge: Cambridge University Press.

Ebersole, Gary L. 1989. *Ritual Poetry and the Politics of Death in Early Japan.* Princeton: Princeton University Press.

Eco, Umberto. 1979. *The Role of the Reader.* Bloomington: Indiana University Press.

———. 1990. *The Limits of Interpretation.* Bloomington: Indiana University Press.

———. 1994. *Six Walks in the Fictional Woods.* Cambridge: Harvard University Press.

Epigraphia Zeylanica [EZ]. 1904. Colombo: Department of Government Printing.

Fabian, Johannes. 1993. "Keep Listening: Ethnography and Reading." In *The Ethnography of Reading*, edited by Jonathan Boyarin. Berkeley and Los Angeles: University of California Press.

Fernando, P.E.E. 1959. "An Account of the Kandyan Mission Sent to Siam in 1750." *Ceylon Journal of Historical and Social Studies* 21.1:37–83.

Fish, Stanley. 1980. *Is There a Text in This Class?* Cambridge: Harvard University Press.

Gatellier, Marie. 1991. *Peintures murales du Sri Lanka: École kandyenne, XVIIIe-XIXe siècles.* 2 volumes. Paris: École Française d'Extrême-Orient.

Geertz, Clifford. 1971. *Islam Observed.* Chicago: University of Chicago Press.

Godakumbura, C. E. 1955. *Sinhalese Literature.* Colombo: Colombo Apothecaries' Company.

———. 1966. "Relations between Burma and Ceylon." *Journal of the Burmese Research Society* 49.2:145–162.

———. 1980. *Catalogue of Ceylonese Manuscripts.* Copenhagen: Royal Library.

Gombrich, Richard. 1971. *Precept and Practice.* Oxford: Clarendon Press.

———. 1988. *Theravada Buddhism.* Routledge and Kegan Paul.

Gombrich, Richard, and Gananath Obeyesekere. 1988. *Buddhism Transformed.* Princeton: Princeton University Press.

Gomez, Luis. 1989. "Buddhism in India." In *Buddhism and Asian History*, edited by Joseph M. Kitagawa and Mark D. Cummings. New York: Macmillan.

Goody, J., ed. 1968. *Literacy in Traditional Societies.* Cambridge: Cambridge University Press.

Goody, J. 1977. *The Domestication of the Savage Mind.* Cambridge: Cambridge University Press.

Goonewardena, K. W. 1958. *The Foundation of Dutch Power in Ceylon 1638–1658.* Amsterdam: Djambatan.

———. 1980. "Ayutthia in the Twilight Years and Its Triangular Relations with the V.O.C. and Sri Lanka." *Sri Lanka Journal of the Humanities* 6.1–2:1–47.

———. 1986. "Muslims under Dutch Rule up to the Mid-eighteenth Century." In *Muslims of Sri Lanka*, edited by M.A.M. Shukri. Beruwala, Sri Lanka: Jamiah Naleemia Institute.

Graham, William A. 1987. *Beyond the Written Word.* Cambridge: Cambridge University Press.

Gunawardana, R.A.L.H. 1979. *Robe and Plough.* Tucson: University of Arizona Press.

———. 1988. "Subtile Silks of Ferreous Firmness: Buddhist Nuns in Ancient and Early Medieval Sri Lanka and Their Role in the Propogation of Buddhism." *Sri Lanka Journal of the Humanities* 14.1–2:1–59.

———. 1990. "The People of the Lion." In *Sri Lanka: History and the Roots of Conflict*, edited by Jonathan Spencer. London: Routledge and Kegan Paul.

———. 1993. "Colonialism, Ethnicity and the Construction of the Past: The Changing 'Ethnic Identity' of the Last Four Kings of the Kandyan Kingdom." In *Institute for Culture and Consciousness: Occasional Papers I*, edited by Susanne Hoeber Rudolph et al. Chicago: University of Chicago, Committee on Southern Asian Studies.

Hallisey, Charles. 1988. "Devotion in the Buddhist Literature of Medieval Sri Lanka." Ph.D. dissertation, University of Chicago.

———. 1990. "Tuṇḍilovāda." *Journal of the Pali Text Society* 15:155–195.

———. 1993. "*Nibbānasutta:* An Allegedly Non-canonical Sutta on Nibbāna as a Great City." *Journal of the Pali Text Society* 18:97–130.

———. 1995. "Roads Taken and Not Taken in the Study of Theravāda Buddhism." In *Curators of the Buddha,* edited by Donald S. Lopez, Jr. Chicago: University of Chicago Press.

Hallisey, Charles, and Anne Hansen. 1996. "Narrative, Sub-ethics, and the Moral Life: Some Evidence from Theravada Buddhism." *Journal of Religious Ethics* 24.2:305–328.

Hardy, R. Spence. 1860. *A Manual of Buddhism in Its Modern Development.* London: Williams and Norgate.

Hēvāvasam, P.B.J. 1966. *Mātara Yugayē Sāhityadharayan hā Sāhitya Nibandhana.* Colombo: Laṃkāṇḍhuvē Mudraṇālayē.

Hobsbawm, Eric, and Terence Ranger, eds. 1983. *The Invention of Tradition.* Cambridge: Cambridge University Press.

Holt, John. 1990. "Sri Lanka's Protestant Buddhism?" *Ethnic Studies Report* 8.2:1–8.

———. 1996. *The Religious World of Kīrti Śrī.* London: Oxford University Press.

Irvine, Martin. 1994. *The Making of Textual Culture.* Cambridge: Cambridge University Press.

Ishii, Yoneo. 1993. "Religious Patterns and Economic Change in Siam in the Sixteenth and Seventeenth Centuries." In *Southeast Asia in the Early Modern Era,* edited by Anthony Reid. Ithaca: Cornell University Press.

Jayatilaka, D. B. 1940. "Sinhalese Embassies to Arakan." *Journal of the Ceylon Branch of the Royal Asiatic Society* 35.93:1–6.

Jeganathan, Pradeep, and Qadri Ismail, eds. 1995. *Unmaking the Nation: The Politics of Identity and History in Modern Sri Lanka.* Colombo: Social Scientist's Association.

Kemper, Steven. 1991. *The Presence of the Past.* Ithaca: Cornell University Press.

Khemānanda, Vērahära, and Venivälkoḷa Indajoti, eds. 1915. *Damsakpävatum Sūtraya.* Colombo: Sanda Kirana Press.

Kotelawele, D. A. 1977. "New Light on the Life of Sangharaja Welivita Saranankara." *Journal of the Vidyalankara University of Ceylon* 1.1:119–124.

———. 1986. "Muslims under Dutch Rule in Sri Lanka 1638–1796." In *Muslims of Sri Lanka,* edited by M.A.M. Shukri. Beruwala, Sri Lanka: Jamiah Naleemia Institute.

Kurē, E., pub. 1897. *Āḷavaka Sūtraya.* Colombo: Sudarśana Yantrāsālāva.

LaCapra, Dominick. 1983. *Rethinking Intellectual History.* Ithaca: Cornell University Press.

Lawrie, Archibald. 1896/1898. *A Gazetteer of the Central Province of Ceylon.* 2 volumes. Colombo: Government Printer.

Leclercq, Jean. 1982. *The Love of Learning and the Desire for God.* New York: Fordham University Press.

Leff, Gordon. 1992. "The *Trivium* and the Three Philosophies." In *A History of the University in Europe,* edited by Hilde de Ridder-Symoens. Volume 1. Cambridge: Cambridge University Press.

Le Goff, Jacques. 1985. *The Medieval Imagination.* Chicago: University of Chicago Press.

Lieberman, Victor. 1993. "Was the Seventeenth Century a Watershed in Burmese History?" In *Southeast Asia in the Early Modern Era,* edited by Anthony Reid. Ithaca: Cornell University Press.

———. 1997. "Introduction." *Modern Asian Studies* 31.3:449–461.

Liyanaratne, Jinadasa. 1983. *Catalogue des manuscripts singhalais* Paris: Bibliothèque Nationale.

Lopez, Donald S., Jr. 1995a. "Introduction." In *Curators of the Buddha,* edited by Donald S. Lopez, Jr. Chicago: University of Chicago Press.

———, ed. 1995b. *Curators of the Buddha.* Chicago: University of Chicago Press.

Ludden, David. 1993. "Orientalist Empiricism." In *Orientalism and the Postcolonial Predicament,* edited by Carol A. Breckenridge and Peter van der Veer. Philadelphia: University of Pennsylvania Press.

Mahāvaṃsa [MV]. 1912. *Cūlavaṃsa: Being the More Recent Part of the Mahāvaṃsa.* Edited by Wilhelm Geiger. London: Pali Text Society.

Mahinda, Deegalle. 1995. "Baṇa." Ph.D. dissertation, University of Chicago.

Malalasekere, G. P. 1938. *Dictionary of Pali Proper Names*. London: Pali Text Society.

———. 1958. *The Pali Literature of Ceylon*. Colombo: M. D. Gunasena.

Malalgoda, Kitsiri. 1972. "Sinhalese Buddhism: Orthodox and Syncretistic, Traditional and Modern." *Ceylon Journal of Historical and Social Studies* (n.s.) 2:156–169.

———. 1976. *Buddhism in Sinhalese Society 1750–1900*. Berkeley and Los Angeles: University of California Press.

Mallikovādasutta. n.d. Manuscript. London: British Library 14098.d.45 (1).

Maṅgala, Godhagama. n.d. *Mahanuvara Sangavuṇu Toraturu*. N.p.

Mani, Lata. 1990. "Contentious Traditions." In *Recasting Women*, edited by Kumkum Sangari and Sudesh Vaid. New Brunswick, N.J.: Rutgers University Press.

Mirando, A. H. 1985. *Buddhism in Sri Lanka in the Seventeenth and Eighteenth Centuries*. Colombo: Tisara Prakāsakayō.

Nardi, Paolo. 1992. "Relations with Authority." In *A History of the University in Europe*, edited by Hilde de Ridder-Symoens. Vol. 1. Cambridge: Cambridge University Press.

Ñāṇamoli Bhikkhu. 1971. *A Thinker's Notebook*. Kandy: Forest Hermitage.

Nattier, Jan. 1991. *Once upon a Future Time*. Berkeley: Asian Humanities Press.

Norman, K. R. 1983. *Pali Literature*. Wiesbaden: Otto Harrasowitz.

———. 1993. *Collected Papers*. Vol. 4. Oxford: Pali Text Society.

Obeyesekere, Gananath. 1970. "Religious Symbolism and Political Change in Ceylon." *Modern Ceylon Studies* 1.1:43–63.

———. 1991. "Buddhism and Conscience." *Daedalus* 120:219–239.

Obeyesekere, Ranjini. 1991. *Jewels of the Doctrine*. Albany: State University of New York Press.

Olson, Grant, trans. 1996. *Buddhadhamma*. Albany: State University of New York Press.

Paññānānda, Induruva. 1887. *Mahāparinirvāna Sūtraya*. Colombo: Lokāthisādhaka Yantrālaya.

Paraṇavitāna, K. D. 1981. *Välivitạ Śrī Saraṇaṃkara Saṃgharāja Svāmīndrayangē Lekhana Tunak*. Colombo: Cultural Affairs Ministry.

Penth, Hans. 1977. "Reflections on the Saddhamma-Saṅgaha." *Journal of the Siam Society* 65.1:259–280.

Perera, S. G. 1942. *Life of Father Jacome Goncalvez*. Madura: De Nobili.

———. 1962. *Historical Sketches*. Colombo: Catholic Book Depot.

Petrucci, Armando. 1995. *Writers and Readers in Medieval Italy*. Translated by Charles M. Radding. New Haven: Yale University Press.

Phukan, Shantanu. 1999. "Through a Persian Prism: Hindi and *Padmavat* in the Mughal Imagination." Ph.D. dissertation, University of Chicago.

Pieris, P. E. 1903. "An Account of King Kirti Sri's Embassy to Siam in 1672 Saka (1750 A.D.). *Journal of the Royal Asiatic Society (Ceylon)* 17.54:17–45.

———. 1929. *The Dutch Power in Ceylon 1602–1670*. London: Curzon.

Piyadassi Thera. 1981. *The Book of Protection*. Kandy: Buddhist Publication Society.

Pollock, Sheldon. 1993. "Deep Orientalism? Notes on Sanskrit and Power beyond the Raj." In *Orientalism and the Postcolonial Predicament*, edited by Carol A. Breckenridge and Peter van der Veer. Philadelphia: University of Pennsylvania Press.

———. 1995. "Literary History, Indian History, World History." *Social Scientist* 23.10–12:112–142.

Prērā, Vikramagē Siyadōris, pub. 1891. *Mahāsamaya Sūtraya.* N.p.

Prothero, Stephen. 1996. *The White Buddhist.* Bloomington: Indiana University Press.

Pruitt, William. 1994. Étude linguistique de nissaya birmans. Paris: École Française d'Extrême-Orient.

Rahula, Walpola. 1956. *History of Buddhism in Ceylon.* Colombo: M. D. Gunasena.

Ratnapala, Nandasena. 1971. *The Katikavatas.* Munich: R. Kitzinger.

Ray, H. C., ed. 1960. *University of Ceylon History of Ceylon.* Colombo: University of Ceylon.

Reid, Anthony. 1988. *Southeast Asia in the Age of Commerce 1450–1680.* Vol. 1. New Haven: Yale University Press.

———. 1993a. *Southeast Asia in the Age of Commerce 1450–1680.* Vol. 2. New Haven: Yale University Press.

———, ed. 1993b. *Southeast Asia in the Early Modern Era.* Ithaca: Cornell University Press.

Reimers, E., trans. and ed. 1935. *Memoir of Steivan Gollennesse for His Successor, 1751.* Colombo: Government Printer.

———. 1946. *Memoir of Joan Schreuder for His Successor, 1762.* Colombo: Government Printer.

———. 1947. *Memoir of Joan Gideon Loten for His Successor, 1757.* Colombo: Government Printer.

Reynolds, C.H.B. 1981. *Catalogue of the Sinhalese Manuscripts in the India Office Library.* London: India Office Library and Records.

Reynolds, Craig. 1972. "The Buddhist Monkhood in Nineteenth-Century Thailand." Ph.D. dissertation, Cornell University.

Reynolds, F. E., and M. B. Reynolds. 1982. *The Three Worlds According to King Ruang.* Berkeley and Los Angeles: University of California Press.

Reynolds, Frank. 1972. "The Two Wheels of Dhamma." In Bardwell L. Smith, ed. *Two Wheels of Dhamma.* Chambersburg, Pa.: American Academy of Religion.

Reynolds, Frank, and Charles Hallisey. 1989. "Buddhist Religion, Culture and Civilization." In Joseph M. Kitagawa and Mark D. Cummings, eds. *Buddhism and Asian History.* New York: Macmillan.

Roberts, Michael. 1982. *Caste Conflict and Elite Formation.* Cambridge: Cambridge University Press.

———. 1997. *Sri Lanka: Collective Identities Revisited.* 2 vols. Colombo: Marga Institute.

Rogers, John. 1987. *Crime, Justice, and Society in Colonial Sri Lanka.* London: Routledge.

Rouse, Richard H., and Mary A. Rouse. 1979. *Preachers, Florilegia, and Sermons.* Toronto: Pontifical Institute of Mediaeval Studies.

Saddhānanda, Nedimāle. 1890. "Saddhamma Saṃgaho." *Journal of the Pali Text Society*, reprint Delhi: Caxton Publications, 1985, 21–89.

Said, Edward. 1978. *Orientalism*. New York: Vintage.

Samaranāyaka, D.P.R., ed. 1966. *Nikāyasaṅgraha* [= *Nikāyasaṅgrahaya*]. Colombo: M. D. Gunasena.

Saṃgharājasādhucariyāva [SSC]. 1969. Edited by Hēnpiṭagedara Piyananda. Colombo: Ratna Pot Prakāsakayō.

Saṃgharājavata [SV]. 1955. Edited by Śrī Charles de Silva. Colombo: M. D. Gunasena.

Sannasgala, P. B. 1964. *Siṃhala Sahitya Vaṃsaya*. Colombo: Lake House.

Sārārthadīpanī [SD]. 1891. Edited by Beligallē Sobhita. Peliyagoda, Sri Lanka: Satya Samuccaya Press.

Sāratthappakāsinī. 1977. Edited by F. L. Woodward. London: Pali Text Society.

Sāratthasamuccaya [SS]. 1929. Edited by Doranägoḍa Ñāṇasena. Colombo: Tripitaka Publication Press.

Schopen, Gregory. 1991. "Archeology and Protestant Presuppositions in the Study of Indian Buddhism." *History of Religions* 31.1:1–23.

———. 1997. *Bones, Stones, and Buddhist Monks*. Honolulu: University of Hawai'i Press.

Seneviratne, H. L. 1976. "The Alien King." *Ceylon Journal of Historical and Social Studies* (n.s.) 6.1:55–61.

———. 1978. "Religion and Legitimacy of Power in the Kandyan Kingdom." In *Religion and Legitimation of Power in Sri Lanka*, edited by Bardwell L. Smith. Chambersburg, Pa.: Anima Books.

———. 1999. *The Work of Kings: The New Buddhism in Sri Lanka*. Chicago: University of Chicago Press.

Silakkhandha, Tumbullē. 1995. "Asgiri Mahavihārayē Prabhavaya, Vikāśaya hā Tadanubuddha Adhyāpanaya." Darśana Viśārada Upādhiya thesis, Colombo University.

Sīlānanda, Telvatte, ed. 1901. *Vimānavastuprakaraṇaya*. Colombo, Jīnalankara Press.

Silva, D. P., pub. 1887. *Damsakpävatum Sūtraya*. N.p.: Śāstrādhāra Yantrālaya.

Sizemore, Russell, and Donald K. Swearer, eds. 1990. *Ethics, Wealth and Salvation*. Columbia: University of South Carolina Press.

Smith, Bardwell L., ed. 1978a. *Religion and the Legitimation of Power in Sri Lanka*. Chambersburg, Pa.: Anima Books.

———. 1978b. *Religion and the Legitimation of Power in Thailand, Laos and Burma*. Chambersburg, Pa.: Anima Books.

Somadasa, K. D. 1959/1964. *Laṇkāvē Puskoḷa Nāmāvaliya*. Colombo: Department of Cultural Affairs.

———, ed. 1987. *Catalogue of the Hugh Nevill Collection of Sinhalese Manuscripts*. 7 vols. London: British Library and Pali Text Society.

Sorata, Väliviṭiyē. 1970. *Śrī Sumaṅgala Śabdhakoṣaya*. Colombo: Anula Mudraṇālaya.

Spencer, Jonathan, ed. 1990. *Sri Lanka: History and the Roots of Conflict*. London: Routledge and Kegan Paul.

Śrī Dharmakīrti, Nivandama. 1961. *Siṃhala Sāhityayē Svarṇayugaya*. Colombo: Vidyālankāra Viśvavidyālaya.

Stock, Brian. 1983. *The Implications of Literacy.* Princeton: Princeton University Press.

Street, Brian. 1984. *Literacy in Theory and Practice.* Cambridge: Cambridge University Press.

Strenski, Ivan. 1983. "On Generalized Exchange and the Domestication of the Saṃgha." *Man* (n.s.) 18:463–477.

Strong, John. 1983. *The Legend of King Aśoka.* Princeton: Princeton University Press.

———. 1992. *The Legend and Cult of Upagupta.* Princeton: Princeton University Press.

Subrahmanyam, Sanjay. 1997. "Connected Histories: Notes Towards a Reconfiguration of Early Modern Eurasia." *Modern Asian Studies* 31.3:735–762.

Suraweera, A. V. 1968. "The Imprisonment of Sangharāja Saranaṃkara." *Vidyodaya Journal of Arts, Sciences and Letters* 1.1:53–57.

Swearer, Donald K. 1995. *Buddhism in Southeast Asia.* Albany: State University of New York Press.

Tambiah, H. W. 1962. "Buddhist Ecclesiastical Law." *Journal of the Ceylon Branch of the Royal Asiatic Society* (n.s.) 8.1:71–107.

Tambiah, S. J. 1970. *Buddhism and the Spirit Cults in North-East Thailand.* Cambridge: Cambridge University Press.

———. 1976. *World Conqueror World Renouncer.* Cambridge: Cambridge University Press.

———. 1984. *The Buddhist Saints of the Forest and the Cult of the Amulets.* Cambridge: Cambridge University Press.

Vācissara, Koṭagama. 1964. *Saraṇaṃkara Saṃgharāja Samaya.* Colombo: Y. Don Edwin et al.

Vibhaṅga-aṭṭhakathā /Sammohavinodanī [Vibh-a]. 1980. Edited by Buddhadatta Thero. London: Pali Text Society.

Vijayaśirivardhana, K.V.A. 1989. "Mahanuvara Yugayē Sāṃpradāyika Siṃhala Bhāsā Adhyayana Kṛti Pilibanda Vimarśanayak." M.A. thesis, Peradeniya University.

Vijayavardhana, G. Hēmapāla, and P. B. Mīgaskumbura. 1993. *Siyam-Śrī Laṃkā Āgamika sambandhanā.* Colombo: Pradīpa Prakāsakayō.

Visuddhimagga [Vm]. 1975. Edited by C.A.F. Rhys Davids. London: Pali Text Society.

von Hinüber, Oskar. 1982. "Pali as an Artificial Language." *Indologia Taurinensia* 10:133–140.

———. 1988. "Remarks on a List of Books Sent to Ceylon from Siam in the 18th Century." *Journal of the Pali Text Society* 12:175–183.

Walters, Jonathan. 1997. "The Mahāyāna Origins of the Theravāda." *Sri Lanka Journal of the Humanities* 23:1–2.

———. 1998. "Buddhist History." In *Querying the Medieval*, edited by Ronald B. Inden. New York and Delhi: Oxford University Press.

———. 1999. "Mahāsena at the Mahāvihāra. In *Invoking the Past: The Uses of History in South Asia*, edited by Daud Ali. London: Oxford University Press.

Whitaker, Mark. 1999. *Amiable Incoherence: Manipulating Histories and Mod-*

ernities in a Batticaloa Hindu Temple. Sri Lanka Studies Vol. 8. Amsterdam: V.U. University.

Wickremasinghe, Sirima. 1960. "Ceylon's Relations with South-East Asia. With Special Reference to Burma." *Ceylon Journal of Historical and Social Studies* 3.1:38–58.

Wyatt, David K. 1969. *The Politics of Reform in Thailand.* New Haven: Yale University Press.

———. 1997. "Southeast Asia 'Inside Out,' 1300–1800: A Perspective from the Interior." *Modern Asian Studies* 31.3:689–709.

Index

Abhayagiri Nikāya (monastery), 36
adigārs, 33
Adikaram, E. W., 142
Adikāri, Abhayaratna, 44, 51, 60
administration, monastic, 60–65
administrative structure, of Kandyan Kingdom, 32–35
advisory letters, 48–49, 57–59, 66, 149–50
Almond, Philip, 199
alms round, monastic, 132, 170
Amarapura Nikāya, 169
Ampiṭiya Vihāraya, 51
Äṇavum, 55
Annales school, 15
anti-Orientalism, 20
anunāyaka, 61
Anurādhapura, royal capital at, 25–26, 42
Anuśāsanā Vaṭṭōruva, 48, 57
Arakan, 31
aristocracy, monks as members of, 37. *See also* caste, role of; patronage
arthavyākhyāna, 166
Asgiri Talpata, 44
Asgiri Upata, 44n.6
Asgiri Vihāraya, 44, 44n.6, 51, 60–61, 63–64
Asoka (Dhammasoka) (king), image of, 102–4
aṣṭakas, 50, 115
Atmahāsthāna Vihāraya, 51
authoritative texts. *See* textual authority; texts, Buddhist; *tipiṭaka*

Bambawa Vihāraya, 100
Bannḍāra, Kobbäkaḍuvē Gaṇe, 37
Batavia (Jakarta), 31
Bechert, Heinz, 6
bhava sannaya, 176n.25
biographies, 88, 91, 171–72
boundaries, monastic, establishment of, 50, 55
Brahmins, in Kandyan Kingdom, 38
Breckenridge, Carol, 8
Buddha, epithets for *(iti pi so gathā)*, 191–93
Buddha Gadya, 56
Buddhaghosa, 80–81, 116, 127
Buddharakkhita, Tibboṭuvāvē, 34–35, 63, 65, 78n.3, 99, 172n.21. See also *Mahāvaṃsa*
Buddhism, 5–9, 24–25, 76–77, 91–93, 201; Lankan, 4–5, 13–14, 23–29, 43, 43n.4, 77–80, 107–8, 139, 197–203; "Protestant," 199–202. *See also* textual community, Buddhist

Cantor, Norman, 15
Carrithers, Michael, 76
Carruthers, Mary, 15, 19, 167–68
Carter, John Ross, 81
caste, role of, 35, 35n.21, 65, 169–70
Catholicism, in Lanka, 28, 38–40, 43
Catholic priests, in Lanka, 30, 35n.19, 39–40
catubhāṇavāra Pāli, 110. *See also* Recitation Sections, Four
characters, use in preaching, 184, 184n.34, 185, 185n.35, 185n.36, 189
Christianity, in Lanka, 17–18. *See also* Catholicism, in Lanka
Clanchy, Michael, 11n.20
Coedès, G., 85n.13
Cohn, Bernard, 113n.9
Collins, Steven, 92–93, 141–42
colonialism: British, 199–203; Dutch, 28–31, 39; Portuguese, 26–28, 38–39, 43, 43n.4
commentaries. See *sannayas*; *Sārārthadīpanī*; *sūtra sannaya* genre
community, monastic, 25, 28, 193. See also *saṃgha; Siyam Nikāya*
composition, commentarial, 114–25, 129–31. See also *Sārārthadīpanī; sūtra sannaya* genre
conservatism, educational, 62–65
Copeland, Rita, 15, 116–17, 117n.15, 121, 128
Copleston, Reginald Stephen, 176n.25

Cūlavaṃsa, 78n.3
curriculum, monastic, 45, 147; four levels of study, 55–58; implementation of, 59–69; Siamese additions to, 58–59. *See also* educational system, monastic

Dagenais, John, 15, 146, 167–68
Daḷada Maligāva, 73
Daṁbadeṇi, royal capital at, 26, 42
Dambulu Vihāraya, 51
Davis, Richard, 89
D'Avray, D. L., 19, 185n.37
de Certeau, Michel, 164–65, 165n.14
decline-and-revival motif, in Buddhist historiography, 8–9, 76–86, 105–6. See also *sāsana*, life of
Degaldoruvē Vihāraya, 51, 101
demon sorcery, 137
description, confidence-inducing, in *sūtra sannayas*, 182–83
devotionalism, Buddhist, 26, 28
Dewaraja, Lorna, 34–35, 35n.20, 38, 103
Dhammadassi, Golahänvattē, 44n.6
Dhammadinna, Vehällē, 63, 73
Dhammajoti, Siṭinâmaluvç, 44, 65
Dhammakkhanda, Moratoṭa, 63, 65, 73–74, 78n.5, 171
Dhammaloka, Varakavē, 45n.7
Dhammapāla, 58–59
Dhammarakkhita, Däramiṭipala, 63, 73, 78n.4, 172
Dhammaratana, Mihiripänna, 169
Dhammasiddhi, Urulävattē, 64
Dharmadasa, K. N. O., 32, 103
Dharmakīrti, Gaṇanāyaka Golahänvattē, 44n.6
dharmāniasṃsa texts, 71, 71n.28, 172, 172n.21
Dharmapāla (king), 43
dialogical interplay, in bilingual commentary, 129–30
disāvas, 33
discipline, monastic, 82–85, 94–95, 147–48, 163–64; in *Sārārthadīpanī*, 150–53. See also *sūtra sannaya* genre
discourse on monasticism, 77–90, 105; effects of, 86–90; influences on, 80–86; royal appropriations of, 98–102; and Siyam Nikāya, 90–98
Duncan, James, 102
Dutch, as colonial power, 28–31, 39
Dutch East Indies Company (V.O.C.), 28–31
Dutch Reformed Protestantism, 39

Eco, Umberto, 146n.6, 157n.10
education, print medium, 171
educational system, monastic, 41, 139; formation of, 46–52; pre-1730, 41–45; and royal patronage, 52–55. *See also* learning, monastic
etymological interpretation *(nirutti)*, in *sūtra sannayas*, 180–81, 192
expository guidance, in *sūtra sannayas*, 183–85
expository patterns, in *sūtra sannayas*, 178

Fabian, Johannes, 11n.20
festivals, Buddhist, 186
First Council, Buddhist, 24
Fish, Stanley, 77, 89, 89n.17
fundamentalism, Buddhist, 200–201

Gaḍalādeṇiyē Saddharmatilaka Vihāraya, 51
Gampola, 42
Gaṇadevi Hälla, 56
Gaṃgārāmaya Vihāraya, 52–53
gaṇinnānse, 37–38, 43–44, 47, 69–70, 137, 153, 172
ganthadhura (responsibility to study and preserve texts), 44–45, 94–96, 198–202
glossing. *See* composition, commentarial
Gombrich, Richard, 6, 80, 94, 200
Goonewardena, K. W., 31, 38
goyigama, 65, 169
Graham, William A., 11n.20
grammars, use of, 57, 67
Gunawardana, R. A. L. H., 33n.15, 93n.23

Hallisey, Charles, 10, 45, 94n.24, 116n.13, 162, 168, 201
handbooks, monastic *(baṇa daham pot)*, 56–57, 67–68, 67n.26, 141–42, 151n.7, 165, 196. *See also* discipline, monastic; *sūtra sannaya* genre
Hansen, Anne, 168
Hēvāvasam, P. B. J., 43, 43n.5, 51, 55, 60, 70–71, 169
hierarchy, monastic, 60–65, 148

higher ordination (Pāli *upasampadā*), 31, 36–37, 44, 46, 50, 59–61, 74–75; and caste exclusion, 65, 169–70
Himi, Irivinnē Vipassi, 79n.6
Hinduism, in Kandyan Kingdom, 38
historiography: Orientalist, 4; post-Orientalist, 4–5
Hōḍiya pota, 55
Holt, John, 19, 35, 102–4, 195–96

identity, monastic, 69–70, 116, 138
Indajoti, Galagedara, 78n.4
influence, literary, 80–87
intercultural mimesis, 201
interpretive communities, 89–90, 89n.17. *See also* textual communities
interpretive strategies, 13, 66, 197
intertextuality, in monastic reading, 164–65
introductory stories: in *sūtra sannaya*s, 181–82; in *sutta*s, 134–36
Irvine, Martin, 12–13, 15, 117–18, 129–30
Ishii, Yoneo, 17n.28

Jaffna Kingdom, 25
jātaka stories, 172
Jetavana Nikāya (monastery), 36
Jotipāla, 185n.36

Kandy (Mahānuvara, the Great City), 30, 33
Kandyan Kingdom, 16–17, 28–30, 32–35, 39–40
*katikāvata*s. *See* regulations, monastic
kingship: and discourse on monasticism, 98–102; images of, 102–4
Kīrti Śrī Katikāvata, 137
Kīrti Śrī Rājasiṃha (king), 32, 34, 44n.6, 50, 61, 78n.2–78n.3; and image of Asoka, 102–4; as patron, 53–55, 62, 96–102
Kīrti Śrī Rājasiṃha Katikāvata, 78–80, 78n.2, 95, 150
Kōṭṭe, 28
Kulatunga family, 46, 65
Kurumburē Vihāraya, 51
Kuruṇägala, 42

LaCapra, Dominick, 145–46
language, local, 113–14, 130
language, Pāli, 26, 42, 56, 96, 114–16, 198–99; in bilingual commentaries, 110–16, 118–25, 129–36; in preaching, 175–77, 177n.28, 178; and Siyam Nikāya, 91–93
language, Sanskrit, 42, 42n.3, 56, 114, 114n.10
language, Sinhala, 26, 42, 42n.3, 55–56, 114–16; in bilingual commentaries, 112–16, 118–25, 129–36; in preaching, 175–77, 177n.28, 178
language, social meanings of, 114–15
languages, literary, 4n.4
Lanka, 16–18, 24, 30–31. *See also* Buddhism
Lawrie, A., 72
lay audience, for monastic preaching, 171–96
lay-monastic relations, 70–72. *See also* patronage
learning, monastic, 64, 126, 172, 177; and life of *sāsana*, 85–88; and Pāli language, 91–93; and prestige, 72–74; and royal patronage, 98–102; and Siyam Nikāya, 93–96; standardization of, 41, 74–75. *See also* discourse on monasticism; *sutra sannaya* genre; texts, Buddhist
learning, religious, 41
Le Goff, Jacques, 15
Leuke, 35, 35n.19, 39
lexicons, use of, 67
Lieberman, Victor, 16, 17n.28
lineage, monastic, 61–65, 91, 116, 197
literacy, 10–11, 11n.20; lay, 48, 70, 194–96; monastic, 55–56
literary culture, 108, 113–14
literary work, defined, 108n.2
Lopez, Donald S., Jr., 7

Mädavela Rajamahavihāraya, 52
Mädavela Siri Ānanda, 63
Magul Lakuṇa, 56
Mahā Dhammarāja II (king), 31n.12
Mahākassapa, 84–85
Mahākāśyapa, Udumbaragiri Āranyavāsī, 83
mahānāyaka, 61
Mahāsāmi, Dhammakitti, 85–86
Mahāsvāmi, Amaragirivāsavāsī Vanaratana, 84

Mahāsvāmi, Āranyaka Medhaṃkara, 84
mahāthera (senior monk), 36
Mahāvaṃsa (The Great Lineage), 52–54, 71, 78–80, 78n.3, 82–84, 91–92, 95, 97–100, 109, 137, 141–42, 172n.21
Mahāvihāra (monastic group), 25
Mahāvihāra Nikāya (the Great Monastery), 36, 83
Mahāvīra (Jain leader), 23
Mahinda, Deegalle, 173–75
Maitreya, Ven. Ānānda, 142n.3
Maitreya, Vīdāgama, 42
Malalgoda, Kitsiri, 30, 37, 60, 65, 75
Mālinbaḍa, 63
Malvatu Vihāraya, 44, 44n.6, 60–61, 63
Manoratthapūraṇī, 81–82
manuscripts, monastic, 140–44, 140n.1, 141n.2, 146, 165–66, 172n.21, 175–76, 176n.25. *See also* printed texts, monastic
manuscript textuality, 41, 146–47, 165n.14. *See also* reading
Mātara Kalugala Ārāmaya, 51
Medhaṃkara, 116
meditation, practice of, 94, 133, 135–36, 168, 186–89
memorization, role of, 55, 58, 167–68, 176–79
mental freedom, 188
metaphor, in *Sārārthadīpanī*, 162–65
Mīgaskumbura, P. B., 71n.28, 116n.13, 172n.21, 175, 183
Milindapraśnaya/Milindapañha, 45
Mirando, A. H., 43n.4, 71n.28, 172n.21
monasticism, 25, 35–38. *See also* discourse on monasticism; monastic practice; Siyam Nikāya
monastic practice, 93–96; and preaching, 171–72; in *Sārārthadīpanī*, 130–38. *See also* discipline, monastic
monks: novice, 37, 54, 158–59, 169–70; visiting, 50, 52, 54–55, 58–59. *See also* Saraṇaṃkara, Väliviṭa
Muhandiram, Āyittāliyaddē, 79n.6
mūla, 36
Mulkirigala Rajamahavihāraya, 51
Muslims, in Kandyan Kingdom, 38

Nampota, 55
Narēndrārāma Vihāraya, 100
Narēndrasiṃha (king), 39, 44n.6, 47, 49–50, 115
ñātiśisya paramparā, 64. *See also* lineage, monastic
Nattier, Jan, 81–82
nāyaka, 61
Nāyakkar dynasty, 32–33, 103
nidāna kāthā. *See* introductory stories
nikāya, 3n.2, 36
Nikāyasaṅgrahāya (The Nikāya Compilation), 83, 84, 85n.13, 86, 87n.15
nirutti, 180–81, 192
nissaya, 59
Nittavela Vihāraya, 51
Niyamakanda, 46, 49–51
Norman, K. R., 161–62
novice monks (Pāli *pabbajā*), 37, 54, 158–59, 169–70. *See also* higher ordination

Obeyesekere, Gananath, 168, 200
oral/aural learning, 141–42. *See also* reading, monastic
Oratorians, 39
Orientalism, 7n.13, 201

padārtha, 166
Pali Text Society, 200
Pälmadullē Vihāraya, 51
Parākramabāhu I (king), 83–84
Parākramabāhu II (king), 83
Parākramabāhu VI (king), 42
Parākramabāhu Katikāvata, 84
paritta (protective texts), 110–11, 141n.2, 188n.40, 192; recitation of, 136–38. See also *catubhāṇavāra Pāli*; texts, Buddhist
paṭipatti. *See* discipline, monastic
patronage: lay, 36, 43, 64–65, 72, 170; royal, 42, 49–50, 52, 72–74, 83, 88, 96–98
Pegu, 31
Penth, Hans, 85n.13
periodization, historical, 14–20; of Lankan history, 24–25
pirit. See *paritta*
piriveṇas (educational institutions), 41–43, 51, 60
plot of 1760, in Kandyan Kingdom, 34–35
pluralism, religious, 17–18

poetic composition, as valued skill, 73, 115
Pollock, Sheldon, 8, 107–8, 108n.2, 113–14, 113n.9
Poḷonnaruva, as royal capital, 26, 42
Portuguese, as colonial power, 26–28, 38–39, 43, 43n.4
post-Orientalism, 7–8, 14
practical canon, 166
preaching, monastic, 71, 99; and creation of textual community, 194–96; styles of, 172–75; and *sūtra sannaya* genre, 171–85. See also *sūtra sannaya* genre
preaching guides, *sūtra sannayas* as, 175–85
prestige, learning and, 72–74
printed texts, monastic, 176n.25, 201–2
print textuality, 202
protection rituals, 136–38
pupillary lineage, 62–65, 91, 91n.19

Rāhula, Toṭagamuva Śrī, 42
Rahula, Walpola, 142
Rājādhi Rājasiṃha (king), 78n.5, 101
Rājaguru Baṇḍāra, Attaragama, 55–56, 67, 71
Rājasiṃha, Kīrti Śrī, 14n.22
Rājasiṃha I (king), 43, 43n.4
Rāḷa, Muṃkoṭūvē Abesiṃha, 78n.5
Ramañña Nikāya, 202
Ratanapāla, Gammüllē, 78n.4. See also *Vimānavastuprakāraṇaya*
raṭērālas, 33
reader, empirical *vs.* model, 157, 157n.10
reader response theory, 77
readers, community of, 165–66
reading: constrained, 147–57; historical, 144–47; monastic, 139–44, 147, 164–71; resistant, 167–71
Recitation Sections, Four, 109, 113, 115, 117–25, 128–30, 134, 138, 150, 154–57, 164, 178, 185. See also *catubhāṇavāra Pāli*
regional networks, 30–31
regulations, monastic (*katikāvatas*), 54, 59, 66–67, 67n.26, 78n.2, 84, 95, 149–50
Reid, Anthony, 15–16, 15n.23, 17n.28
repetition/association, in sūtra sannayas, 178–79
Ridī Vihāraya, 51
rivalry, among monasteries, 36

Saddhammasaṅgaha (Compendium of the Excellent Teaching), 85–86, 85n.13
Saddharmālankāra, 81
Saddharmāvavāda Saṅgrahaya, 71n.28
Śaiva *bhakti*, 26
Śaivism, in Kandyan Kingdom, 38
Sakaskaḍaya, 55
Sakka (lord of the gods), 189–91
Sakyamuni Buddha, 23, 23n.1
samaṇa (follower of Buddha), 23
Samanakkoḍi, 35n.19, 39
sāmaṇera piriveṇa, 49
saṃgha (monastic community), 23
saṃgharāja, 61
Saṃgharājānuśāsanaya (The Instructions of the Lord of the Monastic Community), 149
Saṃgharājasādhucariyāva, 47–50, 63, 71–74, 78–80, 78n.6, 91–92, 132, 142, 171–73
Saṃgharājavata (Activities of the Lord of the Monastic Community), 3–4, 78–80, 78n.5, 91, 97, 137–38
Saṃgharājāvavādaya, 149
Saṃgharakīrti, Kokunnävē, 63
Saṃkicca, 185n.36
Sammohavinodanī, 81
Saṃskṛta Nāmavaranāgilla, 56
sannasas, 52, 100–101
Sannasgala, P. B., 42, 57, 73, 78n.4–78n.5, 79n.6, 175
sannayas, 68–69. *See also sūtra sannaya* genre
Saraṇaṃkara, Välivița, 14n.22, 35n.19, 39, 57, 61, 78n.2, 115, 171; advisory letters to students, 48–49, 57–59, 66, 149–50; background and early life, 46–49; as commentator, 108–10, 115–16, 119–29, 150–57; erudition of, 72–73, 138; as founder of pupillary lineage, 91, 91n.19; and monastic practice, 95–96, 130–38; and plot of 1760, 34–35; and royal patronage, 49–50. See also *Saṃgharājasādhucariyāva*; *Sārārthadīpanī*; Siyam Nikāya
Sārārthadīpanī (Illuminator of Excellent Meaning), 45, 108–16, 129, 139–40; dialogical interplay in, 129–36; as preaching guide, 175–85; resistant readings of, 167–71; structure and content of, 112–13, 118–29, 129n.23, 150–57;

Sārārthadīpanī (*cont.*)
study/reading of, 140–47; use of metaphor in, 162–65; use of simile in, 158–62; views on monasticism, 130–38, 150–53
Sārārthasaṅgrahaya, 45, 127, 184, 187–88
Sāratthasamuccaya, 111–12, 112n.7, 119, 122–23, 122n.19, 134
Sāriputta, 84
sāsana, life of, 80–86, 88–91, 102–4, 109
Śāsanikasandeśaya (The Letter Relating to the Sāsana), 149–50
Sāsanopakāra Saṇgrahavastuva (Account of Accumulated Support for the Sāsana), 78n.4
śāstrāyatana, 49
*śataka*s, 56
schools, of Buddhism, 24
self-questioning, 154–55, 162
Seneviratne, H. L., 19, 32–33, 35
Senkaḍagala, 28, 43
Siam (Ayutthaya), 29, 31, 34; visiting monks from, 50, 52, 54–55, 58–59
Silakkhandha, T., 44, 44n.6
Silaratana, Hendiyagala, 177, 182
Śīlavaṃsa Dharmakīrti, Samgharāja, 86
Silvat Samāgama (Disciplined Community), 46–50, 109, 132, 142. *See also* Siyām Nikāya
simile: in *Sārārthadīpanī*, 158–62; in *sūtra sannaya*s, 179–80
Sītāvaka, 28, 43
Siṭinārnaluvē, 169
Sivali, 185n.35
Siyāmika pota, 59
Siyam Nikāya (Siamese Order), 3, 14n.22, 41, 46, 50–52, 64, 69–70, 109–10, 139; administrative structure, 61–62; caste exclusivity, 65, 169–70; and centralization of higher ordination, 60–61; and creation of Buddhist textual community, 194–96; curriculum of, 55–59; and discourse on monasticism, 77–80; and *paritta* recitation, 136–38; and plot of 1760, 34–35; and royal patronage, 52–55; use of historical narratives, 87–90. *See also* Saraṇaṃkara, Välivita
Smith, Bardwell L., 90n.18
Somadasa, K. D., 176n.25, 177n.28, 182
Sotabbamālinī, 85n.13
South Asia, Lankan ties to, 30–31
Southeast Asia, Lankan ties to, 30–31
Sri Lanka. *See* Lanka
Śrī Saddharmāvavāda Saṅgrahaya, 85
Śrī Vijayarājasiṃha (king), 32, 39, 109, 136
Śrī Vikrama Rājasiṃha (king), 169
Śrī Vīraparākrama Narēndrasiṃha (king), 32, 50; and preaching activity, 71, 171–72, 175–78
Stock, Brian, 10–11, 11n.20, 15
Street, Brian, 11n.20
student-teacher relationship, 58, 62–63, 142, 142n.3, 148. *See also* pupillary lineage
Subramanyam, Sanjay, 16, 16n.25
succession, monastic, 37, 61–62
Sūduhumpola Vihāraya, 51
Sumaṇgala, Hikkaḍuvē, 59
Suriyagoḍa Unnansē, 46
sūtra pada änuma, 165, 165n.15
sūtra sannaya genre, 60, 68–69, 107–8, 108n.3, 139–40, 199, 202; and Buddhist textual community, 194–96; and monastic reading, 165–66, 166n.17; as preaching guides, 175–85; use of confidence-inducing description in, 182–83; use of etymological interpretation in, 180–81; use of expository guidance in, 183–85; use of repetition/association in, 178–79; use of simile in, 179–80. See also *Sārārthadīpanī*
*sutta*s, introductory stories for, 134–36. See also *sūtra sannaya* genre; texts, Buddhist
symbolic capital, 107

teacher, role of, 58, 142, 142n.3, 148. *See also* student-teacher relationship
teaching. *See* educational system, monastic
technical subjects, study of, 49, 58
temples, Buddhist: construction and restoration of, 50, 52–53, 62, 99–100; as educational centers, 50–52, 70–71; royal patronage of, 52–53
texts, Buddhist. See also *paritta; tipiṭaka*
Aṭanāṭiya Discourse (Aṭaṇātiyasutta), 111, 183
Discourse on Appropriate Acts of Loving Kindness (Karaṇīyamettā sutta),

110, 124–25, 149–53, 158–59, 168–70, 180
Discourse on the Benefits of Friendship (Mittāniasṃsasutta), 111, 126, 184–85
Discourse on the Benefits of Loving Kindness (Mettāniasṃsasutta), 111, 127, 133–36, 182, 184–89
Discourse on the Simile of the Mountain of Fire (Aggikkhandpamasutta), 184, 187
Discourse on the Standard's Tip (Dhajaggasutta/Dhajaggaparitta), 111, 186, 189–93
Discourse on the Ten Elements (Dasadhammasutta), 110, 119–21, 123, 132–33, 149–50, 156–57, 163
Discourse on What Is Auspicious ([Mahā]maṅgalasutta), 110, 121–23, 127, 163–64, 179, 181, 184
Going for Refuge (Saraṇagamana), 110, 154
Jewel Discourse (Ratanasutta), 110, 123, 158, 179–80, 182
Protective Account of the Moon (Chandaparitta), 111, 125–26
Questions for a Novice (Sāmaṇerapañha), 110, 154–55
Reflections (Paccavekkhaṇā), 110, 131–32, 156–57, 185
Ten Training Precepts (Dasasikkhāpada), 110, 154, 184
Thirty-two Characteristics (Dvattiṃsākāra), 110, 155–56
texts, monastic, 42, 55–59, 65–69; preservation of, 44–45, 94–96, 198–202; production of, 49–50, 54. *See also* handbooks, monastic; manuscripts, monastic; printed texts, monastic; *sūtra sannaya* genre
textual authority, 194, 198–99
textual communities, 5, 9–13, 105, 107. *See also* interpretive communities
textual community, Buddhist, 140, 171, 194–96, 198–203
textual hybridity, 130, 130n.24
textuality. *See* manuscript textuality; print textuality
textual transmission, 62
Thero, Śrī Narēndrasiṃhārāma Rajamahāvihārayē Adhipati Paññāsāra, 129n.23
tipiṭaka (authoritative texts of the Theravāda), 25, 25n.7, 57, 85–86, 110–11, 114, 117–18, 166, 198, 200. See also *paritta;* texts, Buddhist
trade, 29–31, 35
translation: access and appropriation in, 128–29; of authoritative texts, 198–99; local-language, 117–18, 121; primary and secondary, 117
tribunal of 1745, 39
Triple Gem, 193

Unnānsē, Maḍabāviṭa, 172
Upāli, 55, 85n.13, 169
upa-saṃgharāja, 61
Urulevatte Vihāraya, 101

Vadankavi Pota, 56
vaṃsa (lineage or chronicle), 24
van der Veer, Peter, 8
Vanniar, the, 25
Vidyōdaya Piriveṇa, 59
vihārādhipati, 61–62
Vijayanagar Empire, 32
Vijayaśirivardhana, K. V. A., 55n.12
Vijayavardhana, G. H., 176
Vimānavastuprakāraṇaya (Explanation of the Vimānavastu), 78–80, 78n.4, 95–97
vipassanādhura (responsibility to meditate), 94, 133, 135–36, 168, 186–89
Visakha Thera, 184n.34, 188
visual arts, and literacy, 195–96, 196n.44
Visuddhimagga, 25, 127, 188, 200
V.O.C., 28–31

wealth, monastic, 170–71
Whitaker, Mark, 146n.6

Yāpahuva, 42

BUDDHISMS: A PRINCETON UNIVERSITY PRESS SERIES

Buddhist Learning and Textual Practice in Eighteenth-Century Lankan Monastic Culture, by Anne M. Blackburn

The Red Thread: Buddhist Approaches to Sexuality, by Bernard Faure